1001:
A Video Odyssey

Movies to Watch For Your Every Mood!

Steve Tatham

lone eagle
PUBLISHING COMPANY

1001: A VIDEO ODYSSEY
Movies to Watch for Your Every Mood!
Copyright © 2000 by Steve Tatham

LONE EAGLE PUBLISHING COMPANY, LLC™
1024 North Orange Avenue
Hollywood, California 90038
Tel: 800-FILMBKS • 310-471-8066
www.loneeagle.com and www.eaglei.com
A division of IFILM Corp., www.ifilm.com

Printed in the United States of America

Cover design by Carla Green
Cover photo artwork by Steve Tatham
Book design by Carla Green
Author's photo by Tom Lasher

Lone Eagle books may be purchased in bulk at special discounts for promotional or educational purposes. Special editions can be created to specifications. Inquiries for sales and distribution, textbook adoption, foreign language translation, editorial, and rights and permissions inquiries should be addressed to: Jeff Black, Lone Eagle Publishing, 1024 North Orange Avenue, Hollywood, CA 90038 or send e-mail to: info@loneeagle.com

Distributed to the trade by National Book Network, 800-462-6420

To Mary and Cole who are even more fun than the movies.

CONTENTS

FEELING LIKE A GIRL

FEELING KINDA GAY

FEELING ARTISTIC

FEELING LIKE GETTING OUTTA TOWN

FEELING LIKE A GENRE MOVIE

FEELING JUDGMENTAL

ACKNOWLEDGMENTS

When my publisher, Jeff Black, called me up to tell me I needed to write an acknowledgment, I thought "well, there's you and then who the hell else?" This was Jeff's project from day one. Jeff was the sure and steady steward of this book through all the rough seas and choppy waves that we encountered.

But, of course there are others to whom I am indebted. They are...

For making my language briefer, funnier, and more tasteful: Editors Lauren Rossini and Steve LuKanic.

For entrusting a first-time author: Joan Singleton.

For her keen artistic eye and skillful design: Carla Green.

For helping to hash out these lists in their formative stages (though don't think that means you get a free book): Paul Duran and Tracy Howard.

For all the writing projects we've worked on together: Connie Johnson, Ross Osterman, Bil Dwyer, Laura Levine.

For everything (including being the only person I know who, at any time of day or night, can eat a whole order of nachos before the opening credits are over): my wife, Mary Manofsky.

For being my family: Cole Tatham, Carol Tatham, Greg Tatham, Jeff Tatham, Linda Tatham, Del and Dick Moen, Tom Tatham, Robert and Bernadine Manofsky.

For being my teachers: Linda Horvath, Larry Minné, Marilyn Fabe, Bertrand Augst.

A special thanks to the three best video stores in Los Angeles for allowing me to give them a ton of my business. They have an amazing stock of videos and between them, shelve pretty much every title in this book—believe me, I've got the blurry eyes and two burnt out VCR's to prove it. *Video Journeys* in Silver Lake where I always check first. *Eddie Brandt's Saturday Matinee* in North Hollywood for hard-to-find videos. And *Dave's Video* in Studio City for lasers and DVDs.

INTRODUCTION

There are 113 lists in this book. Each list has ten films on it. If you're clever, you've already figured out that's 1,130 movies...which is a lot. If the average movie lasts 100 minutes, that equals 113,000 minutes worth of movies. 113,000 minutes equals 1,884 hours, which, in turn, equals 78.47 days. Is there a point to all this? Not really. If there was a point, I would have included it inside the book and not stuck it in the introduction. But just know that if you watched every movie in this book back to back, twenty-four hours a day, without stopping, it would take three months to watch them all. If, on the other hand, you watched just one a week, it would take you twenty-three and a half years. And if a train leaves for Chicago six hours after a train from Pittsburgh, it would *still* take you the same amount of time to watch these movies. The bottom line? I'm providing you with twenty-three and a half years of entertainment tips. You can thank me later.

I've scoured thousands of movies to find the best films of the twentieth century. The best films of all time! The best films of the movies' first 100 years! You'll find them all listed within these pages (along with a little slop thrown in for fun). And they're all listed according to mood. Why? Because most of the time when you rent a movie, you're not looking for a particular title but rather you're feeling a particular way. You're depressed or excited or romantic or angry, and you'd like to watch a movie that will either reinforce or diminish how you're feeling. So, here are the answers to those "wandering-the-video-store-aisle-aimlessly" blues. It's like therapy, only cheaper. It's like a relationship, only simpler. It's like having a friend, but not as good. It's like a book, only...well, it *is* a book.

So go forth to your local video store armed with this book and a glow of confidence that you're the kind of person who knows what he or she wants and gets it. I'm not saying your whole life will take a turn for the better, but I'm certainly implying it.

A note about DVDs: New DVDs come out every day and while I have listed the most current information available, even more DVDs will be hot off the presses by the time you read this. So keep your eyes peeled (ouch!) because your favorite movie is probably coming to DVD just as fast as the DVD elves can get to it.

FEELING ROMANTIC

Sometimes you're feeling romantic—and then it passes, and you realize it's just nausea. Sometimes it is romance but it still passes. Sometimes it's nausea but it passes for romance, and that'll do for the moment.

Everyone has a different notion of what constitutes "romance." For some, it's flowers and champagne and late night walks on the beach. For others, it's piña coladas and getting caught in the rain (that is, if you're not into yoga and you have half a brain, to quote the lyrics from Rupert Holmes' 1979 "Piña Colada" song).

The point is, there is no clear-cut definition of romance, but everybody needs love. So, to quote the lyrics of another old song…"Birds do it, bees do it. Let's do it. Let's fall in love."

Perfect Date Movies

WHEN YOU'RE FEELING ROMANTIC

Here are the ultimate date movies. Watch these with someone you love. By the way, there is, as you are probably painfully aware, a discrepancy between what men and women consider to be romantic. Although men generally don't have any idea what romantic is (take it from me), so it's really hard to say for sure. These movies will probably get under the skin of any feeling person who has a romantic streak—however deep it's buried.

1. Titanic
Leonardo DiCaprio, Kate Winslet (1997, PG-13, 194m, DVD)
As far as romantic movies go, this is the King of the World. Action and romance in equal doses makes the perfect "something for everybody" movie. The best part is that everyone's already seen it so you can make out during the slow parts.

2. Wuthering Heights
Merle Oberon, Laurence Olivier (1939, NR, 104m, DVD)
If you've read the book, you'll notice the movie only covers the first half of this classic tragic love story. Not that I'm complaining, but it's been over sixty years...where the hell is the sequel?

3. A Room with a View
Helena Bonham Carter, Daniel Day-Lewis (1986, NR, 117m)
A veddy, veddy tasteful Merchant-Ivory production. For all you travel-junkies, this is also a nice travelogue of a European vacation.

4. Moonstruck
Cher, Nicolas Cage (1987, PG-13, 103m)
Back when Cher still had most of her ribs, she won an Oscar® for her role in this romantic gem which won over the hearts of millions. You'll never look at a full moon again without singing "That's Amoré."

5. The African Queen
Humphrey Bogart, Katharine Hepburn (1951, NR, 105m)
The two biggest stars in the history of the world team up for an unlikely love story between a drunk and a spinster. I'll let you guess who plays whom.

6. Much Ado About Nothing
Kenneth Branagh, Emma Thompson (1993, PG-13, 110m, DVD)
In this witty take on Shakespeare, former real-life couple Branagh and Thompson trade barbs so fast and furious, it has to be love. At least in the movie.

7. Ever After
Drew Barrymore, Anjelica Huston (1998, PG-13, 122m, DVD)
Barrymore, the quintessential Gen-Ex'er (ex-child star, ex-party girl) stars in this romantic fairytale that girls will have to talk guys into watching and guys will have to pretend not to like.

8. Breakfast at Tiffany's
Audrey Hepburn, George Peppard (1961, NR, 114m)
Let me guess, you love Audrey Hepburn, right? Well, take a number.

9. An Officer and a Gentleman
Richard Gere, Debra Winger (1982, R, 126m)
Way before the legendary gerbil story, Gere teamed up with Winger in this military heartwrencher. He, in that crisp white uniform; she, being whisked away as Joe Cocker croons "Love lift us up where we belong..."

10. Somewhere in Time
Christopher Reeve, Jane Seymour (1980, PG, 103m, DVD)
The ladies love this time-travel romance.

SEE ALSO:
Casablanca ("Pity Party: The Tear-jerkers")
Gone with the Wind ("Pity Party: The Tear-jerkers")
Bringing Up Baby ("King of All Genres: Howard Hawks")
Roman Holiday ("Some Movies Are from Venus... ")
When Harry Met Sally ("Romantic Movies for Jews")

WHEN TO WATCH
February 14. Valentine's Day.

WHAT TO EAT
Something romantic like a bottle of Dom Perignon and some shellfish. Or, instead of a big traditional romantic meal of meat and heavy desserts, try something a little different, like Indian food.

GREAT DIALOGUE
from *Moonstruck* by John Patrick Shanley

DANNY AIELLO as JOHNNY
In time, you'll see that this is the best thing.

CHER as LORETTA
In time, you'll drop dead and I'll come to your funeral in a red dress.

Love Conquers All

WHEN YOU FEEL HOPELESSLY ROMANTIC

Love conquers all. These movies really test that theory to the max. The essence of storytelling is conflict, so lovers have to have some obstacles to overcome to make a movie interesting. These movies are chock full of obstacles, and you're guaranteed to be left feeling overly optimistic that love is possible no matter what—and I do mean *no matter what*.

You'll learn that you can find true love with someone EVEN IF that person is...someone you hate, someone with a penis you didn't know about, Amish, a gorilla, a mermaid, your rapist, your sister, gay and you're not, an alien, or Gérard Depardieu.

1. It Happened One Night
Clark Gable, Claudette Colbert (1934, NR, 105m)
The good old screwball comedies (and this is one of the first and best) generally start out with the couple—typically from different social classes—hating each other. But despite—or because of—the many obstacles, they still manage to fall in love.

2. The Crying Game
Forest Whitaker, Jaye Davidson (1992, R, 112m, DVD)
Is that a penis under your skirt or are you just glad to see me?

3. Witness
Harrison Ford, Kelly McGillis (1985, R, 112m)
An absorbing peek into the world of the Amish which serves as a backdrop for this story about a cop in hiding who falls for local woman. If I can sound like a real girlie-girl here for a second, I just want to say, this film has some really lovely moments.

4. King Kong
Fay Wray, Robert Armstrong (1933, NR, 105m)
Is that a banana...

5. Splash
Tom Hanks, Daryl Hannah (1984, PG, 109m, DVD)
He's human, she's a fish. But as the Captain and Tennille so eloquently warbled, "Love will keep us together."

6. Tie Me Up! Tie Me Down!
Victoria Abril, Antonio Banderas (1990, NC-17, 105m)
You sure can't accuse Spanish director Pedro Almodóvar of being too politically correct. Here's the story: mental case kidnaps and ties up porn actress and they fall in love.

7. *Fool for Love*
Sam Shepard, Kim Basinger (1986, R, 108m)
The family that sleeps together...

8. *Object of My Affection*
Jennifer Aniston, Paul Rudd (1998, R, 112m)
Well gals, for those of you convinced all of the good men out there are either married or gay, here's the movie to prove it. Written by playwright Wendy Wasserstein, heroine and role model for all strong, single and desperate women over thirty.

9. *Starman*
Jeff Bridges, Karen Allen (1984, PG, 115m, DVD)
A woman falls in love with a handsome hunk/alien from another planet. (And you think *your* boyfriend seems distant.)

10. *Green Card*
Gérard Depardieu, Andie MacDowell (1990, PG-13, 108m)
With his girth and her hair, it's a wonder these two can fit into the same apartment. The "opposites attract" theory gets a full treatment in this "let's-have-fun-violating-the-immigration-laws-for-our-own-selfish-reasons-and-maybe-we'll-fall-in-love" comedy.

WHEN TO WATCH
If you're a hopeless romantic, you might try May 7. National Prayer Day.

WHAT TO EAT
How about some aphrodisiacs like oyster shooters or strawberries dipped in chocolate? Mmmmm.

GREAT DIALOGUE
from *It Happened One Night* by Samuel Hopkins Adams and Robert Riskin

WALTER CONNOLLY as ALEXANDER ANDREWS
Do you love her?

CLARK GABLE as PETER WARNE
A normal human being couldn't live under the same roof with her without going nutty! She's my idea of nothing!

ALEXANDER ANDREWS
I asked you a simple question! Do you love her!

PETER WARNE
YES! But don't hold it against me, I'm a little nutty myself!

Splitsville Hits

WHEN YOU'RE FEELING PISSED OFF AT YOUR EX

Here are some very messy divorces with a lot of bitterness on both sides. These movies are designed to make you feel good about dumping your ex. Let the animosity begin!

1. The War of the Roses
Michael Douglas, Kathleen Turner (1989, R, 116m)
What's great about this movie is that it's so filled with hate right up until the very end. Douglas, Turner and Director Danny DeVito never waver in their commitment to nastiness and big laughs.

2. The Women
Joan Crawford, Norma Shearer, Rosalind Russell (1939, NR, 133m)
Hilarious! The all-woman cast spends most of their time berating the men in (and out of) their lives. It's just so sassy! Watch for a bizarre Technicolor fashion show in the middle of this black and white film. Catty with a capital "C"!

3. An Unmarried Woman
Jill Clayburgh, Alan Bates (1978, R, 124m)
Clayburgh is so good in this film—as a suddenly single woman after being shattered by her husband's affair—one has to wonder what life choices led her to squandering her considerable talent in a string of forgettable TV projects.

4. Husbands and Wives
Woody Allen, Mia Farrow (1992, R, 107m)
This was the film Woody's fans were waiting for after his break-up with Farrow—to see what, if any, effect his real-life experience had on his work. As anticipated films go, this has a pretty good pay-off. We see characters come in and out of relationships with agony and joy; it is especially moving, and even difficult, to watch Farrow, knowing this would be her last collaboration with Allen. My only gripe: there ought to be some kind of National Day of Mourning commemorating the fact that the brilliant Judy Davis' work was beat out for the Oscar® by Marisa Tomei's role in *My Cousin Vinny*.

5. Shoot the Moon
Albert Finney, Diane Keaton (1982, R, 124m)
This portrayal of a nasty marital break-up is so bitter, it's actually painful to watch. Really takes all the fun out of divorce.

6. Living Out Loud
Holly Hunter, Danny De Vito, Queen Latifah (1998, R, 102m, DVD)
Hunter, whom I love, is the jilted ex-wife of a doctor who left her high and dry after she sacrificed everything for him. Is she bitter? Damn straight she is. This quirky comedy drama is the directorial debut of the obscenely gifted screenwriter Richard LaGravenese (*Fisher King, Bridges of Madison County, A Little Princess, Unstrung Heroes, The Horse Whisperer*).

7. Betrayal

Jeremy Irons, Ben Kingsley, Patricia Hodge (1983, R, 95m)

This movie goes backwards—starting with the ugly split of a relationship and working back toward the happy first blush of love. Don't you wish life could work that way? I haven't tried it, but I bet there are other movies that would be better if you watched them on rewind.

8. The First Wives Club

Bette Midler, Goldie Hawn, Diane Keaton (1996, PG, 104m, DVD)

The three comedy divas (notice the redhead, blonde, brunette thing) team up with some pretty funny results in this revenge comedy.

9. Faces

Gena Rowlands, John Marley (1968, R, 129m)

Another Cassavetes exercise in free-form improvisational film making with brilliant acting. It's the story of a bored middle-aged couple whose marriage is coming apart at the seams.

10. Interiors

Woody Allen, Diane Keaton, Sam Waterson (1978, R, 95m)

Woody thinks he's his idol Ingmar Bergman in this brooding film which will kill the joy in any viewer's life for an hour and a half. In fact, if you're feeling depressed about your divorce, this one may just finish you off.

SEE ALSO:
Kramer vs. Kramer ("Fathers and Sons")
The Philadelphia Story ("Delusional Cinema")

WHEN TO WATCH
April 26. The anniversary of the Chernobyl disaster (1986).

WHAT TO EAT
You can have half of everything.

GREAT LINE
from *Husbands and Wives* by Woody Allen

"It's the second law of Thermodynamics: sooner or later everything turns to shit. That's my phrasing, not the Encyclopedia Britannica's."
                    —JUDY DAVIS as SALLY

Delusional Cinema

WHEN YOU'RE FEELING LIKE GETTING BACK TOGETHER WITH YOUR EX

Many people either divorced or on the verge of breaking up labor under the delusion that their marriage or relationship will be perfect if they just try again. I say, it's your life...screw it up as you see fit! The films on this list are sure to give you false hope and feed those unhealthy fantasies about your failed love life. They're all stories where divorced couples are reunited and in most cases live happily ever after. Or at least until the sequel.

1. The Philadelphia Story
Jimmy Stewart, Cary Grant, Katharine Hepburn (1940, NR, 112m, DVD)
This is just one of the most clever, enjoyable and funniest movies ever made. As if Stewart, Grant and Hepburn aren't enough, there are divorces, high society weddings, drunken midnight swims and a foxhunt.

2. His Girl Friday
Cary Grant, Rosalind Russell (1940, NR, 92m)
They talk so rapid-fire fast in this screwball comedy, you'll have to listen close or miss out on one of the funniest films of all time. Based on the play *The Front Page*.

3. The Palm Beach Story
Claudette Colbert, Joel McCrea (1942, NR, 88m)
Don't miss this Preston Sturges delight. Why have broken marriages provided some of the funniest movies in the history of the Western world? Because when given the choice of laughing or crying, I'll take laughter for $1000, Alex.

4. Mr. and Mrs. Smith
Carole Lombard, Robert Montgomery (1941, NR, 95m)
Hitchcock's purely screwball comedy is a gas. It's the story of a couple who discover they were never legally married and have to discover each other all over again—with some complications.

5. The Awful Truth
Irene Dunne, Cary Grant, Ralph Bellamy (1937, NR, 92m)
Quintessential screwball comedy. Grant is getting divorced again, just like in the two movies at the top of the list, but as caddish as he may be, the women always seem to come back for more.

6. Irreconcilable Differences
Ryan O'Neal, Shelley Long, Drew Barrymore (1984, PG, 112m)
Am I the only one who still loves Shelley Long? Okay, so leaving *Cheers* was probably a mistake, but let's give her a break! In this movie, she shines.

7. My Favorite Wife

Cary Grant, Irene Dunne, Randolph Scott (1940, NR, 88m)

Grant and real life "roommate" Scott vie for the attentions of Dunne, as Grant's movie wife. She is stranded on a desert island with Scott so long that Grant divorces her—and then, oops! she shows up one day.

8. A Guide for the Married Man

Walter Matthau, Robert Morse (1967, NR, 91m)

Jammed with comedy stars and lots of laughs this is about a faithful husband being lured into adultery by his lecherous friend.

9. Mrs. Doubtfire

Robin Williams, Sally Field (1993, PG-13, 120m)

Williams puts on a dress, ten pounds of make-up, a bad Irish accent and acts like a nanny in order to win back his family. It's *Tootsie* meets *Kramer vs. Kramer*.

10. Liar Liar

Jim Carrey, Maura Tierney (1996, PG-13, 87m, DVD)

Here's the high concept: a lawyer has to tell the truth for twenty-four hours. That alone is enough to get Carrey into a whole range of facial tics and body contortions as he woos his ex-wife and son.

WHEN TO WATCH
October 24. International Kiss & Make Up Day.

WHAT TO EAT
First, you have to eat your words if you're getting back together with your ex. But allow me to recommend something a lot more palatable: a nice pot of soup for one.

GREAT LINE
from *The Philadelphia Story* by Philip Barry (play), Donald Ogden Stewart (screenplay)

CARY GRANT as C. K. DEXTER HAVEN
Sometimes, for your own sake, Red, I think you should have stuck to me longer.

KATHARINE HEPBURN as TRACY LORD
I thought it was for life, but the nice judge gave me a full pardon.

To Have and to Watch

WHEN YOU'RE FEELING LIKE YOU WANT TO GET MARRIED

You might want to watch these before you commit to planning a wedding. When you see how much agony you're in for you might want to consider eloping to Vegas for the Dennis Rodman-style drive-through wedding of your dreams.

1. The Wedding Banquet
Winston Chao, May Chin (1993, R, 111m)
Gay man agrees to marry woman in name only so she can get her green card. Then his parents decide to wing on over from Taiwan. Let the mayhem and meshugas begin!

2. Father of the Bride
Spencer Tracy, Elizabeth Taylor (1950, NR, 106m)
One thing this original has over the 1991 remake is a great surrealistic nightmare in which Tracy can't manage to make it up the aisle. It alone is well worth the price of admission (or video rental, as the case may be).

3. My Best Friend's Wedding
Julia Roberts, Durmot Mulroney, Cameron Diaz (1997, PG-13, 105m, DVD)
Admit it, girls: the appeal of this movie is seeing Roberts as the loser. That's okay; it doesn't make you a bad person. But this infectious comedy has several other winning qualities, like Rupert Everett's showstealing turn as her best friend. He's like an Eve Arden of the '90s.

4. Muriel's Wedding
Toni Collette, Bill Hunter (1994, R, 105m)
Muriel's just a little bit depraved, and that's exactly what we love about the poor, pudgy, ABBA-singing bride-wannabe in this Australian dark comedy.

5. A Wedding
Celebrity ensemble cast, directed by Robert Altman (1978, PG, 125m)
I'll bet you didn't know Carol Burnett, Desi Arnaz Jr., Lillian Gish, Pam Dawber, Lauren Hutton and Mia Farrow all worked together on the same film. How does Robert Altman *do* that?

6. Betsy's Wedding
Alan Alda, Madeline Kahn, Molly Ringwald (1990, R, 94m)
Writer/director/star Alda is determined to give Ringwald the wedding of her dreams, even if it ruins everything. Including her career.

7. Hobson's Choice
Charles Laughton, John Mills (1953, NR, 107m)
British comedy about a shoemaker and his daughters who rebel against his wish for them to never marry.

8. In and Out

Joan Cusack, Kevin Kline (1997, PG-13, 92m, DVD)

Cusack has found the perfect groom for her dream wedding with only one little problem to work out: the groom just might be gay.

9. Father of the Bride

Steve Martin, Diane Keaton (1991, PG, 105m, DVD)

It's not the original, but a very life-like simulation. Martin Short is priceless as the wedding coordinator.

10. You Can't Take it With You

Jimmy Stewart, Jean Arthur (1938, NR, 127m)

Stewart and Arthur have in-law issues that drive them apart as they try to create a life together in the classic Capra screwball comedy. Their biggest problem is her crazy family. So, if you think your family is nuts, remember: when you get married it can always get worse.

WHEN TO WATCH

June is always a good month.

WHAT TO EAT

Wedding cake and maybe some Jordan almonds.

GREAT LINE

from *Muriel's Wedding* by P. J. Hogan

"You're terrible, Muriel."

—RACHEL GRIFFITHS as RHONDA

Marital Bliss

WHEN YOU'RE FEELING LIKE YOU'RE IN WEDDED BLISS

Sometimes, but very rarely, a happy couple in a movie has a great love life, respect for each other, lots of laughs, and they're married. Even rarer is they're married to each other. If *you're* married and you're having one of those days when you're so glad to have a life partner who nurtures, supports, loves you and generally makes life worth living—don't snicker, it could happen—and you want to share a marriage-affirming movie with them, pick one from the list below.

1. On Golden Pond
Katharine Hepburn, Henry Fonda (1981, PG, 109m, DVD)
By the time Hepburn warbles, "You're my knight in shining armor," to Fonda (in his last performance), there won't be a dry eye in the house.

2. The Madness of King George
Nigel Hawthorne, Helen Mirren (1994, R, 110m)
With their "Hello, Mr. King" and "Hello, Mrs. King," Hawthorne and Mirren make the sweetest old married couple ever. Even if he is completely loony.

3. After the Thin Man
William Powell, Myrna Loy (1936, NR, 113m)
If every marriage was like Nick and Nora Charles', divorce lawyers would go broke. In all six *Thin Man* films, husband and wife are equal partners in every way, especially in wit. They even match each other martini for martini, proving that marriage can be a lot of fun, especially if you're drunk half the time. Nick and Nora were the inspiration for the Cybill Shepherd/Bruce Willis series, *Moonlighting*.

4. Rob Roy
Liam Neeson, Jessica Lange (1995, R, 144m, DVD)
Lange and Neeson make quite a team as wife and warrior who, through trials and much adversity, embody the definition of "soul mates."

5. Four Weddings and a Funeral
Hugh Grant, Andie MacDowell (1994, R, 118m, DVD)
Prior to getting arrested in Hollywood, Hugh Grant starred in this charming comedy about a staunch bachelor who slowly warms up to the idea of commitment as he attends wedding after wedding. One question: what's with Andie MacDowell's humongous hat?

6. Mr. and Mrs. Bridge
Paul Newman, Joanne Woodward (1990, PG-13, 127m)
This slice-of-life study of a long-lasting marriage is given resonance by the long-lasting real-life marriage of Newman and Woodward who play the title characters.

7. Country
Jessica Lange, Sam Shepard (1984, PG, 109m)
Anyone can be happy under the best of circumstances but this marriage is truly tested when Mother Nature unleashes a torrent of troubles on the couple.

8. An Ideal Husband
Rupert Everett, Minnie Driver, Cate Blanchett (1999, PG-13, 96m)
This breezy adaptation of Oscar Wilde play with an all-star cast features a husband and wife that hold each other up to high moral and ethical standards and guess what?—their marriage is all the richer for it. Who'd have guessed?

9. That's Life!
Jack Lemmon, Julie Andrews (1986, PG-13, 102m)
Lemmon and Andrews spend the weekend of his 60th birthday dealing with some of life's messy realities, but at least they're doing it together.

10. The Hairdresser's Husband
Jean Rochefort, Anna Galiena (1992, R, 84m)
A boy obsessed with the local hairdresser grows up, falls passionately in love with a woman just like the woman of his dreams and has a torrid affair—with his own wife.

SEE ALSO:
What Dreams May Come ("The Future Looks Weird")

WHEN TO WATCH
April 28. Kiss Your Mate Day (when they least expect it).

WHAT TO EAT
Pull that saved piece of wedding cake from the back of the freezer and eat it. Like you, it's not getting any younger.

GREAT LINE
from *Four Weddings and a Funeral* by Richard Curtis

> *"Marriage is just a way of getting out of an embarrassing pause in conversation."*
> —HUGH GRANT as CHARLES

Romantic Movies for Jews

WHEN YOU'RE FEELING LIKE A ROMANTIC JEW

There are so many incredible movies about the Jews and the Holocaust. And don't get me wrong, I love *Schindler's List* and *Sophie's Choice*. But what about a story about a nice Jewish girl or a nice Jewish boy who falls in love? Well, guess what, bubbie? You're in business!

1. Annie Hall
Woody Allen, Diane Keaton (1977, PG, 94m, DVD)
It's only the greatest movie ever made, that's all.

2. Fiddler on the Roof
Haim Topol, Norma Crane (1971, G, 184m)
Topol's portrayal of Tevye (or is it the other way around?) is one of the main reasons this big movie musical holds up so well.

3. The Way We Were
Robert Redford, Barbra Streisand (1973, PG, 118m, DVD)
If your "misty, water-colored memory" bank serves you correctly, you'll remember this was one of the biggest tear-jerkers of the '70s.

4. The Goodbye Girl
Richard Dreyfuss, Marsha Mason (1977, PG, 110m, DVD)
If you can avoid the temptation to fire a bullet at the screen whenever the precocious Quinn Cummings appears, you'll probably love this Neil Simon comedy.

5. Crossing Delancey
Amy Irving, Peter Riegert (1988, PG, 97m)
What's the matter with you? Why can't you settle down with a nice Jewish movie like this one? It's a sweet story about a matchmaker and her reluctant client. Would I lie to you? Go on...rent it.

6. Enemies, a Love Story
Anjelica Huston, Ron Silver (1989, R, 119m)
Smart, stylish movie about the many loves of a Holocaust survivor making up for lost time with a very hectic social calendar.

7. Brighton Beach Memoirs
Jonathan Silverman, Blythe Danner (1986, PG-13, 108m, DVD)
Neil Simon's nostalgic memoirs. The play was good and so is the movie.

8. *Dirty Dancing*
Jennifer Grey, Patrick Swayze (1987, PG-13, 97m, DVD)
Joel Grey's daughter, Jennifer, made a huge splash in this movie about a girl who learns to dance while on a family vacation (yes, that is the whole story). Then Jennifer disappeared from the radar until she reemerged a decade later with a new nose on the sitcom *It's Like, You Know*.

9. *Yentl*
Barbra Streisand, Mandy Patinkin, Amy Irving (1983, PG, 134m)
This is a good story, but c'mon...Babs as a young Jewish girl disguised as a young Jewish boy? Not even James Brolin would buy it.

10. *When Harry Met Sally...*
Billy Crystal, Meg Ryan (1989, R, 96m)
It wishes it were *Annie Hall*.

 WHEN TO WATCH
Any Sabbath is good, unless you're Orthodox, in which case you can't use any electronic equipment.

 WHAT TO EAT
If you're going to have "what she's having," let me remind you what Meg Ryan was eating in that scene from *When Harry Met Sally...*: a chef salad with oil and vinegar on the side and the apple pie á la mode.

 GREAT DIALOGUE
from *Annie Hall* by Woody Allen

DIANE KEATON as ANNIE
You know, I can't get over that this is really Beverly Hills.

WOODY ALLEN as ALVY
Yeah, the architecture is really consistent, isn't it? French next to—Spanish, next to Tudor, next to Japanese.

ANNIE
God, it's so clean out here.

ALVY
It's that they don't throw their garbage away. They make it into television shows.

The Love that Dare Not Speak Its Name

WHEN YOU'RE FEELING LIKE A GAY ROMANCE

Movies with gay love stories often end up portraying the characters as offensive stereotypes. Butch women and limp-wristed men who are routinely preyed upon, ostracized, beaten up or worse. But there *are* a few "Girl-Meets-Girl" and "Boy-Meets-Boy" stories that focus on the fun part of romance:

For the girls:

1. Entre Nous
Jacqueline Doyen, Isabelle Huppert (1983, PG, 112m, DVD)
Two married women form a friendship that over the years grows into something much more.

2. High Art
Ally Sheedy, Radha Mitchell (1998, R, 102m)
In this gritty drama, Sheedy graduates from the "Brat Pack" to the "Smack Pack" playing a lesbian heroin junkie.

3. Desert Hearts
Helen Shaver, Audra Lindley (1986, R, 93m)
Professor goes to 1950s Nevada for a divorce and feels dissatisfied. Could it be, I don't know... because she's a lesbian? Bingo! Luckily she makes up for lost time with some steamy lesbian love action.

4. Lianna
Linda Griffiths, Jane Hallaren (1983, R, 110m)
John Sayle's entry into the lesbian love story derby. A well-written story that has the bonus of featuring *Cabin Boy* star Chris Elliott in a minor role.

5. Personal Best
Mariel Hemingway, Scott Glenn (1982, R, 126m)
Two female runners prepare for the Olympics and occasionally have sex with each other.

For the boys:

1. Another Country
Rupert Everett, Colin Firth (1984, NR, 90m)
British political figures who spied for Russia are the inspiration for this play-turned-movie in which Everett plays the spy as a gay school boy.

2. Maurice
Hugh Grant, James Wilby (1987, R, 139m)
A guy falls in love with Grant, who just can't seem to close the deal, so the guy does the logical thing and falls for the stable boy in this upper crust Merchant-Ivory production.

3. My Beautiful Launderette
Daniel Day-Lewis, Gordon Warnecke (1985, R, 93m)
Race, politics, class struggle and homosexuality are all themes well-explored and done with comedy and insight in this impressive work.

4. Gods and Monsters
Ian McKellan, Lynn Redgrave, Brendan Fraser (1998, R, 105m, DVD)
Excellent screenplay based on completely fictional book about real life director James Whale's waning years. Both Redgrave and McKellan earned Oscar® nominations for their rich performances.

5. Billy's Hollywood Screen Kiss
Sean P. Hayes, Brad Rowe (1998, R, 92m, DVD)
Hey, isn't that the guy from that *Will and Grace* sitcom?

WHEN TO WATCH
First week in June. Orlando's semi-official and Disney World's unofficial Gay Pride Days.

WHAT TO EAT
Something gourmet, appropriately garnished.

GREAT LINE
from *Maurice* by E. M. Forster (novel), Kit Hesketh-Harvey, James Ivory

"England has always been disinclined to accept human nature."

—BEN KINGSLEY as LASKER JONES

Ghostly Romances

WHEN YOU'RE FEELING IN MOURNING

Any of these movies is great to watch with someone you love. Even if that someone isn't there.

1. Heaven Can Wait

Warren Beatty, Julie Christie (1978, PG, 101m)

Beatty was nominated for an unprecedented four Oscars® for writing, directing, producing and acting in this delightful gem of a remake of *Here Comes Mr. Jordon*.

2. The Sixth Sense

Bruce Willis, Haley Joel Osment (1999, PG-13, 106m, DVD)

The "I see dead people" smash is Hollywood movie-making at it's finest. M. Night Shyamalan wrote and directed this cleverly crafted script. But, whatever you do, don't give away the secret—just this hint: unlike the *Crying Game,* it doesn't have anything to do with anybody's surprise package.

3. Blithe Spirit

Rex Harrison, Constance Cummings, Margaret Rutherford (1945, NR, 96m, DVD)

Who else but Noel Coward could really even use a word like "blithe"? Harrison's dead wife shows up to haunt his second marriage.

4. Truly, Madly, Deeply

Alan Rickman, Juliet Stevenson (1991, PG, 107m)

It's the thinking person's *Ghost.*

5. Death Takes a Holiday

Fredric March, Evelyn Venable (1934, NR, 79m)

1998's *Meet Joe Black* was based on this movie. But the original version is actually interesting and worth watching.

6. Ghost

Patrick Swayze, Demi Moore, Whoopi Goldberg (1990, PG-13, 127m)

It's the stupid person's *Truly, Madly, Deeply.*

7. Topper

Cary Grant, Constance Bennett (1937, NR, 97m)

This movie spawned a minor industry with a number of sequels and a TV series. Grant and Bennett are high-living ghosts who try to breathe some life into a stuffy banker. See the irony? The ghosts are the lively ones, get it?

8. The Ghost and Mrs. Muir
Gene Tierney, Rex Harrison (1947, NR, 104m)
If you're old enough, and God knows I'm not, you'll remember this as a TV series with Charles Nelson Reilly. This is a love story about a woman who's in love with the sea captain who once lived in her house.

9. Always
Richard Dreyfuss, Holly Hunter, John Goodman (1989, PG, 123m, DVD)
Steven Spielberg's romantic remake of *A Guy Named Joe* features Dreyfuss as a guardian angel. This was Audrey Hepburn's final film.

10. I Married a Witch
Veronica Lake, Fredric March (1942, NR, 77m)
Sultry Lake plays a witch burned at the stake in the Salem Witch Trials who comes back to life to haunt the descendants of her persecutors and ends up marrying a mortal. Inspired the TV show *Bewitched*. From a book by Thorne Smith, who wrote *Topper*...and seems to have quite a fetish for dead people.

WHEN TO WATCH
October 16. The Sweetest Day.

WHAT TO EAT
Something warmed-over. Chili is always good the second time around.

IRRITATINGLY MEMORABLE DIALOGUE
from *Ghost* by Bruce Joel Rubin

DEMI MOORE as MOLLY JENSEN
I love you.

PATRICK SWAYZE as SAM WHEAT
Ditto.

FEELING SEXY

Sex in contemporary society is a very complicated issue. For starters, there's AIDS. Recently, scientists discovered a higher incidence of AIDS transmissions among monkeys performing oral sex. Of course, I'm thinking if you're experimenting with oral sex and monkeys, maybe disease isn't you're biggest problem. Maybe sex is your biggest problem, and if it is, you have something in common with a whole lot of people.

Even if you don't actually have sex, you have to worry about getting sued for talking about it. We've become a grossly over-litigious society with people suing each other over every little thing. A woman sued her employer because a guy at the office described to her a racy episode of "Seinfeld." Now, this doesn't have anything to do with sexual harassment, but I'd like to collect damages for that time I had to endure listening to someone recount an entire episode of "Nash Bridges."

Like romance, we each have our own idea of what is "sexy." If you're the Artist Formerly Known as Prince, sexy means wearing a purple suit with the butt cut out of it. That doesn't work for me. Hard as I try, I just can't see me in a pair of butt-less khakis. But who am I to judge?

The good news is that whatever you're into, there's probably someone out there who's into it, too. And with increasing frankness, filmmakers are exploring various sexual attitudes and appetites so that soon, not only will there be someone for everyone's desire, but a movie for every proclivity as well. For now, you might want to rent one of these. Or take a cold shower and go to bed.

Not in Front of Your Parents

WHEN YOU DON'T WANT TO FEEL EMBARRASSED

Don't get me wrong, these are all good movies worth watching. And you'll definitely want to see all of these movies. Most have rather candid sexual content. So, just don't, and I mean Do Not, watch these with your parents in the room. Unless, of course, you have some hippie-dippy parents who are all about free love and expression and communication—but then you have bigger problems than I can help you with.

1. La Luna
Jill Clayburgh, Matthew Barry (1979, R, 142m)
About a guy having sex with his mom—enough said.

2. Spanking the Monkey
Jeremy Davies, Alberta Watson (1994, R, 99)
See the film above. Except, in addition to the mother-son sex scenes, you get the added bonus of several scenes of masturbation.

3. Short Cuts
Celebrity ensemble cast, directed by Robert Altman (1993, R, 189m)
Sure, the most talked-about scene is when Julianne Moore is stomping around her house without her panties on. But there's also Jennifer Jason Leigh as a phone sex operator. Good movie, but not for that after-Thanksgiving dinner crowd.

4. Priest
Linus Roache, Robert Carlyle, Cathy Tyson (1994, R, 98m)
You're a good Catholic, at least when your parents are around, so you decide to watch a movie called *Priest* because you think it's something you can all enjoy together. Well, maybe, if you can all enjoy homosexual love scenes together. Oh yeah, did I mention there's an incest sub-plot?

5. Chasing Amy
Ben Affleck, Joey Lauren Adams, Jason Lee (1997, R, 113m)
My wife made this mistake. In front of both parents and a carpet installer she got to listen to the er, uh, colorful language of this boy-meets-girl, girl-loves-girl, does boy-love-boy romance.

6. Matador
Antonio Banderas, Assumpta Serra (1986, NR, 90m)
Twisted. Fun.

7. 'night Mother
Anne Bancroft, Sissy Spacek (1986, PG-13, 97m)
This movie is based on a play and I didn't know much about the play when I took my mom to see it for Mothers' Day. Bad idea. The play and the movie are about a daughter who decides to kill herself in her mother's house. Suffice to say, it's not much of an upper.

8. 9 1/2 Weeks

Mickey Rourke, Kim Basinger (1986, R, 114m, DVD)

The horny classic with the messy eating and the bondage and the Oscar® winning Basinger. And just when you least expect it, there's Christine Baranski.

9. Crash

James Spader, Rosanna Arquette, Holly Hunter (1995, NC-17, 98m)

David Cronenberg explores what I can only hope is a fictional psychological disorder in which people become sexually aroused by getting into car wrecks. I don't know on which planet that happens, but they don't make very good movies there. Interesting maybe, but not good. If you insist on seeing this movie because it's rated NC-17 and it won a special prize for artistic merit at the Cannes Film Festival, just don't watch it when anyone else is around, mostly because you'll be embarrassed by your taste in movies.

10. American Pie

Jason Biggs, Thomas Ian Nicholas, Natasha Lyonne (1999, R, 95m, DVD)

This Porky's-for-the-'90s features a whole lot of moments no seventeen-year-old is going to want to share with Mom and Dad, not the least of which is the famous "getting intimate with baked goods" scene.

WHEN TO WATCH
Fourth Sunday in July. National Parents' Day.

WHAT TO EAT
As long as your parents aren't around you can have whatever you want—how about a couple microwave dinners and some vodka from their liquor cabinet—just remember to top the bottle off with some tap water so they won't notice it's missing.

DIALOGUE WHICH PROVES MY POINT
from *Chasing Amy* by Kevin Smith

> *"All every woman really wants, be it mother, senator, nun, is some serious deep dickin'."*
> —JASON LEE as BANKY EDWARDS

Peeping Toms

WHEN YOU'RE FEELING LIKE A VOYEUR

Watching movies, in general, is an act of voyeurism. You are sitting in the dark, peeping at the most intimate details of characters' private lives. In fact, if you want to get Freudian, movies are like fantasies where you can experience wish-fulfillment in a dream-like state. Yeah, I took Psych 101, what about it? Anyway, I have included movies on this list that are not only metaphorically about voyeurism but are literally about that dirty little theme. Here are some very interesting movies about Peeping Toms. That's right, just you watching others watching others. Put on your rubber raincoat and nothing else and watch these while you're alone.

1. Vertigo
Jimmy Stewart, Kim Novak (1958, PG, 126m, DVD)
Stewart, as a detective, is hired to tail a woman he falls for. There's a lot more—involving a fear of heights and Stewart's obsession with a make-over (Novak's, not his own).

2. Rear Window
Jimmy Stewart, Grace Kelly (1954, NR, 112m)
Stewart likes to spy on his neighbors with his binoculars, but then everyone needs a hobby, especially when wheelchair bound. Grace Kelly is her most luminescently Grace and Thelma Ritter is at her sassiest.

3. Atlantic City
Susan Sarandon, Burt Lancaster (1981, R, 104m)
I'm thinking about the scene where Sarandon is washing herself with cut lemons to get the stink of fish off of her while she's being watched. This movie—about a crumbling Atlantic City, N.J. making way for the future—is the kind of perceptive American tableau which is sometimes seen best through the fresh eyes of a foreigner; in this case, French Director Louis Malle.

4. Blue Velvet
Dennis Hopper, Isabella Rossellini, Laura Dern, Kyle MacLachlan (1986, R, 121m)
This movie seemed subversive and funny when it first came out. Now, with the irony epidemic that has washed over our great land, it seems almost normal—but, not quite. It is still a great film about all the twisted little things that get some odd people off.

5. Red
Iréne Jacob, Jean-Louis Trintignant (1994, R, 96m)
The final film in the much-ballyhooed (there's a word I've never used before) Polish filmmaker Krzysztof Kieslowski's (how'd you like to have to spell that your whole life?) French-language trilogy. The film is about an old judge who has become, as you might guess by the fact that this film appears on this list, a voyeur.

6. The Conversation

Gene Hackman, Harrison Ford, Robert Duvall, Teri Garr (1974, PG, 113m)

1974 was a good year for Coppola. Not only did he win the Academy Award® for *The Godfather II*, but he also made this absorbing film about a morally conflicted professional eavesdropper.

7. Body Double

Melanie Griffith, Craig Wasson, Dennis Franz (1984, R, 114m, DVD)

Brian DePalma has spent his career trying to be Alfred Hitchcock. He comes closest here. For you architecture buffs, the house featured in the film is designed by Los Angeles Modernist and Frank Lloyd Wright protégé John Lautner.

8. Peeping Tom

Karl-Heinz Boehm, Moira Shearer (1960, NR, 88m)

Although there's nothing graphic at all in this movie, its themes and story are so kinky that an outraged reaction in 1960 all but ruined the career of accomplished Director Michael Powell.

9. Monsieur Hire

Michel Blanc, Sandrine Bonnaire (1989, PG-13, 81m)

A creepy old French Peeping Tom may be a killer.

10. A Man of Flowers

Norman Kaye, Alyson Best (1984, NR, 91m)

A creepy old Australian Peeping Tom.

WHEN TO WATCH
September 28. National Good Neighbor Day.

WHAT TO EAT
I know. You'll have what they're having.

GREAT LINE
from *Vertigo* by Pierre Boileau (novel), Thomas Narcejac (novel),
Samuel A. Taylor, Alec Coppel

"Only one is a wanderer. Two together are always going somewhere."

—KIM NOVAK as MADELEINE ELSTER/JUDY BARTON

Dirty Movies for the Art House Crowd

WHEN YOU'RE FEELING HORNY

Pretentious people like to watch sex too. If you're one of those people who don't like to get caught in the adult aisle of the video store with a copy of *Sperms of Endearment* in your hot little hands but have no qualms about renting NC-17 rated art films, then have I got some recommendations for you. When you watch these, two thumbs aren't the only body parts that'll be up. So, watch these in bed—for art's sake.

1. Belle de Jour
Catherine Deneuve, Jean Sorel (1967, R, 100m)
Is it true, as I once heard on *Hollywood Squares,* that Deneuve once referred to herself as "the most beautiful woman in the world"? I don't know if it is, but after seeing this (housewife by night, hooker by day) film, no one is going to disagree with her.

2. Henry and June
Uma Thurman, Fred Ward, Maria de Madeiros (1990, NC-17, 136m, DVD)
You want to see this because you're interested in literature—I know. The fact that this NC-17 rated story of writer Henry Miller just happens to have a three way sex scene with Thurman is just gravy.

3. The Cook, the Thief, His Wife and Her Lover
Tim Roth, Helen Mirren (1990, NC-17, 123m)
Of course, you'll want to get the NC-17 version of this artsy movie with all kinds of sex, brutality and bodily functions. An orgiastic movie about the relationships of the above mentioned characters who carry on in a gourmet restaurant.

4. Last Tango in Paris
Marlon Brando, Maria Schnider (1973, R, 126m, DVD)
Pass the butter!

5. White Palace
Susan Sarandon, James Spader (1990, R, 103m, DVD)
The tamest film on this list, but for me, the sexiest.

6. Crimes of Passion
Kathleen Turner, Anthony Perkins (1984, NR, 101m)
You know the type: "fashion designer by day, hooker by night." This one is wall-to-wall kink.

7. Spetters
Renée Soutendijk, Maarten Spanjer (1980, R, 108m)
A dirty little Dutch movie with three young motorcycle guys all after the same carny worker girl. Sex scenes are pretty graphic if you like that sort of thing and really, doesn't everyone, way deep down in their filthy little hearts?

8. Betty Blue
Beatrice Dalle, Jean-Hugues Anglade (1986, R, 121m)
You're so cultured renting this artsy French movie. I'm sure the fact that the first five minutes contain nothing but explicit sex is just something you have to wade through to get to the deeper meaning of this story of a mentally unstable love affair.

9. Sea of Love
Ellen Barkin, Al Pacino (1989, R, 113m, DVD)
What's sexier than serial killers?

10. Damage
Jeremy Irons, Juliette Binoche (1992, R, 111m, DVD)
Irons plays another aloof character who can't seem to control his naughty impulses in this steamy European import.

SEE ALSO:
Swept Away ("Desert Island Movies")

WHEN TO WATCH
July 31. The anniversary of the closing of the last Playboy Club (1988).

WHAT TO EAT
Cover each other with chocolate and whipped cream, then roll in some chocolate and strawberries and take it from there. If you need more ideas, consult *9 1/2 Weeks* or the book *Everything You Always Wanted to Know about Sex but Were Afraid to Ask.*

MEMORABLE DIALOGUE
from *Crimes of Passion* by Barry Sandler

ANTHONY PERKINS AS REVEREND SHANE
Save your soul, whore.

KATHLEEN TURNER AS CHINA
Save your money, shithead.

Adulterous Faves

WHEN YOU'RE FEELING LIKE BREAKING EVERYONE'S FAVORITE COMMANDMENT

Isn't infidelity romantic? At least that's the way Hollywood portrays it. In some of film's greatest romances, the paramours were married to other people. Believe me, it is a lot easier to make a list of great romances featuring adulterous couples than a list in which romantic couples are actually married to each other—go ahead, try it. I did notice an alarming trend: Meryl Streep is in a lot of these films—three to be exact (don't forget to check out the "See Also's") and that's not even counting her adulterous affairs in the movies *Falling in Love* and *She-Devil*. America's most beloved actress is a home wrecker—or at least she plays one in the movies. Sit back and watch these with someone to whom you're not married.

1. *Brief Encounter*
Celia Johnson, Trevor Howard (1946, NR, 86m)
A real heartbreaker, beautifully told.

2. *Prince of Tides*
Nick Nolte, Barbra Streisand (1991, R, 132m)
Nolte rolls around a park with his therapist, Streisand, while his wife waits back home for him to be "cured."

3. *The English Patient*
Kristin Scott Thomas, Ralph Fiennes (1996, R, 162m, DVD)
Seems there isn't anything more romantic to Hollywood than adultery, and here's a classic example of a film that received all kinds of prizes—including the Oscar® for best picture of 1996.

4. *Out of Africa*
Meryl Streep, Robert Redford (1985, PG, 161m)
Another best picture winning adulterous romance. A lyrical movie that begins its biographical tale of Isak Dineson with the famous Streep voice-over, "We had a farm in Africa...," and soars from there.

5. *Body Heat*
Kathleen Turner, William Hurt (1981, R, 113m)
This is a hot, sexy, 1980s film-noir. Turner's first movie. Not a bad start.

6. *The Return of Martin Guerre*
Gérard Depardieu, Nathalie Baye (1983, NR, 111m, DVD)
This was remade in the United States with Richard Gere and Jodie Foster as *Sommersby*, which was pretty good, too. But, I'd stick with the original French version of the intriguing story of a man who returns from war and either is or is not the same man who left a woman alone years earlier.

7. Doctor Zhivago
Omar Sharif, Julie Christie (1965, PG-13, 197m)
Three hours of Russian sets, costumes, war and adultery.

8. A Touch of Class
Glenda Jackson, George Segal (1973, PG, 105m)
Five-star comedic adulterous romance.

9. The French Lieutenant's Woman
Meryl Streep, Jeremy Irons (1981, R, 124m)
Meryl Streep again. That bad, naughty lady.

10. Anna Karenina
Greta Garbo, Fredric March (1935, NR, 85m)
Not only does Garbo speak, she also fools around on her husband.

SEE ALSO:
Casablanca ("Pity Party: The Tear-jerkers")
The Bridges of Madison County ("Book Reports Made Easy")

WHEN TO WATCH
May 1. Loyalty Day.

WHAT TO EAT
I'm sure you will want to splurge on champagne and caviar and anything else that pops into your head that you would never buy for your spouse.

GREAT LINE
from *Body Heat* by Lawrence Kasdan

"You're not very bright, are you? I like that in a man."
—KATHLEEN TURNER as MATTY WALKER

FEELING THOSE OL' FAMILY VALUES

In this day and age where so many people measure their degree of happiness by the size of their bank account and the kind of car they drive, it's easy to see why some (not me) say that good old fashioned family values have become almost obsolete. Fortunately, there *is* a contingent of people out there who still believe the American Dream isn't just owning Barbie's Dream House...it's settling down with Barbie (or Ken) in that Dream House, having lots of little Skippers, and instilling in them the real, non-materialistic virtues of life. Hell, even Warren Beatty's got a wife and family now, and why? Because at the end of the day, he realized what really matters in the short time we're on this planet has to do with home and family and nothing to do with fame or fortune or anything related to Madonna.

Warren found what works for him and you have to do the same. You can't let Madison Avenue design your American Dream for you, you have to solve that little Rubik's cube yourself. Now don't worry, I'm not going Tony Robbins on you. I just want you to be happy! Maybe marriage and family will be the answer for you...maybe they won't. The quality of life is what's important. And unlike Warren's sister, Shirley MacLaine, we've each only got one life, and it's that life over which we have any quality control.

As for me, I wanted a family for the longest time, but my wife, a sketch comedy actress, was too busy collecting wigs for her characters. Any free time we had we spent carousing wig shops, so instead of becoming a father, I was the Wig Master of Hollywood Boulevard. But all that changed recently when the stork finally dropped a bundle of joy on our doorstep (I thought it was our Sunday paper) and life, my friends, has never been better. I've also never been more interested in family films, and if you are too, take a gander at these family-friendly gems.

Good, Wholesome Family Adventures (Or, Movies Even a Mormon Could Love)

WHEN YOU FEEL LIKE TAKING AN ADVENTURE WITH YOUR FAMILY

For the most part, they sure don't make 'em like this anymore. Here are some movies to watch with the whole family. The good news is that these movies are actually good enough that you won't just tolerate them, you'll enjoy them. You don't have to turn on the movie and leave the kids in front of the glowing baby-sitter box. You can actually share some quality time with them—this will give them less to talk about when they are in therapy.

1. Babe
James Cromwell, Christine Cavanaugh (1995, G, 91m, DVD)
Better than the *Wizard of Oz,* this is destined to be a classic for the ages. I mean, who doesn't love this little talking pig?

2. The Court Jester
Danny Kaye, Angela Lansbury (1956, NR, 101m)
Kaye tries to pass himself off as a court jester in this wonderfully entertaining family musical comedy.

3. The Four Musketeers
Raquel Welch, Richard Chamberlian, Michael York (1975, PG, 108m, DVD)
This riotous romp of a sequel to *The Three Musketeers* is even better than the original.

4. The Princess Bride
Cary Elwes, Robin Wright Penn (1987, PG, 98m)
One scene to treasure after the next as this big, schticky adventure yarn unfolds.

5. The Adventures of Robin Hood
Errol Flynn, Olivia de Havilland (1938, NR, 102m)
A beautiful, lavish Technicolor® swashbuckler with Flynn starring as the definitive Robin Hood. Co-directed by Michael Curtiz (*Casablanca, Mildred Pierce, Yankee Doodle Dandee, Life with Father, White Christmas*).

6. Time Bandits
John Cleese, Sean Connery, Shelley Duvall (1981, PG, 110m, DVD)
A story of a boy and six dwarves who travel through time and space and meet important historical figures (just like *Bill and Ted's Excellent Adventure,* but without the phone booth and with dwarves).

7. The Thief of Bagdad
Sabu, John Justin, Conrad Veidt (1949, NR, 106m)
This is basically the live action version of Disney's animated *Aladdin*. And this one is just as much fun. Amazing photography, sets and effects for 1940. Your jaded little kids might even like it.

8. The Bear
Bart the bear (1989, PG, 92m)
Marvelous nature footage in this film which stars a bear as he makes a trek in the wilderness after losing his mom. This terrific film has no dialogue but plenty of heart-warming adventure.

9. Star Wars quadrilogy
Star Wars; The Empire Strikes Back; Return of the Jedi; Star Wars: Episode I—The Phantom Menace;
all directed by George Lucas
These don't really do a whole lot for me but I defer to you, the movie-going public, who seem to like 'em just fine, especially the kids. But then, kids can be entertained by an empty cardboard box.

10. 20,000 Leagues Under the Sea
Kirk Douglas, James Mason (1954, NR, 127m, DVD)
Jules Verne as told by Disney. These are the many adventures in Captain Nemo's futuristic submarine.

WHEN TO WATCH
Second Sunday in October, National Children's Day.

WHAT TO EAT
Flavored popcorn

GREAT LINE
from *Babe* by Dick King-Smith (novel), George Miller, Chris Noonan

"That'll do, pig. That'll do."
—JAMES CROMWELL as FARMER HOGGETT

The Wonderful World of Animation

WHEN YOU'RE FEELING LIKE A KID

If you have kids, you probably already own all of the Disney animated movies ever made and are so sick of seeing them eight times a day that you probably hate me for even bringing these titles up, but here they are. Maybe one or two have slipped through your fingers. And, be sensitive, there might be someone out there who has never seen these and so let's not deny them the pleasure of watching them for the very first time. Also, other people out there make animation besides Disney. A lot of it isn't very good, but some of it is interesting because it doesn't stick to the tried-and-true formula and the requisite comical familiar anthropomorphic sidekicks. Oh, and by the way, you're allowed to watch these even if you don't have kids.

1. Beauty and the Beast
Robby Benson, Paige O'Hara (1991, G, 84m)
A tale as old as time. The only animated film ever to be nominated for a best picture Oscar®.

2. The Lion King
Jonathan Taylor Thomas, James Earl Jones (1994, G, 88m)
The first animated film ever to generate a billion dollars in revenue (box office, merchandise, sequels and spin-offs). This thing is a phenomenon and it happens to be a terrific movie—part *Hamlet*, part Broadway musical (it spun off its own hugely successful Broadway musical which took home the Tony for Best New Musical of 1997).

3. A Grand Day Out / The Wrong Trousers / A Close Shave
Peter Sallis (1992, NR, 23m, DVD / 1993, NR, 30m, DVD / 1995, NR, 30m, DVD)
I love Wallace and Grommit. These three short claymation films are some of those most delightful films you'll ever see.

4. Toy Story
Tom Hanks, Tim Allen (1995, G, 84m)
The first all-computer-generated feature film is another landmark in animation you can chalk up to the Disney empire—with special thanks to Pixar. This is one of Disney's funniest animated films (the sequel, *Toy Story 2*, is just as entertaining).

5. Snow White and the Seven Dwarfs
Adriana Caselotti, Harry Stockwell (1937, G, 83m)
The one that started it all is still watchable, lo, these many decades later.

6. The Jungle Book
Bruce Reitherman, Phil Harris (1967, NR, 78m)
This one's a bare necessity.

7. My Neighbor Totoro
Hitoshi Takagi, Noriko Hidaka, Chika Sakamoto (1993, G, 76m)
Hayao Miyazaki is known as the Walt Disney of Japan for gentle kiddie-friendly stories like this one. He's also the creator of the artistic, but brutal, *Princess Mononoke*.

8. A Nightmare Before Christmas
Chris Sarandon, Catherine O'Hara (1993, PG, 75m, DVD)
Tim Burton's ambitious stop-action animation creation. Catchy Danny Elfman songs and some dark edges make this an awesome adventure.

9. The Iron Giant
Vin Diesel, Eli Marienthal (1999, PG, 86m, DVD)
You've been hypnotized into buying every Disney video ever made, now why don't you check out this wonderful animated film from Warner Bros. that went largely ignored upon its initial release.

10. What's Opera Doc?
Mel Blanc (1957, NR, 7m)
This seven minute Bugs Bunny cartoon opera spoof from Chuck Jones represents the pinnacle of Warner Bros. animation and as such has earned a place on the select list of the National Film Registry at the Library of Congress. Included on the laserdisc "Looney Toons Curtain Calls" with another Chuck Jones classic: *The Rabbit of Seville*.

SEE ALSO:
Tarzan ("Desert Island Movies")

WHEN TO WATCH
Last Sunday in October, National Family Day in Australia. (But you might want to get together with your family more than once a year.)

WHAT TO EAT
I'd say that there's going to be some junk food involved.

GREAT LINE
from *Beauty and the Beast* by Linda Woolverton

> *"There's the usual things: flowers, chocolates, promises you don't intend to keep."*
> —DAVID OGDEN STIERS as COGSWORTH

Girl Power

WHEN YOU FEEL LIKE SHOWING YOUR DAUGHTER A POSITIVE ROLE MODEL IN THE MOVIES

Hollywood doesn't have a great record of putting forward strong, positive female role models. All you have to do is count the number of Oscar® nominated portrayals of hookers (see "Oscar® Whores") and you'll quickly discover that they far outstrip (pun intended) the number of award winning depictions of women as scientists, inventors, nuns, athletes, or stay-at-home moms. But not to jump on the "the sky is falling" bandwagon when it comes to Hollywood morality, there have been some excellent examples of positive young female characters for girls to look up to, and here are the best:

1. Little Women
Susan Sarandon, Winona Ryder (1994, PG, 118m, DVD)
A great movie that should be required viewing for every girl as she grows up. It's a positive story that deals with family, work, love and the meaning of life. I like this version even better than the classic 1933 Katharine-Hepburn-as-Jo version—which is certainly no slouch.

2. A Little Princess
Liesel Matthews, Eleanor Bron (1995, G, 97m, DVD)
Magical tale of a high-spirited girl who survives a wicked head mistress at a boarding school.

3. The Secret Garden
Kate Maberly, Heydon Prowse, Andrew Knott (1993, G, 102m, DVD)
Sumptuous version of the children's classic about a girl who comes to live in a mysterious Victorian manor and discovers its secrets which include a garden that she brings back to life.

4. The Sound of Music
Julie Andrews, Christopher Plummer (1965, NR, 174m)
Known for its sappy elements, this picture was dubbed "The Sound of Mucus" upon its 1965 release. About singing nun, spunky Maria (the perennially spunky Andrews) and the Von Trapp family's musical escape from the Nazis, will likely please many youngsters and those with a high tolerance for sweets.

5. Fly Away Home
Jeff Daniels, Anna Paquin (1995, PG, 107m, DVD)
What a nice sweet story. A father and daughter teach a family of geese to migrate south for the winter. Hey, if they say it's based on a true story, who am I to doubt it?

6. National Velvet
Elizabeth Taylor, Mickey Rooney (1944, G, 124m, DVD)
A wholesome film about a girl who is driven to compete in a national steeplechase. And you can imagine, a young and headstrong Taylor is like an unbroken mare; there are no "Liz Whisperers" who can stop her.

7. My Brilliant Career
Judy Davis, Sam Neill (1979, G, 101m)

Though about an adult woman, this G-rated eighteenth century Australian story of woman trying to find her way by bucking society's expectations, is good material for any mature girl to watch.

8. Freaky Friday
Jodie Foster, Barbara Harris (1976, G, 95m)

After Foster nabbed an Oscar® nomination for playing a pubescent prostitute in *Taxi Driver*, she returned to the Disney fold in this body-switch comedy in which mother and daughter swap roles for a day. So much better than all those '80s body-switch comedies like *Vice Versa*.

9. FairyTale: A True Story
Florence Hoath, Elizabeth Earl, Peter O'Toole (1997, PG, 99m)

Two girls photograph fairies and make national headlines thus receiving a visit from Sherlock Holmes author, Sir Arthur Conan Doyle, who proclaims the pictures the real thing. They're not. Okay, so they perpetrated a fraud—at least they've got spunk.

10. The Miracle Worker
Anne Bancroft, Patty Duke (1962, NR, 107m)

The inspirational screen version of the play retelling how blind, deaf and mute Helen Keller came to become educated. Bancroft stars in her first decent role after a string of schlocky movies.

WHEN TO WATCH
August 11. Daughters' Day.

WHAT TO EAT
Some Easy Bake cookies.

GREAT LINE
from *Little Women* by Louisa May Alcott (book), Robin Swicord

> *"Oh, Jo. Jo, you have so many extraordinary gifts; how can you expect to lead an ordinary life? You're ready to go out and - and find a good use for your talent. Tho' I don't know what I shall do without my Jo. Go, and embrace your liberty. And see what wonderful things come of it."*
> —SUSAN SARANDON as MARMEE MARCH

Stories for Boys

WHEN YOU FEEL LIKE A BOYISH ADVENTURE

Boys will be boys—which isn't such good news if you have to clean up after them. A lot of movies featuring boys' stories are nasty, disgusting, violent and demonstrate immoral behavior—which is why we love them. But, if you would like to show your son some movies where boys go on nice, wholesome adventures, check out these:

1. The Black Stallion
Kelly Reno, Mickey Rooney, Teri Garr (1979, PG, 120m, DVD)
A beautiful poem of a movie about a young boy and his horse.

2. Stand By Me
River Phoenix, Jerry O'Connell, Wil Wheaton, Corey Feldman (1986, R, 87m, DVD)
A coming-of-age story about a group of boys growing up in the '50s. Based on a Stephen King novella, this R-rated nostalgic treat may be more for more mature teens, however.

3. Willy Wonka and the Chocolate Factory
Gene Wilder, Jack Albertson (1971, G, 100m, DVD)
Charlie and Chocolate Factory is the Roald Dahl book, *Willy Wonka and the Chocolate Factory* is the movie based on the book. I don't know why, but I think it's important for you to know the difference. The cool sets were designed by Harper Goff who went on to design theme parks for Walt Disney.

4. Oliver!
Mark Lester, Jack Wild, Ron Moody (1968, G, 145m, DVD)
I don't know your kid, but when I was a kid, I loved this movie musical adaptation of Dicken's *Oliver Twist* (and I walked seven miles to the movie theater in the snow, dammit).

5. Searching for Bobby Fisher
Max Pomeranc, Joe Mantegna, Joan Allen (1993, PG, 111m)
A brilliant seven-year-old chess prodigy (as opposed to a moronic chess prodigy) is forced into the world of competitions by an eager father in this thoughtful adaptation of the book by the same name.

6. King of the Hill
Adrien Brody, Jessie Bradford (1993, PG-13, 102m)
This original and beguiling period piece, which is a bit dark around the edges, is the story of a boy abandoned by his incapable parents and is forced to use his own tenacity to survive the Great Depression.

7. Wargames

Matthew Broderick, Dabney Coleman, Ally Sheedy (1983, PG, 110m, DVD)
A whiz kid taps into government computers bringing us to the brink of World War III, a seemingly implausible plot that seems more believable with every real world technological advance.

8. James and the Giant Peach

Paul Terry, Pete Postlethwaite, Miriam Margolyes (1996, PG, 80m)
This one is also based on a book by Roald Dahl. (How many times in Roald's life do you think someone wanted to stick an "n" right in the middle of his name?) This part live action, but mostly stop motion movie is sweet, fresh, funny and fun. *Absolutely Fabulous'* Joanna Lumley is a hoot.

9. An Indian in the Cupboard

Hal Scardino, Litefoot (1995, PG, 97m)
Directed by Muppeteer Frank Oz and written by E.T.'s Melissa Mathison, this is a wise tale of an Indian toy come to life.

10. Jumanji

Robin Williams, Kirsten Dunst (1995, PG, 104m, DVD)
A board game becomes a "Stargate" to another world in this adventure filled with a terrific computer generated menagerie.

WHEN TO WATCH
February 8. Boy Scouts' Day (assuming that you don't object to their discrimination against gays and atheists).

WHAT TO EAT
Snakes and snails and puppy dog tails, of course.

GREAT DIALOGUE
from *Wargames* by Lawrence Lasker, Walter F. Parkes

MATTHEW BRODERICK as DAVID L. LIGHTMAN
Is this a game, or is it real?

JAMES ACKERMAN as JOSHUA THE COMPUTER
What's the difference?

Fathers and Sons

WHEN YOU'RE FEELING EITHER PATERNAL OR WHATEVER THE WORD IS FOR FEELING LIKE A SON

Cats in the cradle and the silver spoon, little boy blue and the man on the moon... **If you can't get this Cat Stevens song out of your head (and now you can't, thanks to me), then maybe you have some "closeness issues" between you and your dad or son. I can't fix 'em, and in fact, I don't even want to try. What I do suggest is that you sit down and watch one of these movies. Maybe you pour yourself a drink and maybe you even have a little cry. Maybe not a three-hanky, two-pints-of-Ben-and-Jerry's cry, but a manly sort of cry. Let's call it a lump in the throat. And then you stuff all those feelings way deep down inside and don't let anyone see them.**

1. Missing
Jack Lemmon, Sissy Spacek (1982, PG, 122m)
This penetrating political drama features Lemmon as the driven father searching for his missing son in a politically volatile Latin American country.

2. Kramer vs. Kramer
Dustin Hoffman, Meryl Streep (1979, PG, 105m)
Hoffman and son Justin Henry find their way to a new, deeper relationship after Streep decides she has to go find herself in this Best Picture winner.

3. The Bicycle Thief
Lamberto Maggiorami, Enzo Staiola (1948, NR, 90m, DVD)
A poignant textbook example of Italian neo-realism about a father and son searching for the person who took their bicycle and consequently their livelihood.

4. Boyz N the Hood
Laurence Fishburne, Cuba Gooding Jr., Ice Cube (1991, R, 112m, DVD)
Fishburne plays "Furious Styles" (you gotta love that name). Furious is the father in the 'hood. This is about fathers and sons but mostly about what happens to sons in the absence of fathers. What happens is, they turn their neighborhoods into war zones. We learn, in the elegant prose of Furious, that, "Any fool with a dick can make a baby, but only a real man can raise his children."

5. The Great Santini
Robert Duvall, Blythe Danner (1980, PG, 118m)
Discipline-crazed Marine spends most of his time drilling his son a new asshole.

6. East of Eden
James Dean, Raymond Massey, Jo Van Fleet (1954, NR, 115m)
Albert Dekker is in this. He is most famous for dying of auto-erotic asphyxia, which is a practice wherein you hang yourself in order to come close to death, without actually killing yourself, for the purpose of sexual pleasure. He, apparently, went too far. But that's not why we're here. We're here to talk about Dean's feature film debut in this picture about two sons vying for the attention of their father in this outstanding screen version of a John Steinbeck novel.

7. A River Runs Through It
Brad Pitt, Tom Skeritt, Craig Sheffer (1992, PG, 123m)
A movie about fly fishing. It's good—I swear.

8. Da
Martin Sheen, Barnard Hughes (1988, PG, 102m)
Sheen's relationship with his father unfolds over a series of flashbacks triggered by his return to Ireland for his father's funeral.

9. Funny Bones
Oliver Platt, Jerry Lewis, Leslie Caron (1994, R, 128m)
I love this Jerry Lewis movie and I'm not even French. Platt stars as a struggling stand-up comic who lives in his successful father's shadow. It's a gem.

10. A Bronx Tale
Chazz Palminteri, Robert De Niro (1993, R, 122m, DVD)
Palminteri's first film as writer and star, and De Niro's first film as director resulted in this well-mounted screen version of Palminteri's one-man play about growing up in the Bronx torn between two role models: his bus driver father and the local mob boss.

WHEN TO WATCH
Father's Day, Third Sunday in June.

WHAT TO EAT
Something a father and son can prepare together, maybe a grilled cheese sandwich.

GREAT SPEECH
from *Kramer vs. Kramer* by Avery Corman (novel) Robert Benton

DUSTIN HOFFMAN as TED KRAMER
The only thing that's supposed to matter here is what's best for Billy...When Joanna said why shouldn't a woman have the same ambitions as a man, I suppose she's right. But by the same token what law is it that says a woman is a better parent simply by virtue of her sex? I guess I've had to think a lot about whatever it is that makes somebody a good parent: constancy, patience, understanding... love. Where is it written that a man has any less of those qualities than a woman? Billy has a home with me, I've tried to make it the best I could. It's not perfect. I'm not a perfect parent. I don't have enough patience. Sometimes I forget he's just a little kid...But I love him...More than anything in this world I love him.

Mothers and Daughters

WHEN YOU'RE FEELING EITHER MATERNAL OR WHATEVER THE WORD IS FOR FEELING LIKE A DAUGHTER

Mothers and daughters have a special bond. Not being either one, that is pure speculation on my part, of course. I have, however, walked down an aisle of greeting cards and have noticed that there are many cards addressed to mothers and daughters. So I do know one thing: mothers and daughters buy a lot of greeting cards for each other.

1. Terms of Endearment

Shirley MacLaine, Debra Winger (1983, PG, 132m)

A beautifully written and acted comedy/drama about the relationship of an irascible mother and independent daughter. This baby is stuffed with notable highlights and Jack Nicholson's "Nearly made a clean get-away" moment is but one.

2. Postcards from the Edge

Meryl Streep, Shirley MacLaine (1990, R, 101m)

A hilarious Carrie Fisher scribed comedy, based on her book of the same name, about her relationship with her mother, Debbie Reynolds. I can't wait to see Carrie's take on her father, Eddie Fisher, whose salacious autobiography made Carrie claim, "I'm going to have my DNA fumigated."

3. Now, Voyager

Bette Davis, Claude Rains (1942, NR, 117m)

Here's the short version: spinster finally asserts her independence apart from her mother with the help of her shrink with whom she has a very famous scene in which two cigarettes are lighted at a time.

4. Secrets and Lies

Brenda Blethyn, Marianne Jean-Baptiste (1995, R, 142m)

A middle class black woman discovers her birth mother is a needy working class white woman with really embarrassing social graces. Director Mike Leigh uses improv with his actors over a long rehearsal time and the effort pays off with characters and performances that really resonate.

5. One True Thing

Meryl Streep, Renée Zewelleger (1998, PG-13, 128m, DVD)

Like *Terms of Endearment*, this has a cancer theme. Cancer is big between mothers and daughters. I guess not so much between fathers and sons. If a man gets cancer he just "sucks it up" and doesn't talk much and there's not a movie in that.

6. Rambling Rose

Laura Dern, Diane Ladd (1991, R, 115m, DVD)

Dern and Ladd become the first mother-daughter team to be nominated for Oscars® for the same movie. Dern, as Rose, is an unabashed sexual fireball unnerving everyone around her in depression-era small town America.

7. Gypsy
Rosalind Russell, Natalie Wood (1962, NR, 144m);
Bette Midler, Cynhtia Gibb (1993, NR, 150m)
I'll give you your choice on this one: there's the Bette Midler version or the Rosalind Russell version. Both tell the story of Mama Rose, who works her tail off for her little darling daughter: stripper Gypsy Rose Lee. If my mom was always belting out a tune at the top of her lungs, I don't imagine I'd be too well-adjusted either.

8. The Joy Luck Club
Tamlyn Tomita, Lauren Tom (1993, R, 136m)
Four mothers born in China, four daughters born in America. That's a lot of characters and a lot of locations. It's a terrific cross-cultural mural.

9. The Mirror Has Two Faces
Barbra Streisand, Jeff Bridges, Lauren Bacall (1996, PG-13, 127m)
Streisand gets a make-over, but Bacall doesn't get an Oscar® (and boy is she surprised).

10. Grey Gardens
Edith B. Beale, Jr., Edith Bouvier Beale (1975, NR, 94m)
Fascinating, if inappropriately voyeuristic, documentary about a mother and daughter who happen to be the aunt and cousin of Jackie O. They also happen to be completely crazy. They prance around as their mansion and their relationship rot around them.

WHEN TO WATCH
Second Sunday in May, Mother's Day.

WHAT TO EAT
Something fancy like you ladies like to make. How about brunch featuring a nice crème fraîche and caviar frittata with a champagne reduction?

GREAT DIALOGUE
from *Terms of Endearment* by James L. Brooks, Larry McMurty (novel)

SHIRLEY MACLAINE as AURORA GREENWAY
You wouldn't want me to be silent about something that's for your own good, even if it might hurt a little?

DEBRA WINGER as EMMA HORTON
Yes, Mom, I certainly would.

Growing Up Foreign

WHEN YOU'RE FEELING LIKE YOU WANT TO KNOW ABOUT CHILDHOOD IN OTHER LANDS

People in foreign countries grow up too. If it's France, they just do it while drinking wine. Here's how some of the world's greatest filmmakers have dealt with the universal "coming-of-age" theme.

1. The 400 Blows
Jean-Pierre Léand, Claire Maurice (1959, NR, 97m, DVD)
Seminal figure of the French New Wave (*nouvelle vogue*) François Truffaut (you know, the guy from *Close Encounters*) directed this, his first film, a poignant story about a young Parisian boy who runs away when no one seems to care about his fate.

2. My Life as a Dog
Anton Glanzélius, Leif Ericson (1985, NR, 101m, DVD)
This charming Swedish film finds a ten-year-old boy shipped out to the country where he meets a village of oddballs.

3. Vigil
Penelope Stewart, Bill Kerr, Fiona Kay (1984, NR, 90m)
Hauntingly photographed and beautifully told story about a young farm girl trying to come to terms with life after the untimely death of her father.

4. Zero for Conduct
Jean Daste, Robert Le Flon (1933, NR, 49m)
One of Truffaut's idols was Jean Vigo, who died at twenty-nine after making this short film about the jubilant rebellion of the students in a boys' school.

5. Au Revoir les Enfants
Gaspard Manesse, Raphael Fejtö (1987, PG, 104m)
Louis Malle's heartbreaking World War II story of Jewish students hiding out in a boarding school who are found out by the Nazis.

6. Fanny and Alexander
Pernilla Allwin, Bertil Guve (1983, R, 197m)
This autobiographical tale, about two kids growing up in Sweden at the turn-of-the-century, is a three hour epic masterpiece from Sweden's greatest director, Ingmar Bergman.

7. I Vitelloni
Alberto Sordi, Franco Fabrizi, Leopoldo Trieste (1953, NR, 104m)
Fellini's take on coming-of-age deals with five young men, in a small Italian town, filled with visions of their own grand futures.

8. Jules and Jim
Jeanne Moreau, Oskar Warner, Henri Serre (1962, NR, 104m)
Ah, young love. Oops, young love triangle. Young love and love triangle mature over the years.

9. My Name Is Ivan
Nikolai Burlyayeu, Valentin Zubkov (1962, NR, 84m)
Nazi's are good for coming-of-age stories because they make you grow up fast, especially when they kill your parents as they do to poor Ivan's in Russian master Andrei Tarkovsky's first film.

10. Europa Europa
Marco Hofschneider, Klaus Abramowsky, Michele Gleizer (1991, R, 115m)
Agnieszka Holland's horrific and humorous adaptation of Solomon Perel's autobiography in which a teenager, in order to escape the horrors of World War II, poses as alternately a Communist and a Nazi.

SEE ALSO:
42 Up ("Middle Age Crazy")

WHEN TO WATCH
October 24. United Nations Day.

WHAT TO EAT
Vin et fromage.

GREAT LINE
from *The 400 Blows* by François Truffaut

> *"He spends hours at the movies ruining his eyes."*
> —CLAIRE MAURIER as ANTOINE DOINEL'S MOTHER,
> complaining about him to a judge.

Pregnant Cinema

WHEN YOU'RE FEELING PREGNANT

You've already bought the book every knocked-up woman carries around like a Bible, *What to Expect When You're Expecting*. But you can't read that all of the time, can you? So while you're getting some much needed bedrest, let me recommend the following movies. In other words, this list lets you know: "What to expect when you're watching movies about expecting."

1. The Opposite of Sex
Christina Ricci, Martin Donovan, Lisa Kudrow (1998, R, 105m, DVD)
When very pregnant Dee Dee downs a Long Island iced tea, you know this is not your typical politically correct, feel-good, take-care-of-yourself, nutty-crunchy '90s movie. Of course, if it took you that long into the movie to figure that out, then pregnancy has really slowed you down.

2. Citizen Ruth
Laura Dern, Swoosie Kurtz, Mary Kay Place (1996, R, 104m)
Dern is nothing short of brilliant in this sharp black comedy about a dim-witted, knocked-up, homeless aerosol-junkie who is used as a pawn by the pro and con factions in the abortion debate.

3. The Snapper
Tina Kellegher, Colm Meaney (1993, R, 95m)
Likable British comedy based on the book that was a kind of sequel to *The Commitments*. This is the story of a pregnant girl who refuses to divulge the name of the baby's father even to her (at times) supportive father.

4. Rosemary's Baby
Mia Farrow, John Cassavetes, Ruth Gordon (1968, R, 134m)
Every pregnant woman's worst nightmare is that her child will grow up to be an idiot, a criminal, a social outcast or go into telemarketing—but any of those are way better than the kid turning out to be the spawn of Satan.

5. Father's Little Dividend
Elizabeth Taylor, Spencer Tracy (1951, NR, 82m)
Appealing warm-hearted sequel to the original *Father of the Bride*.

6. Look Who's Talking
Kirstie Alley, John Travolta (1989, PG-13, 90m, DVD)
A cutesy talking baby movie that some can stomach more easily than others. A Lamaze instructor once told me that this is the most popular video for expectant or new parents to watch while in the hospital having a baby.

7. Immediate Family
Glenn Close, James Woods, Mary Stuart Masterson (1989, PG-13, 112m)
A wealthy couple buy the baby of a pregnant teenager.

8. Home Fries
Drew Barrymore, Luke Wilson (1998, PG-13, 94m, DVD)
Black comedy with white trash characters, featuring that cute little Barrymore all knocked up and oh-so-confused.

9. The Baby Dance
Laura Dern, Stockard Channing (1998, NR, 95m)
This made-for-cable Showtime movie about a well-to-do middle aged couple trying to buy the baby of the brilliantly white trash Dern (again!), features superb writing and acting with a twist that raises compelling issues. Warning: it is a real downer, so if you are skittish or nervous about your impending pregnancy, delivery or adoption, you might want to avoid this one until your kid is safe. Like maybe until he's about eighteen and on his own.

10. For Keeps
Molly Ringwald, Randall Batinkoff, Kenneth Mars (1988, PG-13, 98m)
Ringwald is a pregnant teenager who decides that she and her boyfriend are going to make a go at raising a family on their fast food wages. That'll work.

SEE ALSO:
The Miracle of Morgan's Creek ("Satire in Style: Films of Preston Sturges")
Fargo ("Independent Spirit: Films of Steve Buscemi")
Parenthood ("Movies to Watch on Thanksgiving")
She's Having a Baby ("Six Degrees of Kevin Bacon")
The Object of My Affection ("Love Conquers All")

 WHEN TO WATCH
While you're going into labor. You might try the first Monday in September, which is Labor Day.

 WHAT TO EAT
Ice chips.

 GREAT LINE
from *The Opposite of Sex* by Don Roos

"I don't have a heart of gold and I don't grow one later, OK? But relax, there's other people a lot nicer coming up—we call them losers."
—CHRISTINA RICCI as DEE DEE TRUITT

FEELING TEEN SPIRIT

If you don't like movies made for a teenage audience, you better get used to it, because Hollywood has a fixation on this demographic. Since the perception is that teens rule at the box office, more and more movies geared to what teens like or what middle-aged studio execs *think* they like are going to get made. Hollywood also seems to be obsessed with remakes, so I'm thinking maybe the formula for a megahit today is to re-make classic movies of yesterday, only gear them to teens. I offer the following examples. Oh, and by the way, if any of these actually get made, I expect my cut of the action:

GONE WITH THE WIN
Basketball rivalry between North and South High schools and a romance between South High cheerleader Scarlett and drop-out Rhett.

THE SILENCE OF THE DORMS
Teen slasher movie about a buxom seventeen-year-old FBI intern who cracks the FBI's toughest case about a serial killer who preys on beautiful co-eds.

ALL ABOUT CAITLIN
Caitlin wants more than anything to be captain of the cheerleading squad, and she doesn't care who's eyes she has to claw out to get there.

LAWRENCE OF ARCADIA HIGH
Enemy gang turf is invaded by heroic high school warrior.

KING DONG
MTV-produced sex comedy about a well-endowed new kid in school who does the nasty with a lot of girls to the sound of some really hot boy bands.

GUESS WHO'S COMING TO THE DINER
Teenage boy brings home his new date to meet his parents and, surprise! She's not only black...she's a he.

IT'S A WONDERFUL SLICE OF LIFE
Teen slasher movie in which a serial killer meets an angel who shows him what his life would be like if he weren't such a bloodthirsty butcher.

REALLY HIGH NOON
'70s drug comedy set in a high school.

THE GRADES OF WRATH
High school drop-out has to get a job in a fast-food joint because of his poor study habits.

EASY MOUNTAIN BIKE RIDER
Extreme sports jock goes on a road trip and meets a lot of girls.

ANNIE HALL PASS
Hall monitor Annie attends a posh boarding school and has a relationship with a neurotic Jewish teacher's aide.

Zit Flicks

WHEN YOU'RE FEELING LIKE YOU'RE GOING THROUGH PUBERTY

These are troubled times: awkward, anxious, embarrassing and cruel and if you're going through puberty right now, I can only say to you: I'm glad it's you and not me. These movies will help you navigate this "Bridge Over Troubled Waters" (which, by the way, was the even-then dated "theme" for my junior high school graduation ceremony) by letting you know that there are others who are going through many of the same issues you're facing right now. And if you're not a teenager, you can just watch these and laugh at those problems that you no longer have to face—and that's always the most fun. (Remember, as we learned in Woody Allen's *Crimes and Misdemeanors*: "comedy = tragedy + time.")

1. Welcome to the Dollhouse
Heather Matarazzo, Matthew Faber (1995, R, 87m)
You've got to love Dawn Wiener. She's the biggest dork to hit junior high since...well, since you.

2. Risky Business
Tom Cruise, Rebecca De Mornay (1983, R, 99m, DVD)
Not a lot of teen angst from Cruise, who occupies the polar opposite of the social spectrum from Dawn Wiener, but you do get a funny and stylish comedy with some insights into the coming-of-age experience.

3. Fast Times at Ridgemont High
Jennifer Jason Leigh, Phoebe Cates (1982, R, 91m)
This classic high school comedy features one of Sean Penn's best performances as substance-ingesting surfer Jeff Spicoli. ("People on 'ludes should not drive.")

4. The Summer of '42
Jennifer O'Neill, Gary Grimes (1971, R, 102m)
Nostalgic World War II-era story about a young guy trying to get into O'Neill's panties. In case you're wondering what Jennifer has been doing the last couple decades, she's been very busy—she's been married nine times!

5. American Graffiti
Richard Dreyfuss, Ron Howard (1973, PG, 112m, DVD)
George Lucas' view of growing up in Modesto, California in 1962, which was a long time ago in a town far, far away.

6. River's Edge
Keanu Reeves, Dennis Hopper (1987, R, 99m)
A chilling tale of a group of apathetic teens who discover one of their friends is a murderer and has the corpse to prove it—he's such a show-off. Based on a real-life incident, but I'm sure no one in real life is as freaky as Crispen Glover is in this.

7. Lucas

Corey Haim, Winona Ryder (1986, PG-13, 100m)

I know it isn't saying much to say that this is the best film Haim has ever starred in (considering the competition is *License to Drive*), but this is a really well-written teenage love story that is worth seeking out.

8. Dazed and Confused

Jason London, Joey Lauren Adams (1993, R, 97m, DVD)

What *American Graffiti* is to the '60s and *Fast Times* is to the '80s, this is to the '70s.

9. Ferris Bueller's Day Off

Matthew Broderick, Jennifer Grey (1986, PG-13, 103m)

The timeless classic about slacking-off which Dan Quayle once called his favorite film.

10. Election

Reese Witherspoon, Matthew Broderick (1999, R, 105m)

Alexander Payne, writer and director of *Citizen Ruth*, again successfully mines for black comedy in this funny story of a good teacher gone bad who tries to rig a high school election.

SEE ALSO:
Heathers ("Hip Flicks")
Clueless ("So Five Minutes Ago: Movies of the '90s")
Say Anything ("Before They Were Stars")

WHEN TO WATCH
June 21. The first day of Summer.

WHAT TO EAT
Order out for a pizza. But don't count on Domino's arriving in thirty minutes any more. Here's the official company reason for changing the policy that had led to many car accidents: "To ensure the safety of our drivers, we replaced the thirty minute guarantee with the Total Satisfaction Guarantee. If you are not completely satisfied with your Domino's Pizza® product, or service, for any reason, we'll make it right or refund your money. Guaranteed."

GREAT LINE
from *Fast Times at Ridgemont High* by Cameron Crowe

"All I need are some tasty waves, a cool buzz and I'm fine."
—SEAN PENN as JEFF SPICOLI

Book Reports Made Easy

WHEN YOU'RE FEELING LIKE READING A BOOK...
BUT WOULD RATHER WATCH A MOVIE

People always say books are better than movies. I say they're full of crap, and to prove it, here is a list of fourteen movies that are better than the books on which they are based. And there are plenty more. One great thing about this list: say you're in high school and you need to do a book report, just rent one of these and save yourself all that boring reading time. And it's even faster than reading the Cliff Notes.

1. The Silence of the Lambs
Jodie Foster, Anthony Hopkins (1991, R, 118m, DVD)
The greatest horror movie ever made with Hollywood's most memorable villain (with apologies to Darth Vadar).

2. The Shawshank Redemption
Morgan Freeman, Tim Robbins (1994, R, 142m, DVD)
Based on a Stephen King short story, the movie, which is headed for classic status, improves upon the original writing.

3. Drugstore Cowboy
Matt Dillon, Kelly Lynch (1989, R, 100m)
Based on an unpublished novel, this is a gritty, realistic and completely excellent portrayal by Dillon as the leader of a band of junkies who prowl the streets looking for liquor stores to knock over to feed their habits.

4. Das Boot
Jürgen Prochnow, Klaus Wennemann (1981, R, 210m)
A tense trip aboard a German U-boat as it sinks to the bottom of the ocean. Your ears almost pop!

5. Psycho
Anthony Perkins, Janet Leigh (1960, NR, 109m, DVD)
This Hitchcock classic kept Leigh, in real life, out of the shower for decades.

6. The Bridges of Madison County
Clint Eastwood, Meryl Streep (1995, PG-13, 135m, DVD)
The fact that this schmaltzy book was made into an excellent movie is a small miracle.

7. The Wizard of Oz
Judy Garland, Ron Bolger, Bert Lahr (1939, NR, 101m, DVD)
C'mon, who would rather read *The Wizard of Oz* than watch the movie?

8. Educating Rita
Michael Caine, Julie Walters (1983, PG, 110m)
This one is based on a play and not a book, but I've included it because it is about reading books and they discuss so many books in this that you'll have enough material for a dozen book reports.

9. Wages of Fear
Yves Montand, Charles Vanel (1953, NR, 141m, DVD)
This lassic French masterpiece of suspense was remade in English as *Sorcerer*.

10. To Live
Gong Li, Ge You (1994, NR, 130m)
A sweeping Chinese epic spanning the lives of a couple as they transition from the 1940s into a life of Communist oppression. OK, I didn't read the book "Lifetimes" on which this is based, but I'm sure it's not more beautiful to look at—and with a book, you don't get the stunning Li.

SEE ALSO:
Raging Bull ("Real Sports Movies")
The Graduate ("Classic Comedies")
Jaws ("Crowd Pleaser: Films of Steven Spielberg")
2001: A Space Odyssey ("The Future Looks Weird")

WHEN TO WATCH
The first week in May: National Teachers' Week.

WHAT TO EAT
May I recommend something from the cafeteria, like a carton of juice, meatloaf surprise and some cubed Jell-O™?

GREAT LINE
from *The Silence of the Lambs* by Thomas Harris (novel) and Ted Tally

"A census taker once tried to test me - I ate his liver with some fava beans and a nice Chianti."
—ANTHONY HOPKINS as DR. HANNIBAL LECTER

It Rocks!

WHEN YOU'RE FEELING LIKE ROCKIN'

These movies rock!

1. *This is Spinal Tap*
Rob Reiner, Christopher Guest (1984, R, 82m, DVD)
This is why the Mockumentary was invented. The funniest rock 'n' roll movie ever.

2. *A Hard Day's Night*
The Beatles, Wilfred Brambell, Norman Rossington (1964, NR, 90m, DVD)
This high-spirited romp, directed by Richard Lester about a "day in the life" of The Beatles presaged MTV by nearly a couple decades.

3. *Woodstock*
Documentary, directed by Michael Wadleigh (1970, R, 180m, DVD)
This documentary really captures the scene and makes great use of flashy multiple images. Joan Baez, Joe Cocker; Crosby, Stills and Nash; Jefferson Airplane, Jimi Hendrix, Janis Joplin, Sly and the Family Stone, Santana, The Who and many more!

4. *William Shakespeare's Romeo + Juliet*
Claire Danes, Leonardo DiCaprio (1996, PG-13, 120m)
A very stylish and entertaining MTV style take on Shakespeare turns the tale of star-crossed lovers into a contemporary music video.

5. *The Last Waltz*
(1978, PG, 117m)
This documentary, directed by Martin Scorsese, who worked as an editor on Woodstock, graduates to director on this film of The Band's final concert.

6. *Jailhouse Rock*
Elvis Presley, Judy Tyler, Vaughn Taylor (1957, G, 96m, DVD)
Elvis is in the big house in the best of his many musicals.

7. *Quadrophenia*
Sting, Phil Daniels (1979, R, 115m)
The Who's rock opera about a teenager growing up in the turbulent '60s.

8. *Tommy*
The Who, Elton John, Tina Turner (1975, PG, 108m)
Demented Director Ken Russell's take on another Who rock opera has some interesting results—like Ann-Margret rolling around in beans spewing from a television set. But hey, it's only rock 'n' roll and I like it.

9. The Decline of Western Civilization

Documentary, directed by Penelope Spheeris (1981, NR, 100m)

Spheeris' first film delves into the Los Angeles punk scene at the end of the '70s. It's awesome, especially when Los Angeles darlings, X, are on the screen. Spheeris would go on to direct not only two sequels to this documentary chronicling the evolution of rock 'n' roll, but also such mainstream fare as *The Beverly Hillbillies* and *Wayne's World* (proving she's now working for The Man).

10. Rock 'n' Roll High School

The Ramones, P.J. Soles, Vincent Van Patten (1979, PG, 94m, DVD)

Lots of Ramones music and The Ramones themselves in this rebellious, rollicking high school comedy. It's a total blast!

SEE ALSO:
Sid and Nancy ("They Sing, They Have Problems")
The Doors ("They Sing, They Have Problems")
Purple Rain ("They Sing, They Have Problems")

WHEN TO WATCH
The date of the annual induction of new rockers into the Rock and Roll Hall of Fame. Of course, since it's rock 'n' roll you can never be sure whether this event is going to take place in January or maybe May. In 1999 the induction was on March 15.

WHAT TO EAT
Some of those *Tommy* baked beans.

GREAT DIALOGUE
from *This is Spinal Tap* by Christopher Guest, Michael McKean, Rob Reiner and Harry Shearer

CHRISTOPHER GUEST as NIGEL TUFNEL
The numbers all go to eleven. Look, right across the board, eleven, eleven, eleven and...

ROB REINER as MARTY DiBERGI
Oh, I see. And most amps go up to ten?

NIGEL
Exactly.

MARTY
Does that mean it's louder? Is it any louder?

(cont'd)

(cont'd)

NIGEL

*Well, it's one louder, isn't it? It's not ten. You see, most
blokes, you know, will be playing at ten. You're on ten here,
all the way up, all the way up, all the way up, you're on ten
on your guitar. Where can you go from there? Where?*

MARTY

I don't know.

NIGEL

*Nowhere. Exactly. What we do is, if we need that extra push
over the cliff, you know what we do?*

MARTY

Put it up to eleven.

NIGEL

Eleven. Exactly. One louder.

MARTY

*Why don't you just make ten louder and make ten be the top
number and make that a little louder?*

NIGEL

[Pause] These go to eleven.

FEELING YOUR AGE

A MESSAGE TO GENERATION X:
In case you're not aware, there's an entire generation of adults out there in their thirties who, like me, waited through the 1980s for our turn in the pop culture spotlight. We were in our twenties and watched as the Thirty-somethings/Baby Boomers/ Yuppies had their turn in the media glare. Then came the '90s and it seemed we had arrived. Finally, it was our turn, right? Wrong. They skipped us entirely and turned their attention to you..."Generation X." You think *you're* lost, *we* didn't even get a letter! Baby Busters, Lost Generation, Gen. X, Twenty-Somethings. You've got your pick of nicknames and we've got zip.

Bill and Hillary are Boomers...the Grunge Rockers are Xer's. But what about those of us stuck somewhere between MTV and VH1? Haven't we done anything interesting enough to merit a cute nickname?

Generation X, my eye! What did you ever come up with? We were wearing platform shoes in high school, so don't try that one. And if you think you invented aimlessness and underemployment, we were doing that in the '80s while all those Baby Boomers were driving off to their power lunches in convertible Beemers. "Downward mobility"? We invented it, so stick that in your floppy disc and spin it!

It's not that we have nothing to offer the world. We're a generation of substance, not to mention style. I remember the girls in their Farrah Fawcett hairdos, saddle seat powder blue Ditto jeans (Feel the Fit), tube tops, wavy soled Famolare shoes and glossy Bonne Bell Lipsmacker lips. Kinda young, kinda now...Charlie! Guys in our Angel's Flights and oh-so-shiny Quiana knit shirts opened to reveal the perfect strand of puka shells. We had Earth shoes, toe socks, and mood rings, too, and we didn't just stand around all day banging our Klick-Klacks together, no siree. We had meaningful hobbies like découpage, macramé and terrariums.

But enough about our past. Today, we're just about old enough to be eligible for the Presidency—the last legal age barrier between here and social security. In our mid-thirties, we're around the age Jesus was when he died. Now *that's* pressure. But since we can't turn water into wine, we have to work for a living.

We're greedy like the Boomers and lazy like you Xers (that's right, *lazy*), so you can just imagine the kind of conflicted angst we live with every day. But who *are* we really? While *Newsweek* and *Time* and every other magazine under the sun are exploring your generation, we're stuck at Starbucks having an identity crisis over a half-caf Venti latte.

Maybe you think you're superior because you're the children of the information age—growing up faxing, beeping, e-mailing, CD-ROMing, interfacing and downloading. Don't get me wrong, I embrace the new technologies. Bring on the Information Superhighway, baby, yeah! But those of us who grew up in the '60s weren't exactly void of technology either. We had inter-active TV and Winkie Dink's rub-on screen, and guess what? "We always had a lot of fun together."

So here's the bottom line: you probably think the world is yours, but don't be so smug, Gen X, because these glory days won't last forever. The minute you hit thirty, they'll drop you like yesterday's nose ring. Didn't you ever see *Logan's Run*? Watch it and learn.

Groovy Flicks: Movies of the '60s

WHEN YOU'RE FEELING VERY 1960s

Hey, all you hep cats and groovy chicks, these movies are video-delic. Invite the gang over to your pad, man. Turn on that hi-fi, pop on one of these flicks, get down and get funky. In other words: turn on, tune in and drop out.

1. Easy Rider
Dennis Hopper, Jack Nicholson (1969, R, 94m)
If you're tired of being hassled by The Man, then maybe you need a hit of this anti-establishment classic.

2. Blow-Up
David Hemmings, Vanessa Redgrave, Sarah Miles (1966, NR, 111m)
Italian Director Michelangelo Antonioni's hip sixties flick about a photographer who believes he has accidentally taken a picture of a crime in progress. Reworked by Brian De Palma as *Blow Out,* in which movie sound engineer John Travolta may have accidentally recorded a crime in progress.

3. The Thomas Crown Affair
Faye Dunaway, Steve McQueen (1968, R, 102m, DVD)
The clever widescreen visuals in this picture contribute to the pleasure of watching this engaging bank heist movie and romance.

4. Hair
Treat Williams, Beverly D'Angelo (1979, PG, 122m)
The ultimate exuberant hippie musical celebrating the '60s as the Age of Aquarius. Particularly fun to watch when the moon is in the seventh house and Jupiter aligns with Mars.

5. Barbarella
Jane Fonda, John Phillip Law, David Hemmings (1968, PG, 98m)
A camp classic. Yes, the band Duran Duran named themselves after this flick's villain.

6. Our Man Flint
James Coburn, Lee J. Cobb (1966, NR, 107m)
Hip spoof of James Bond films.

7. Alice's Restaurant
Arlo Guthrie, Patricia Quinn, Pete Seeger (1969, PG, 111m)
Guthrie's song made into a counterculture treatise.

8. The President's Analyst

James Coburn, Godfrey Cambridge (1967, NR, 104)

We've had a recent President or two who could use a good analyst. This out-there tale in which Coburn plays the president's shrink is a clever conspiratorial comedy that deserves to be seen.

9. The Wild Angels

Peter Fonda, Nancy Sinatra (1966, PG, 124m)

Cool leather-clad motorcycle dude Fonda is at it again. This time he hooks up with "These Boots Are Made for Walkin'" diva Sinatra in a low-budget '60s camp classic.

10. Austin Powers, International Man of Mystery

Mike Myers, Elizabeth Hurley (1997, PG-13, 88m, DVD)

Although made in the 1990s, this comedy about a swinging '60s super spy is shagadelic, baby!

SEE ALSO:
Medium Cool ("Vidiots")
The Party ("Cocktail Cinema")

 WHEN TO WATCH
May 17. Aging hippie Dennis Hopper's birthday (1936).

 WHAT TO EAT
Tofu is always groovy. What you lace it with is your business.

 GREAT LINE
from *Our Man Flint* by Hal Fimburg, Ben Starr

LEE J. COBB as CRAMDEN
You have your own code?

JAMES COBURN as DEREK FLINT
I know it already. It's a mathematical progression, 40-24-36.

A Bad Hair Decade: Movies of the '70s

WHEN YOU'RE FEELING VERY 1970s

There is a contingent of critics out there who think the '70s were the Golden Age of movie-making. With the emergence of Coppola and Scorsese, and the free-thought spirit of the decade, artistic expression in cinema reached a kind of zenith. Of course, you'd never know that from watching some of these movies on this list. But if you're having a '70s party and you want to turn everyone's mood ring bright blue, slap one of these into the Beta player.

1. Nashville
Keith Carradine, Lily Tomlin, Shelley Duvall (1975, R, 159m)
Robert Altman's *chef d'oeuvre* is a tapestry of American characters as seen through the microcosm of the country music scene.

2. Shampoo
Warren Beatty, Julie Christie (1975, R, 112m)
Beatty co-wrote (with Robert Towne) this film in which he plays a bad boy who gets laid a lot.

3. Lenny
Dustin Hoffman, Valerie Perrine (1974, R, 111m)
Brilliant black and white biopic of controversial-in-his-day comedian Lenny Bruce. More provocative than funny—but then, so was Lenny Bruce.

4. Five Easy Pieces
Jack Nicholson, Karen Black (1970, R, 98m)
There is more here than the chicken salad scene. This is an in-depth portrayal of Nicholson as a gifted-pianist-who-chucks-it-all-and-becomes-an-oil-worker, testing the theory that "you can never go home again."

5. The China Syndrome
Jane Fonda, Jack Lemmon, Michael Douglas (1979, PG, 123m, DVD)
Few things were more scary in the '70s than the threat of a nuclear incident. Now we have boring stuff to worry about, like the threat of biochemical terrorism.

6. Carnal Knowledge
Jack Nicholson, Art Garfunkel (1971, R, 96m)
Nicholson and Garfunkel are college roommates who plow through a series of women.

7. Boogie Nights
Julianne Moore, Mark Wahlberg (1997, R, 155m, DVD)
Made in 1997, this remarkable film seemingly faithfully chronicles the porn industry boom in Los Angeles' San Fernando Valley in the '70s.

8. Bob & Carol & Ted & Alice
Natalie Wood, Robert Culp, Elliott Gould (1969, R, 104m)
Sex, drugs and Dyan Cannon! It's the eve of the '70s and the Sexual Revolution has begun, baby!

9. The Towering Inferno
Steve McQueen, Paul Newman, Faye Dunaway (1974, PG, 165m, DVD)
The '70s were the Golden Age of the disaster movies and this one is the best of the disastrous bunch.

10. The Last of Sheila
James Coburn, Joan Hackett, Raquel Welch (1973, PG, 119m)
The '70s dream cast, and again...Dyan Cannon! This is a very clever murder mystery that you are sure to enjoy if you are a fan of the whodunit genre.

SEE ALSO:
Saturday Night Fever ("Dancers")
Love Story ("Pity Party: The Tear-jerkers")

WHEN TO WATCH
January 4. Loopy and lovely Dyan Cannon's birthday (1937).

WHAT TO EAT
The quintessential '70s party meal is fondue. Wash it down with a Tab or a Fresca.

GREAT DIALOGUE
from *Five Easy Pieces* by Carol Eastman, Joyce Rafelson (story), Bob Rafelson (story)

> JACK NICHOLSON as BOBBY DUPEAU
> *I'd like an omelet, plain, and a chicken salad sandwich on wheat toast, no mayonnaise, no butter, no lettuce. And a cup of coffee.*
>
> LORNA THAYER as the WAITRESS
> *A #2, chicken salad sand. Hold the butter, the lettuce, the mayonnaise, and a cup of coffee. Anything else?*
>
> BOBBY
> *Yeah, now all you have to do is hold the chicken, bring me the toast, give me a check for the chicken salad sandwich, and you haven't broken any rules.*
>
> WAITRESS
> *You want me to hold the chicken, huh?*
>
> BOBBY
> *I want you to hold it between your knees.*

Me Movies:
Movies of the '80s

WHEN YOU'RE FEELING VERY 1980s

Here are some movies for the "Me Generation." Those who got left behind at the end of the '80s like an old coke spoon, replaced by the pluckier, more interesting, newer, Pepsi Generation. It's precarious to be on top, like being Hef's favorite: you know your shelf life is limited, so enjoy it while you can. Here are some very '80s movies showing those '80s characters living it up while they can. Play these movies at your nostalgic '80s party between your favorite Terence Trent d'Arby videos.

1. Desperately Seeking Susan
Madonna, Rosanna Arquette (1985, PG-13, 104m)
Madonna *is* the '80s.

2. Wall Street
Michael Douglas, Charlie Sheen (1987, R, 126m)
The money-obsessed '80s (because, in the '90s, we were on a spiritual plane so far above all that) are summed up well in this paean to greed.

3. Down and Out in Beverly Hills
Bette Midler, Nick Nolte (1986, R, 103m)
Upscale comedy remade from the French film *Bodu Saved from Drowning*.

4. Valley Girl
Nicolas Cage, Deborah Foreman (1983, R, 95m)
If you don't like this movie, then, as Cage says in the film, "Well fuck you, for sure, like totally!"

5. Diva
Frederic Andrei, Rolma Bertin (1982, R, 123m)
The '80s were so new wave. This is an artsy French film that shows you what that looks like.

6. St. Elmo's Fire
Rob Lowe, Demi Moore, Andrew McCarthy, Ally Sheedy (1985, R, 110m)
The Brat-Pack classic. The neon Billy Idol on the wall of Demi Moore's loft apartment says everything there is to say about the '80s.

7. The Big Chill
Glenn Close, William Hurt, Jeff Goldblum (1983, R, 108m, DVD)
Baby Boomer nostalgia piece. '80s characters sit around and reminisce about the '60s while a lot of old songs play on the soundtrack.

8. Bill and Ted's Excellent Adventure
Keanu Reeves, Alex Winter (1989, PG, 105m)
This film took the slot I had reserved for *Breakin' 2 - Electric Boogaloo* which couldn't have been made at any time other than the '80s. If you don't believe me, just try to set up a meeting to pitch the remake. But I have to admit *Electric Bugaloo* doesn't have much going for it other than the title. *Bill and Ted*, on the other hand, is breezy fun.

9. Grand Canyon
Danny Glover, Steve Martin (1991, R, 134m)
Takes itself so very seriously—perfect for the '80s.

10. Mr. Mom
Michael Keaton, Teri Garr (1983, PG, 92m)
Parental gender role-reversal was a fresh new thing in 1983.

SEE ALSO:
Sid and Nancy ("They Sing, They Have Problems")
Heathers ("Hip Flicks")

WHEN TO WATCH
August 16. Middle-aged material mom Madonna's birthday (1958).

WHAT TO EAT
A wheel of brie, endive salad, some Dom Perignon and tiramisu for dessert.

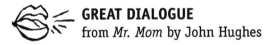

GREAT DIALOGUE
from *Mr. Mom* by John Hughes

      MICHAEL KEATON as JACK BUTLER
Wanna beer?

      MARTIN MULL as RON RICHARDSON
It's seven o'clock in the morning.

      JACK
Scotch?

So Five Minutes Ago: Movies of the '90s

WHEN YOU'RE FEELING VERY 1990s

If you are ready to turn the 1990s into a nostalgia movement, I'm with ya. If you don't think the '90s are already passé, I've got three words for you: Achy. Breaky. Heart. These movies are so '90s, I'm sure they will age deliciously—so let's be the first to crack open that '90s time capsule and revel in our history.

1. Primary Colors
Kathy Bates, Emma Thompson, John Travolta (1998, R, 138m, DVD)
What are the '90s if not the Clinton years? This bull's eye depiction of the beloved and despised forty-second President of the United States is wickedly funny and provocative. Based on the book by Anonymous. Tune in for some bravura performances.

2. Contact
Jodie Foster, Matthew McConaughey (1997, PG, 150m, DVD)
Spirituality and technology were very hot topics in the '90s. This film fuses those two themes as Foster first searches for signs of extra-terrestrial life via radio waves and then she decides to go and check it out in person. A terrific journey with top-notch production values.

3. The People vs. Larry Flynt
Woody Harrelson, Courtney Love (1996, R, 130m, DVD)
Larry Flynt, porn-peddler and civil rights crusader, came into his own in the '90s and here's how he got there.

4. Metropolitan
Carolyn Farina, Edward Clements, Taylor Nichols (1990, PG-13, 98m)
A chatty group of prep school debs and preps offer some funny insights into the upper echelons of Manhattan society once you get used to the stilted way in which they speak.

5. Longtime Companion
Campbell Scott, Patrick Cassidy (1990, R, 100m)
You can't talk about the '90s without talking about AIDS, and this is the definitive AIDS movie.

6. The New Age
Judy Davis, Peter Weller (1994, R, 106m)
A downwardly mobile Los Angeles couple in the age of down-sizing. Some pointed topical humor.

7. Clueless

Alicia Silverstone, Paul Rudd (1995, PG-13, 113m)

Based on Jane Austin's *Emma*, this movie became dated about its second week in release. Good movie, lots of fun and it captures a certain 1995-ness.

8. Jurassic Park

Sam Neill, Laura Dern, Richard Attenborough, Jeff Goldblum (1993, PG-13, 127m, DVD)

People are sure to marvel at how these special effects turned the movie world upside down. I bet you can't wait 'til your kids see this movie and ask you, "Is that what passed for special effects in the olden days?"

9. Two Days in the Valley

Danny Aiello, Jeff Daniels, Charlize Theron (1996, R, 105m, DVD)

I just realized there is a film set in the San Fernando Valley to define any recent era. The *Boogie Nights* '70s, the *Valley Girl* '80s and now this film, which is a good example of a very '90s genre: the Tarantino knock-off. If you want to know what's timely, head on out to the Valley.

10. Swingers

Vince Vaughn, Jon Favreau (1996, R, 96m, DVD)

Swing music came back in the '90s as did cigars, hanging out in supper clubs and lounge music. A group of single guys hang out in Los Angeles on the fringes of the in-crowd thinking themselves cooler than they are in this breezy comedy.

SEE ALSO:
Pulp Fiction ("Copycat Crimes")
The Crying Game ("Love Conquers All")

WHEN TO WATCH
October 4. Slippery-lipped Alicia Silverstone's birthday (1976).

WHAT TO EAT
You might want to try this menu suggested by Alicia Silverstone as Cher in *Clueless*: "I feel like such a heifer. I had two bowls of Special K, three pieces of turkey bacon, a handful of popcorn, four peanut butter M&M's and like five pieces of licorice."

GREAT LINE
from *Clueless* by Amy Heckerling, Jane Austen (novel)

"Dionne and I are both named after great singers of the past who now do infomercials."
—ALICIA SILVERSTONE as CHER

'Nam

WHEN YOU WANT TO FEEL STIRRED UP ABOUT 'NAM

The best of the "Hendrix, hemp, and hump-hump war" genre. These movies are so good, you'll have Post Cinematic Stress Syndrome.

1. The Deer Hunter
Robert De Niro, Christopher Walken, Meryl Streep (1978, R, 183m, DVD)
An intense Vietnam epic following friends from a Pennsylvania steel mill town whose lives are ripped apart by the war. Superb Hollywood filmmaking.

2. Apocalypse Now
Marlon Brando, Robert Duvall, Martin Sheen (1979, R, 153m)
This is a twist on Joseph Conrad's allegorical (or is it metaphorical? You don't know, why am I asking you?) novel *Heart of Darkness,* that I read in high school but didn't get until this artistic portrait of Vietnam appeared on the screen. Beautifully explores the theme of war's descent into madness. And yes, that is Laurence Fishburne as the young pothead.

3. Full Metal Jacket
Matthew Modine, Vincent D'Onofrio (1987, R, 116m)
Kubrick's 'Nam picture. What's the deal with a 'Nam picture being made in the UK? And furthermore, this whole movie was shot in Europe. Well, OK, even though he was an ex-pat American, he was Stanley God Damn Kubrick, so we'll let him have his 'Nam movie since it is so engrossing and brilliant.

4. Platoon
Charlie Sheen, Willem DaFoe, Tom Berenger (1986, R, 113m)
This Oliver Stone opus earned more awards than anyone who served in Vietnam. It was described as the grunt's eye view of the war. This was the high-water mark of capturing the reality of battle carnage until *Saving Private Ryan* came along.

5. Coming Home
Jane Fonda, Jon Voight, Bruce Dern (1978, R, 130m)
A compelling human drama dealing with the aftermath of war when the soldiers felt tossed aside by an ungrateful country.

6. Birdy
Matthew Modine, Nicolas Cage (1984, R, 120m)
Hospitalized Vietnam vet suffering from post traumatic stress syndrome and who knows what else, imagines he's a bird so he can fly away from all his troubles (now that's an allegory, not a metaphor, right?) Anyway, love this movie.

7. Born on the Fourth of July
Tom Cruise, Kyra Sedgewick (1989, R, 145m, DVD)
Biopic of patriot and anti-war activist Ron Kovic, effectively played by Cruise.

8. Casualties of War
Michael J. Fox, Sean Penn (1989, R, 120m)
The insanity of war is dealt with in this film which gets a surprisingly rich performance from Fox and a predictably great one from Penn.

9. Dear America: Letters Home from Vietnam
Tom Berenger, Willem DaFoe, Robert De Niro (1988, PG, 84m)
Gripping documentary with simple premise: well-known actors read aloud actual letters written by soldiers in Vietnam.

10. Who'll Stop the Rain
Nick Nolte, Tuesday Weld (1978, R, 126m)
A powerful film dealing with the destructive psychological effect of war on Nolte, as a vet whose life implodes around him.

SEE ALSO:
The Killing Fields ("One Hit Wonders")
Hearts and Minds ("War Movies: Movies Are Hell")

WHEN TO WATCH
September 15. King of paranoia Oliver Stone's birthday (1946).

WHAT TO EAT
Rations. Something like Spam.

GREAT LINE
from *Full Metal Jacket* by Gustav Hasford, Michael Herr, Stanley Kubrick

> *"I wanted to meet stimulating and interesting people of an ancient culture, and kill them. I wanted to be the first kid on my block to get a confirmed kill."*
> —MATTHEW MODINE as PRIVATE JOKER

Life During World War II
WHEN YOU'RE FEELING NOSTALGIC

These movies remind us that soldiers aren't the only casualties of battle. The Second World War was fought in the trenches and also by those left at home. Since the most recent event to capture the American public's attention was the Clinton/Lewinsky fiasco, maybe it's worth a look at a time when everyday everyone had to consider life and death and good and evil. Even if you weren't born yet, let one of these make you a little nostalgic for life on the homefront.

1. Life Is Beautiful
Roberto Benigni, Nicoletta Braschi (1998, PG-13, 122m)
Benigni's magical fairy tale is something you don't see everyday: an uplifting film about a father's love for his son, set in a Nazi concentration camp.

2. Cabaret
Liza Minelli, Joel Grey (1972, PG, 119m, DVD)
Even then, Liza was a magnet for men of questionable sexuality.

3. Hope and Glory
Sebastian Rice-Edwards, Geraldine Muir (1987, PG-13, 97m)
It may sound depressing, but it's not. A boy grows up during World War II. The tone is light, nostalgic, amusing and warm.

4. The Great Dictator
Charlie Chaplin, Paulette Goddard (1940, NR, 126m)
Chaplin creates one for the ages in this satire in which the Little Tramp transforms himself into Adolph Hitler.

5. Distant Voices/Still Lives
Pete Postlethwaite, Freda Dowie (1988, NR, 87m)
A moody, poetic film about the troubles of an ordinary English family ruled by an abusive father during and after World War II. Lots of brown tones—which is great, because I think they're "in" now.

6. To Be or Not to Be
Jack Benny, Carole Lombard (1942, NR, 102m)
Benny shines as a renowned Polish actor whose troupe gets caught up in World War II and applies their acting skills toward espionage. This was Lombard's final film before she died in a plane crash at thirty-three.

7. Mrs. Miniver
Greer Garson, Walter Pidgeon (1942, NR, 134m)
This sappy story of a family trying to survive on the British homefront collected a ton of Oscars®. It was also very effective propaganda, bolstering American support for involvement in WWII.

8. Swing Shift

Christine Lahti, Goldie Hawn (1984, PG, 100m)
Terrific performances from Lahti and Hawn as housewives who become factory workers holding down the American homefront in this homage to Rosie the Riveter.

9. Julia

Jane Fonda, Vanessa Redgrave (1977, PG, 118m)
Streep didn't waste any time on her way to becoming America's finest screen actress by making her film debut in this prestigious 1977 adaptation of Lillian Hellman's autobiographical story of her involvement in the Nazi resistance movement.

10. For the Boys

Bette Midler, James Caan (1991, R, 120m)
Midler and Caan play two USO entertainers who keep the troops happy over the years.

SEE ALSO:
The Best Years of Our Lives ("One Hit Wonders")

WHEN TO WATCH
May 8. Victory Day.

WHAT TO EAT
Shit on a shingle.

GREAT LINE
from *Hope and Glory* by John Boorman

> *"All my life nothing ever quite matched that moment. My school lay in ruins. The river beckoned with a promise of stolen days."*
>
> —SEBASTIAN RICE EDWARDS as BILL ROHAN

Movies Even Older Than Your Grandparents

WHEN YOU'RE FEELING QUIET

These movies are old. Older than rotary phones; older than the first IBM Selectric™. These movies don't even have sound. So check out the best silent movies ever made.

1. Sunrise
George O'Brien, Janet Gaynor (1927, NR, 110m)
Stunning! Deservedly won the Oscar® for "Artistic Quality of Production" in the very first Academy Awards® which were given to films released in 1927-28. German director F. W. Murnau created this hauntingly beautiful story of a man who plans to kill his wife with the encouragement of another woman.

2. The Last Laugh
Emil Jannings, Hans Unter Kircher (1924, NR, 77m)
From the director of *Sunrise* comes one of the most beautiful films of all time. It's the heart-breaking story of a doorman at a luxury hotel who is demoted to the humiliating job of washroom attendant.

3. Metropolis
Bridgette Helm, Alfred Abel (1926, NR, 115m, DVD)
The seminal futuristic nightmare. This film about the alienation of the modern worker is a landmark in film history.

4. The Gold Rush
Charlie Chaplin, Georgia Hale (1925, NR, 85m)
Chaplin at his comic best.

5. The General
Buster Keaton, Marion Mack (1926, NR, 78m)
Keaton at his comic best.

6. Napoléon
Albert Dieudonné, Antonin Artaud (1934, NR, 140m)
This expansive and awe-inspiring French epic tells the story of the Emperor on three screens.

7. Birth of a Nation
Lillian Gish, Mae Marsh (1915, NR, 175m, DVD)
This controversial film about the Civil War, told from the Southern point of view, is actually sympathetic to the Ku Klux Klan. But it also represents an important film landmark as the first-ever narrative feature film.

8. The Sheik
Rudolph Valentino, Agnes Ayres (1921, NR, 80m)
Valentino plays the great Latin Lover.

9. The Cabinet of Dr. Caligari
Conrad Veidt, Werner Krauss (1919, NR, 92m)
This influential surrealistic German horror film, about a somnambulist who kills in his sleep, is a favorite on the art house circuit even today.

10. The Battleship Potemkin
Beatrice Votoldi, Vladimir Barsky (1925, NR, 71m, DVD)
Studied by every film student, this Sergei Eisenstein landmark film about the rebellion aboard a Russian battleship in 1905, was designed to shore up revolutionary fervor in Russia. Its most notable sequence—the famed Odessa Steps scene, in which citizens are massacred by the Cossacks—has been copied in several films, including *The Untouchables* and *Brazil*.

SEE ALSO:
The Passion of Joan of Arc ("One Hit Wonders")
Male and Female ("Desert Island Movies")

WHEN TO WATCH
Second Sunday in September: National Grandparents' Day.

WHAT TO EAT
Something you can afford on a fixed income.

GREAT LINE
from *Sunset Boulevard* by Billy Wilder, Charles Brackett, D. M. Marshman, Jr.

"We didn't need talking, we had faces."
—GLORIA SWANSON as NORMA DESMOND

FEELS LIKE A HOLIDAY

Don't you just love holidays? They provide so many wonderful opportunities to max out your credit cards purchasing gifts for people you normally wouldn't even speak to (let alone hang out with), but since they're family you don't have a choice. Sometimes, after a long day at one of those holiday family gatherings, don't you just want to lock yourself in the bathroom and ask...who are these people? Is this DNA thing a myth? How can I possibly have anything in common with these freaks? Mind you, as a matter of full disclosure (for personal and legal reasons) I'm not talking about *my* family of course. No, no, no...this is a *hypothetical* family we're talking about here.

For this *hypothetical* family, it seems the most stressful holiday of them all (for those that observe) is Christmas. It can be really loathsome. I hate Christmas shopping. The traffic, the malls, the mauls. One time, I was so stressed out by all the hustle and bustle, I stopped dead in my tracks in the middle of the mall, dropped all my shopping bags on the floor and screamed at the top of my lungs, "I wish Jesus had never been born!" Not that it was exactly a stress-reliever.

Here's a tip on how to put a stop to all those probing, nagging questions relatives who haven't seen you for awhile like to ask. Questions like: When are you going to get married? When are you going to get a job? When are you going to sell that crappy car? When are you going to release those hostages? Whatever the question, just pop in a video or DVD and sit there in silence. You don't have to talk to them, they don't have to pretend to be interested in you, and you can both have a shared experience. But which movie? Ah, just turn the page and all your holiday problems are solved. (For a couple of hours, anyway).

Irish Movies to Watch On St. Paddy's Day

WHEN YOU'RE FEELING A WEE BIT IRISH

Everyone is Irish on St. Patrick's Day. That is, everyone who wants an excuse to choke down green beer and corned beef and cabbage for lunch. These movies are not specifically about St. Patrick, known best for chasing the snakes out of Ireland (which isn't terribly cinematic), but are about Irish people and their experience.

1. Waking Ned Devine
Ian Brennan, David Kelly (1998, PG, 91m, DVD)
An infectiously charming Irish comedy in which whole scheming population of a seaside Irish town conspires to deceive lottery officials.

2. In the Name of the Father
Daniel Day-Lewis, Pete Postlethwaite (1993, R, 127m, DVD)
Based on a true story, this political drama is set in the volatile milieu of Northern Ireland's on-going Catholic/Protestant tug-of-war, in which father and son are persecuted for crimes which they did not commit.

3. The Brothers McMullen
Ed Burns, Mike McGlone, Jack Mulcahy (1994, R, 98m)
Set in Long Island, in a house shared by three brothers from an Irish Catholic family, this low-budget comedy is mostly about how these guys are defined by the women in their lives.

4. Michael Collins
Julia Roberts, Liam Neeson (1996, R, 117m, DVD)
The historic annals of the founding of the Irish Republican Army are revealed in this well-done political period epic, in which the success of passionate idealism leads dispiritedly to diplomatic compromise.

5. Ryan's Daughter
Sarah Miles, Robert Mitchum (1970, PG, 194m)
This David Lean film was not as critically well-received as most of his other films but this has the best Irish scenery of any film that I have seen. It was shot on the beautiful Dingle Peninsula.

6. Dancing at Lughnasa
Meryl Streep, Michael Gambon (1998, PG-13, 92m, DVD)
Quiet—very quiet, almost inaudible—yet moving family drama about poor middle-aged Irish sisters and their crazy brother who live together in rural Ireland.

7. The Field
Richard Harris, Tom Berenger, John Hurt (1990, PG-13, 113m)
A petty dispute over land ownership leads to turmoil in an Irish community and earns Harris an Oscar® nomination.

8. The Quiet Man
John Wayne, Maureen O'Hara (1952, NR, 129m, DVD)
The Duke goes to Ireland in search of his roots and finds redheaded O'Hara in this scenic John Ford classic.

9. The Secret of Roan Inish
Jeni Courtney, Michael Colly (1994, PG, 102m)
A John Sayles parable about a selky, the legendary half-human, half-seal creature who apparently lives in the waters off the west coast of Ireland, and its coy relationship with a believing little girl.

10. The Boxer
Daniel Day-Lewis, Emily Watson (1997, R, 113m, DVD)
Fresh out of prison, a boxer tries to avoid his past, but it seems anxious to catch up with him as he again is inexorably entangled with the Irish Republican Army.

SEE ALSO:
My Left Foot ("Writers")

WHEN TO WATCH
March 17. St. Patrick's Day.

WHAT TO EAT
Corned beef and cabbage.

GREAT LINE
from *The Quiet Man* by Frank S. Nugent, Maurice Walsh (story)

> *"There'll be no locks or bolts between us, Mary Kate, except those in your own mercenary little heart."*
> —JOHN WAYNE as SEAN THORTON to
> new wife MAUREEN O'HARA as MARY KATE THORTON

Spiritual Movies to Watch On Easter

WHEN YOU'RE FEELING SPIRITUAL

You've found all the cracked eggs you're gonna find until the lost ones start stinking up the couch cushions. You've bitten heads off chocolate bunnies like a sugar-addicted Ozzy Osborne. Now what do you do? I know, how 'bout a movie? Faith is a subject a lot of filmmakers shy away from; it's a subject I shy away from and I'm not even a filmmaker. It is possible, though not too easy, to explore deeply spiritual questions in a serious way on film. These are some of the best examples:

1. The Ten Commandments
Charlton Heston, Yul Brenner (1956, G, 219m)
This movie is almost as long as the Old Testament but it is a splashy spectacle, as colorful as a basket of Easter eggs. It's the Bible as Vegas review—not a lot of depth, but very showy.

2. Resurrection
Ellen Burstyn, Sam Shepard (1980, PG, 103m)
Original tale of a woman who acquires the power of faith healing. Life-affirming performances from Burstyn and Eva Le Gallienne.

3. Easter Parade
Fred Astaire, Judy Garland (1948, NR, 103m)
How can this Astaire-Garland vehicle with peppy tunes like "Stepping Out with My Baby" not make you reflect on themes of crucifixion and resurrection?

4. Dead Man Walking
Susan Saradon, Sean Penn (1995, R, 122m, DVD)
You might think a movie about a convicted rapist on death row is an odd Easter choice, but what better time to think about life, death, redemption, and salvation? And, as a bonus, you get Sarandon in her Oscar®-winning nun role added to the mix.

5. Jesus Christ, Superstar
Ted Neeley, Carl Anderson (1973, G, 108m, DVD)
Jesus Christ, hep pacifist cat, is the tone set by this now-classic rock opera.

6. Lilies of the Field
Sidney Poitier, Lilia Skala (1963, NR, 94m)
Simple story of a handyman who builds a church for a bunch of nuns. Poitier won an Academy Award® for his understated work.

7. Diary of a Country Priest
Claude Layou, Leon Arnel (1950, NR, 120m)

Moving, by virtue of its spare story and slow pace (if I've lost you there, I understand), this is just as the title describes, the story of a country priest who happens to be dying of cancer. Directed by great French auteur Robert Bresson who answered the question "Why cinema?" with the pithy retort "To live!" The French are so existential.

8. Jesus of Montreal
Lothaire Bluteau, Gilles Pelletier (1989, R, 119m)

It's in French, it's Canadian and it's about Jesus. If that sounds enticing, you might want to check out this very provocative movie about an actor who really commits to his part.

9. The Rapture
Mimi Rogers, David Duchovny (1991, R, 100m)

An odd, deep little film about a swinging telephone operator who becomes a Jesus freak and then along comes the Rapture and she's just not so sure anymore.

10. Andrei Roublev
Anatoli Solonitsyn, Ivan Lapikov (1966, NR, 185m, DVD)

This is a very serious film, but you're the one who's looking at a list of ten films dealing with the heavy subject of religious faith, so I think you can handle it. This three hour Russian movie is about a fifteenth century painter and his struggle with the social, religious and political issues of his day and how they intertwine.

 WHEN TO WATCH
Easter Sunday.

 WHAT TO EAT
Easter eggs and chocolate bunnies, of course. Or, if you want to go full-tilt Catholic, I suggest a wafer and some wine.

 **GREAT LINE**
from *Dead Man Walking* by Helen Prejean (book), Tim Robbins

> *"I want the last face you see in this world to be the face of love, so you look at me when they do this thing. I'll be the face of love for you."*
>
> —SUSAN SARANDON as SISTER HELEN PREJEAN

Political Movies to Watch On the 4th of July

WHEN YOU'RE FEELING PATRIOTIC

This year, skip the picnics and fireworks and stay in and rent a movie. What more patriotic way to show your American spirit than to support the economy by giving your local video store a few greenbacks? What the hell, return 'em late and support the economy even more, after all, you are a real, red-blooded American, aren't you?

1. Bulworth

Warren Beatty, Halle Berry (1998, R, 107m, DVD)

One of the bravest and funniest political satires ever made. Beatty pulls off the near-impossible in this razor sharp story of a disillusioned liberal Senator who puts a contract out on his own life and then turns into a hip-hop, truth-telling machine. To further illustrate just how unprecedented this film is: Beatty doesn't even have sex in this movie.

2. Mr. Smith Goes to Washington

Jimmy Stewart, Jean Arthur (1939, NR, 130m)

On the other end of the cynical/idealistic spectrum from *Bulworth*, this Capra-esque (because it is, in fact, a Frank Capra film) about a naive, newly elected Senator, played by the lovable Stewart, offends no one because it doesn't really deal with any political issues, but it does rally against corruption, which is a cause we can all get behind.

3. All the President's Men

Robert Redford, Dustin Hoffman (1976, PG, 135m, DVD)

A real life thriller in which you learn everything you always wanted to know about Watergate.

4. The Candidate

Robert Redford, Peter Boyle (1972, PG, 105m, DVD)

Redford's eyes get opened to some political realities as he takes his big sideburns on the road in California to campaign for the U. S. Senate.

5. Wag the Dog

Dustin Hoffman, Robert De Niro (1997, R, 96m, DVD)

This film was mentioned during the Monica Lewinsky escapade by more people than had actually seen it. It does seem eerily prescient and it's also damn funny.

6. Meet John Doe

Gary Cooper, Barbara Stanwyck (1941, NR, 123m, DVD)

Capra again. The story of a common drifter who is elevated to hero status by manipulative members of the media.

7. Dave
Kevin Kline, Sigourney Weaver (1993, PG-13, 110m, DVD)
A guy impersonates the President of the United States and just about fixes the whole damn government. Lots of amusing cameos from real life Washington types.

8. The Right Stuff
Sam Shepard, Scott Glenn, Ed Harris (1983, PG, 193m, DVD)
Now, this will make you proud to be American. This chronicle of the early days of the space program has some very bright, shining moments.

9. Primary
Documentary, directed by Robert Drew (1960, NR, 60m)
Attention all political junkies. This is like eavesdropping on history as we follow Hubert Humphrey and John Kennedy through a 1960 Democratic presidential primary in this engrossing documentary.

10. City of Hope
Vincent Spano, Tony LoBianco, Angela Bassett (1991, R, 132m)
A complex multi-character drama about the political alliances and compromises that make a big city run. Not the cheeriest celebration of democracy, but an interesting one.

SEE ALSO:
Saving Private Ryan ("Crowd Pleaser: Films of Steven Spielberg")
Primary Colors ("So Five Minutes Age: Movies of the '90s")
Medium Cool ("Vidiots")

WHEN TO WATCH
July 4. And wave a flag while you watch.

WHAT TO EAT
Hot dogs and apple pie.

GREAT LINE
from *Bulworth* by Warren Beatty and Jeremy Pikser

> *In response to the question "Are you saying the Democratic Party don't care about the African American community?":*
> *"Isn't that obvious? I mean, you don't put down that malt liquor and chicken wing and get behind somebody other than a running back who stabs his wife, you're never gonna get rid of somebody like me."*
> —WARREN BEATTY as SENATOR BULWORTH

Movies to Watch on Thanksgiving

WHEN YOU'RE FEELING THANKFUL

The list contains films about families. Many are about such Thanksgiving topics as family gatherings and American history. Depending upon how you feel about your own family and its gatherings you will be drawn to different films on this list. Some of the families have some semblance of normalcy, but most do not. You probably won't be able to get to the TV anyway because somebody's watching the damn game.

1. Avalon
Aidan Quinn, Armin Mueller-Stahl (1990, PG, 126m)
The story of a half century in the lives of immigrant families growing up in Baltimore is a beautiful celebration of the trials and tribulations that define what it means to live in America.

2. Dances with Wolves
Kevin Costner, Mary McDonnell (1990, PG-13, 181m, DVD)
A beautiful, politically correct sort-of-Western about a white military officer getting in touch with his inner-Native American. It's really a great movie and the perfect Thanksgiving day guilt trip about our forefathers' mistreatment of the American indigenous peoples.

3. Local Hero
Peter Riegert, Burt Lancaster (1983, PG, 112m)
A very nice story to remind you what's really important in life.

4. Rocket Gibraltar
Burt Lancaster, Macauley Culkin (1988, PG, 92m)
A sentimental family, headed by Lancaster as the dying patriarch, has a reunion in the Hamptons.

5. Parenthood
Steve Martin, Dianne Wiest (1989, PG-13, 124m, DVD)
An insightful character comedy about the trials and tribulations of raising children as seen from the perspectives of characters who are at every stage of their lives.

6. The Celebration
Henning Moritzen, Ulrich Thomsen (1998, R, 105m)
A Danish movie in which a majorly dysfunctional family gathers for the patriarch's 60th birthday and much dirt is aired. Could be very uncomfortable to watch in the presence of your family, but might be just the thing to watch to make you feel good if you decided to skip seeing them this year. So, stick that in your cornucopia and smoke it.

7. Pocahontas
Mel Gibson, Irene Bedard (1995, G, 90m)
I'm pretty sure the historical accuracy on this animated film is a little fuzzy. But the spirit is nice, and they left out that messy part where Pocahontas went off to England with John Smith but ended up with a different guy.

8. The Ice Storm
Kevin Kline, Joan Allen, Sigourney Weaver (1997, R, 113m)
Gene Siskel's favorite film of 1997 is a great '70s period piece in which an ice storm reflects the chilly relations amongst the members of two upscale East Coast families as they grapple with sexual expression.

9. The Myth of Fingerprints
Noah Wylie, Julianne Moore (1997, R, 91m)
Sometimes Thanksgiving is really nasty and when people aren't talking, maybe it's for the best.

10. Planes, Trains, and Automobiles
Steve Martin, John Candy (1987, R, 93m)
Businessman Martin is trying to get home to Chicago for Thanksgiving when he ends up with an unlikely traveling companion—a shower ring salesman, played by Candy.

WHEN TO WATCH
Thanksgiving.

WHAT TO EAT
Things that the pilgrims ate, like one of those Marie Calendar's pies with Cool-Whip™.

MEMORABLE DIALOGUE
from *Parenthood* by Lowell Ganz, Ron Howard, Babaloo Mandel

KEANU REEVES as TOD
Ms. Buchman, do you know what a boner is?

DIANNE WIEST as HELEN
If memory serves.

Christmas Movies

WHEN YOU'RE FEELING SO NOEL

What brings a family together more than Christmas? A Christmas spent gathered around the TV, staring at a movie for two hours without ever having to even look at one another. Generally after a big meal, even if people are still speaking to one another, they've long run out of things to talk about. So, watch one of these movies where happy families demonstrate what you and yours are not like, but should be.

1. It's a Wonderful Life
Jimmy Stewart, Donna Reed (1946, NR, 125m)
Here's how much I'm a sucker for this sentimental Christmas story: I could watch it in August.

2. Miracle on 34th Street
Edmund Gwenn, Natalie Wood (1947, NR, 97)
An old man goes to court to prove he's the real Santa Claus. And you thought there was something new about frivolous law suits. The 1994 remake is worth a look, too.

3. A Christmas Carol
Alastair Sim, Mervyn Johns (1951, NR, 86m, DVD)
This is the definitive version of Charles Dickens oft-told tale.

4. Boys' Town
Spencer Tracy, Mickey Rooney (1938, NR, 93m)
Sticky sweet story of Tracy as a priest who gives wayward boys a new lease on life.

5. The Bishop's Wife
Cary Grant, David Niven, Loretta Young (1947, NR, 109m, DVD)
Grant plays an angel who is the answer to Niven's prayers. The kids in this movie are the same kids as in *It's a Wonderful Life*—talk about a niche career.

6. The Preacher's Wife
Whitney Houston, Denzel Washington, Courtney B. Vance (1996, PG, 124)
A 1996 re-make of *The Bishop's Wife*.

7. Holiday Inn
Bing Crosby, Fred Astaire (1942, NR, 101m)
Light and flaky snow and script are hallmarks of this Crosby and Astaire "White Christmas" charmer.

8. White Christmas
Bing Crosby, Danny Kaye (1954, NR, 120m)
A remake of *Holiday Inn* with Crosby and Kaye, but without Fred Astaire.

9. A Christmas Story

Peter Billingsly, Jeff Gillen (1983, PG, 95m, DVD)

The only decent film to be directed by Bob Clark, who has had a singularly undistinguished track record. Lowlights include: *Baby Geniuses, Turk 182, Rhinestone, Porky's, Porky's 2: the Next Day, From the Hip* and something called *She-Man*. Most of that celluloid, as they say, would be better used as guitar picks. But all is forgiven because he directed this charming Christmas classic.

10. Cocoon

Don Ameche, Jessica Tandy (1985, PG-13, 117m)

Old people really like this movie. I guess it makes them feel like maybe an alien will show up some day and give them the power to break dance. Since there are usually a fair number of oldsters around at Christmas, pop this one in and you'll score some points.

WHEN TO WATCH

December 25. Christmas.

WHAT TO EAT

Ham, goose, turkey or some other animal whose entire carcass you can put at the center of your table.

GREAT LINE

from *It's a Wonderful Life* by Philip Van Doren (story), Frances Goodrich, Albert Hackett, Frank Capra, and Jo Swerling

> *"What do you want, Mary? Do you want the moon? If you want it, I'll throw a lasso around it and pull it down for you. Hey! That's a pretty good idea! I'll give you the moon, Mary."*
> —JIMMY STEWART as GEORGE BAILEY

African-American Movies to Watch on Kwanzaa

WHEN YOU'RE FEELING THAT BLACK PRIDE

African Americans have had a rough going in Hollywood movies. Having been relegated to some degrading roles in the early days of the medium, only now are things beginning to look up and even that is a controversial matter. What I want to know is when is a big screen biography of Martin Luther King Jr. going to be made? Until then, here are some African American gems that are worth seeing for their historical or aesthetic value.

1. Malcolm X
Denzel Washington, Spike Lee (1992, PG-13, 194m, DVD)
Lee's expansive, yet beautifully controlled, biopic of slain black activist Malcolm X has, at its center, a riveting performance by Washington.

2. Sounder
Paul Winfield, Cicely Tyson (1972, G, 105m)
A timeless classic about the struggles of a sharecropper's family. If you haven't seen it, it's not that you're a bad person, it's just that maybe there's something a little wrong with you.

3. Glory
Denzel Washington, Morgan Freeman, Matthew Broderick (1989, R, 122m)
More Denzel. A resplendent record of a black volunteer company that fought for the Union during the Civil War. A great untold history lesson that rises above being a mere chronicle and becomes soaring drama.

4. In the Heat of the Night
Sidney Poitier, Rod Steiger (1967, NR, 109m)
Racial tension between southern redneck small-town sheriff and big-city black cop brought in to help solve a crime form the dramatic spine of this enthralling, relevant drama.

5. Sarafina!
Whoopi Goldberg, Leleti Khumalo (1992, PG-13, 98m)
Of all the many interesting films about the struggle against apartheid in South Africa, astonishingly this is one of the few that is not told from the viewpoint of a white man. And to make it all the more interesting, it is a musical! It soars to great heights and depressing lows as it tells the absorbing story of a school girl who fights the power, and features one of Whoopi's greatest performances as the girl's teacher.

6. A Raisin in the Sun

Sidney Poitier, Lou Gossett Jr., Ruby Dee (1961, NR, 128m)

Poitier heads a family trying to escape inner-city apartment life by contemplating a move to the white suburbs in 1961 with invariably complicated results.

7. Once Upon a Time...When We Were Colored

Phylicia Rashad, Al Freeman Jr., Léon (1995, PG, 112m, DVD)

Warmhearted scrapbook of an African American family growing up on the Mississippi Delta during the mid-20th century.

8. Shaft

Richard Roundtree, Charles Cioffi (1971, R, 98m)

"Who's the black private dick that's a sex machine to all the chicks?"

9. A Family Thing

James Earl Jones, Robert Duvall (1996, PG-13, 109m)

Jones and Duvall discover, and reluctantly accept, the fact that they are half-brothers of different races.

10. The Long Walk Home

Whoopi Goldberg, Sissy Spacek (1989, PG, 95m)

Whoopi as a maid again. This is a film with quiet resonance in its account of a bus strike in the south during the mid '50s that puts the awakening conscious of Spacek between her businessman husband and her loyal maid.

SEE ALSO:
Eve's Bayou ("Hidden Treasures")
Do the Right Thing ("Films that Should've Won the Best Picture Oscar®")
Devil in a Blue Dress ("Los Angeles Noir")

WHEN TO WATCH
December 26 through January 1. Kwanzaa.

WHAT TO EAT
Some good down-home cookin' like Southern fried okra, sweet potato fritters, black-eyed peas with ham, peanut soup and sweet potato pie.

GREAT LINE
from *Malcolm X* by Spike Lee, Arnold Perl, James Baldwin

"We didn't land on Plymouth Rock, Plymouth Rock landed on us."
—DENZEL WASHINGTON as MALCOLM X

TRIUMPHS OF THE HUMAN SPIRIT

Feel-good movies usually have some spiritual aspect about them. Let me just take a second to tell you what I think about spirituality and New Ageism and reincarnation and Eastern and Western religion and all the other fringe beliefs: I don't buy it. Like Gladys Kravitz's husband, Abner, on *Bewitched*, I don't believe anything unless I see it for myself. Not parapsychology. Not ghosts. Not UFO's. Not spoon-bending Uri Geller. Not old wives or new age. But that's just me. You're free to believe whatever it takes to get you through the day. Line up your chakras if you must. I've tried visualizing and channeling, but I still can't get MTV without cable. So what good is it?

Of course, a lot of people are always looking for the answers (with their third eye), and for a price, other people are more than happy to supply them. It's big business. The advice is everywhere: twelve steps, ten stupid things women do to mess up their lives, eight days of Chanukah, seven habits of highly effective people, get clear, visualize, get centered, find your inner child, stay in town during pilot season, etc. But what is the path back to the spirit? Transcendental meditation? Tae Bo? A Gordita at Taco Bell?

Look, I'm not some inbred revival tent preacher trying to tell you there's only one way to believe. I realize there are many paths up the same mountain. I'm just asking you to take a look around. If you're locked in a basement with a year's supply of provisions and Janet Reno is calling your name over a bullhorn while some charismatic fry cook is jumping your wife because he's "The Leader," maybe this isn't quite God's plan. Every religion worth its karma preaches love and tolerance. Beyond that, your dogma is your holy ATM number—it only works when you keep it to yourself.

Just thank God (or Buddha) the following filmmakers have shared their inspirational, spiritual and revelatory thoughts with us, because without them, we'd be void of some very rich and inspiring films. So, if you ever find yourself held up in a compound in Waco or anywhere else, have some of these films on hand. They just might help you snap out of it, and at the very least, you'll be entertained until the FBI shows up.

Inspirational Movies

WHEN YOU'RE FEELING LIKE YOU NEED INSPIRATION

Rent these movies when you're procrastinating on some big project, like making the world a better place to live or adopting a third world refugee, and maybe their characters will inspire you with their determination. But then, you probably won't get around to returning a rented tape or disc to the store and the late fees will pile up. And if you buy a copy of the movie, you'll probably never get around to watching it. So, what do you say you just forget it. Really, we all know you mean well—isn't that enough?

1. Cry Freedom
Kevin Kline, Denzel Washington (1987, PG, 157m, DVD)
Crusading against apartheid is the theme of this moving story that will make you want to go out and save the world—for at least a couple of hours.

2. Dead Poets Society
Robin Williams, Robert Sean Leonard, Ethan Hawke (1989, PG, 128m, DVD)
Williams as an earnest teacher railing against the establishment is something I'm sick of now. (Sick of it? Yeah. Have you seen *Awakenings, Good Will Hunting, Patch Adams* or *Jakob the Liar*?) But the first time he did it was really something special.

3A. Fitzcarraldo
Klaus Kinski, Claudia Cardinale (1982, PG, 157m)
An astonishing feat is attempted as a driven visionary hauls boat over rugged Amazonian terrain, up a mountain and through hostile locals in effort to open up a shipping route. If you can dream it, you can do it.

3B. Burden of Dreams
Documentary, directed by Les Blank (1982, NR, 94m)
A documentary about the making of *Fitzcarraldo* that is just as astonishing as its subject.

4. Lorenzo's Oil
Susan Sarandon, Nick Nolte (1992, PG-13, 135m)
Professional do-gooder Sarandon does good here in the story of a woman fighting the medical establishment to save her son's life.

5. Children of a Lesser God
John Hurt, Marlee Matlin (1986, R, 119m)
Love means never having to say anything out loud in this love story between a deaf woman and a teacher.

6. The Green Mile
Tom Hanks, Michael Clarke Duncan (1999, R, 188m)
Unnecessarily long (the first hour devotes a good chunk of its time to developing the character of a mouse), this sometimes gruesome prison movie is based on a Stephen King story (as was Director Darabont's *The Shawshank Redemption*), but does manage eventually to have a brazenly uplifting point of view.

7. Hear My Song
Ned Beatty, Adrian Dunbar (1991, R, 104m)
Charmingly offbeat British comedy about a nightclub owner's search for a reclusive Irish tenor.

8. The Jackie Robinson Story
Jackie Robinson, Rudy Dee (1950, NR, 76m)
Inspirational tale of Robinson, who finally broke the color barrier in professional sports when he suited up for the Brooklyn Dodgers. Robinson plays himself in this terrific movie.

9. October Sky
Jake Gyllenhaal, Laura Dern (1999, PG, 108m, DVD)
A rare movie that communicates a real passion for learning and encourages you to want to make something of your life. And having Dern in a movie is always a good thing.

10. The Mission
Jeremy Irons, Robert De Niro (1986, PG, 125m)
That scene of the guy tied to a cross going over that massive waterfall is one of the most memorable shots in the history of movies. Loved the shot, loved the billboard. If they had it on a mug and T-shirt, I'd buy it. The rest of the movie ain't bad either. Irons goes into the South American rain forest to convert the locals to Christianity while De Niro just wants to capture them to sell as slaves. But are these two so different? Deep, huh? It's a film that may inspire you to think about your commitment to ideals.

SEE ALSO:
To Kill a Mockingbird ("One Hit Wonders")
Sounder ("African American Movies to Watch during Kwanzaa")
The Miracle Worker ("Girl Power")

WHEN TO WATCH
The last week in October. Peace, Friendship and Good Will Week.

WHAT TO EAT
How about some Sunday you go down to your local soup kitchen (and not on Thanksgiving, because that's the one day that they don't need any more fair-weather volunteers) and then come home and catch one of these feel-good movies.

GREAT LINE
from *Dead Poets Society* by Tom Schulman

> *"Carpe, carpe diem, seize the day boys, make your lives extraordinary."*
> —ROBIN WILLIAMS as JOHN KEATING

Cinema Savant

WHEN YOU'RE FEELING KINDA DUMB

The main characters in these movies sure do mean well. Dumb as tree sap, some of 'em, but awfully nice. Some of them have special talents, like counting things or playing the piano. We all love these kinds of characters in movies because they're sort of like pets—too dumb to challenge or question anything you say and doggedly loyal. Why can't everyone be more like my dog?

1. Being There
Peter Sellers, Shirley MacLaine (1979, PG, 130m)
A total idiot who knows nothing except what he sees on TV becomes a TV star and important political figure. It would be even more hilarious if you didn't see it everyday in real life.

2. Rain Man
Dustin Hoffman, Tom Cruise (1988, R, 128m, DVD)
Hoffman plays a character who's really good at counting matches but not good at much else.

3. Forrest Gump
Tom Hanks, Sally Field, Robin Wright Penn (1994, PG-13, 142m)
People love stupid people cause they're non-threatening and cuddly—as proven by the enormous popularity of this movie.

4. A Simple Plan
Billy Bob Thornton, Bridget Fonda, Bill Paxton (1998, R, 121m, DVD)
Dig-your-nails-into-the-chairs tense, this is a well-crafted story about what trouble one can get into by committing a crime, regardless of how easy and tempting it seems, particularly if one's partners-in-crime are idiots. Thornton plays one of those idiots brilliantly.

5. Charly
Cliff Robertson, Claire Bloom (1968, NR, 103m)
Based on the novel, *Flowers for Algernon*, this is the story of a retarded man who is turned into a genius through the miracle of modern science.

6. Shine
Geoffrey Rush, Armin Mueller-Stahl, Lynn Redgrave (1995, PG-13, 105m, DVD)
All the fuss was about Rush's portrayal of pianist David Helfgott. Noah Taylor gives an equally great performance of the character as an adolescent.

7. Simon
Alan Arkin, Madeline Kahn (1980, PG, 97)
Woody Allen screenwriting collaborator Marshall Brickman directs this Sci-Fi comedy in which a group of think tank scientists brainwash a normal schlub to make him think he's from another planet. What they didn't count on was that they were creating a monster.

8. Benny & Joon

Mary Stuart Masterson, Johnny Depp, Aidan Quinn (1993, PG, 98m)

Movies can make even mental illness look pretty good. Just ask Masterson, who is able to have a relationship with quirky, offbeat Depp, who may be dim-witted in this, but he is also the reincarnation of Buster Keaton and a comic genius.

9. Nell

Jodie Foster, Liam Neeson, Natasha Richardson (1994, R, 114m)

Blowin' in the wind. Chickapee. Chickapee. What the hell is she saying?!

10. The Mighty

Sharon Stone, Gillian Anderson, Harry Dean Stanton (1998, PG-13, 100m, DVD)

A tender story—maybe a little too precious—about two kids, a deformed brainiac and a hulking idiot, teaming up to do the job of one.

WHEN TO WATCH

The second Sunday in October. World Mental Health Day.

WHAT TO EAT

In honor of *Forrest Gump*, may I recommend shrimp-kabobs, shrimp Creole, shrimp gumbo, pan fried, deep fried, stir-fried shrimp, pineapple shrimp, lemon shrimp, coconut shrimp, pepper shrimp, shrimp soup, shrimp stew, shrimp salad, shrimp and potatoes, shrimp burger or a shrimp sandwich?

GREAT LINE

from *Benny and Joon* by Barry Berman

> JOHNNY DEPP as SAM
>
> *How sick is she?*
>
> AIDAN QUINN as BENNY
>
> *Oh, she's plenty sick.*
>
> SAM
>
> *Oh. Because, you know, it seems to me that, aside from being a little mentally ill, she's pretty normal.*

Hooray for Capitalism

WHEN YOU'RE FEELING RICH

Don't you love capitalism? I mean, just look around you at all the things you have: videos, VCR's, that new DVD player. You can thank capitalism for all that. If you don't believe it, you can just move to Russia, buddy. Okay, Russia isn't communist anymore so maybe I should have said, "You can just move to Havana, buddy." But then you'd say, "Havana? Piña coladas, beaches, cigars, those cool old Chevys—and how much longer can Fidel Castro hold out anyway?" Maybe you'd have a point, but capitalism is still great. Next time you get a new job or a promotion or are just feeling especially rich, celebrate the moment by watching one of these movies which celebrate the glory that is capitalism, big business and wealth.

1. Modern Times
Charlie Chaplin, Paulette Goddard (1936, NR, 87m)
Chaplin, the film icon, is amazing as the Little Tramp takes on the evils of modern industrialization in his last silent film.

2. Howards End
Emma Thompson, Helena Bonham-Carter, Anthony Hopkins (1992, PG, 143m, DVD)
This study of the relationship of three families from different classes of turn-of-the-century British society is a very tasteful, winsome and well-made drama which earned Thompson a Best Actress Oscar®.

3. The Man in the White Suit
Alec Guiness, Joan Greenwood (1951, NR, 82m)
Guiness invents an indestructible fabric that can't get dirty and becomes the biggest enemy of big business since Karl Marx.

4. It Could Happen to You
Bridget Fonda, Nicolas Cage, Rosie Perez (1994, PG, 101m, DVD)
A lot of modern movies like to think of themselves (if, indeed, movies are able to think for themselves at all) as Capra-esque. For my money, this feel-good winner is one of the few that really earns the description.

5. Big
Tom Hanks, Elizabeth Perkins (1988, PG, 98m)
The sweetest movie ever made about a twelve-year-old boy getting laid by a thirty-something woman.

6. Mr. Deeds Goes to Town
Gary Cooper, Jean Arthur (1936, NR, 118m)
Cooper inherits a fortune and the all the creeps show up on his doorstep. This is even more Capra-esque than *It Could Happen to You*—which makes sense since this movie was actually made by Frank Capra.

7. How to Succeed in Business Without Really Trying

Robert Morse, Michele Lee, Rudy Vallee (1967, NR, 121m)
Musical corporate climbing comedy.

8. Glengarry Glen Ross

Al Pacino, Jack Lemmon, Alec Baldwin (1992, R, 100m)
David Mamet's scorching adaptation of his own play about a day in the life of a group of cutthroat salesmen.

9. The Hudsucker Proxy

Tim Robbins, Jennifer Jason Leigh, Paul Newman (1993, PG, 115m)
The Coen Brothers' wacky take on the evils of big business.

10. Trading Places

Eddie Murphy, Dan Aykroyd (1983, R, 118m)
Social science experiment results in an opportunistic street hustler and a stock broker swapping places. Funny, but my question is, who can tell the difference between an opportunistic street hustler and a stock broker?

SEE ALSO:
Citizen Kane ("Films that Should Have Won the Best Picture Oscar®")
Chinatown ("Los Angeles Noir")
Wall Street ("Me Movies: Movies of the '80s")
The Jerk ("Movie Morons")

 WHEN TO WATCH
October 24. The anniversary of the 1929 "Black Thursday" stock market crash that led to the Great Depression.

 WHAT TO EAT
A two-martini lunch.

 GREAT LINE
from *Glengarry Glen Ross* by David Mamet

> *"We're adding a little something to this month's sales contest. As you all know, first prize is a Cadillac Eldorado. Anybody want to see second prize? Second prize is a set of steak knives. Third prize is you're fired."*
> —ALEC BALDWIN as BLAKE

Working Class Heroes

WHEN YOU'RE FEELING LIKE STICKING UP
FOR THE REGULAR GUY

Go ahead, root for the little guy. Even if he works for a living. I know you run the risk of being labeled a (gasp!), liberal; maybe even a "bleeding heart liberal." But these movies about union members and their struggles are so compelling I bet even a dyed-in-the-wool conservative (shriek!) with no heart, bleeding or otherwise, could enjoy them.

1. The Grapes of Wrath
Henry Fonda, John Carradine (1940, NR, 129m)
This dust bowl drama is so important that there ought to be a law requiring everybody to watch it. I guess we can all see why I'm not in charge.

2. How Green Was My Valley
Walter Pidgeon, Maureen O'Hara (1941, NR, 118m)
The film that won Oscars® for picture, directing and cinematography over none other than *Citizen Kane*! This is the downbeat but moving story of a Welsh mining family.

3. Matewan
Chris Cooper, James Earl Jones, David Strathairn (1987, PG-13, 130m)
This is a wonderful film that too few people have seen. This based-on-a-true-story film is a moving story about the struggles of 1920s West Virginia striking coal workers.

4. All the King's Men
Broderick Crawford, Mercedes McCambridge (1949, NR, 109m)
A Huey Long-type politician, a champion of the common man, rises through the ranks using every underhanded trick in the book, as well as some new ones all his own.

5. Bound for Glory
David Carradine, Randy Quaid (1976, PG, 149m)
Bio of folk singer Woody Guthrie who wanders around via freight trains during the depression.

6. Norma Rae
Sally Field, Beau Bridges (1979, PG, 114m)
Field stars as union provocateur Norma Rae. You'll like her, you'll really like her.

7. Roger & Me
Documentary, directed by Michael Moore (1989, R, 91m)
Moore's confrontational documentary about trying to get a meeting with the president of GM so he can whine about the treatment of auto workers.

8. Silkwood
Meryl Streep, Kurt Russell, Cher (1983, R, 131)
True story of union activist Karen Silkwood's attempt to expose misdeeds in the nuclear power industry. And, oh yeah, I almost forgot the best part—Cher as a lesbian.

9. Man of Marble
Krystyna Janda, Jerzy Radziwilowicz (1976, NR, 160m)
Call me crazy, but this Polish film kinda reminds me of *Citizen Kane*. A woman tries to piece together the mysteries in the life of a simple bricklayer who was made into a national hero.

10. Harlan County, U. S. A.
Documentary, directed by Barbara Kopple (1976, PG, 103m)
An absorbing documentary about a West Virginia coal miners' strike.

SEE ALSO:
On the Waterfront ("Best Performances by a Male Actor")

WHEN TO WATCH
May 1. International Workers' Day.

WHAT TO EAT
TV dinner and a six-pack.

GREAT LINE
from *Grapes of Wrath* by John Steinbeck (novel), Nunnally Johnson

> *"Then it don't matter. I'll be all around in the dark. I'll be everywhere, wherever you can look. Wherever there's a fight so hungry people can eat, I'll be there. Wherever there's a cop beatin' up a guy, I'll be there. I'll be in the way guys yell when they're mad. I'll be in the way kids laugh when they're hungry and they know supper's ready and where people are eatin' the stuff they raise and livin' in the houses they build. I'll be there, too."*
> —HENRY FONDA as TOM JOAD

FEELING SORRY FOR YOURSELF

Feel like a loser? Have you ever considered the possibility maybe it's because you are one? Whether you're a loser or not, I've got some advice for you. Everyone, from time to time, feels blue, so here's what you do: own your pain, baby. Because at times, it's all you've got. And not only own it, but use it—at every opportunity. Pain is a very useful device. You can use it to manipulate others into feeling guilty. You can use it to excuse your slovenly behavior. And if you're really clever, you can use it to get others to do what you want them to.

Of course, if you really and truly are a great, big, goose-egg loser, you have to learn to accept that. You can't let stuff bother you. You know that old cliché, live every day as if it's your last? (Which I've never completely understood. I mean, if it's my last day, that means I probably should be strapped into an iron lung and drooling on myself until I'm comatose.) But I guess the message is "savor every moment." You have control over only one life, so make good use of it. As for the rest, Karma awaits. Not in any spiritual sense, but if you screw over enough people, odds are you're not going to make it out unscathed and you're going to have very few advocates in your corner.

But why must you be a loser? What is God's plan? Over the course of our lives, we all ask ourselves at one time or another, what's it all about? What does it all mean? And that's usually when we're listening to Ross Perot explain the economy. I've searched for answers. I've looked in the cushions of my couch (where I found eighty-seven cents and a pizza coupon). But then it hit me: turn to those who have found life's answers and learn from them. And where can you find these enlightened souls, you ask? Well, if you answered Nobel prize winners, clergy, or any philosopher, you're in the wrong section—science and philosophy are on aisle five.

No, the answers, my friend, are right in front of your glassed-over eyeballs—in the movies!

Pity Party: The Tear-jerkers
WHEN YOU'RE FEELING LIKE YOU NEED A GOOD CRY

Sometimes you just want to cry, damn it. Usually, you're a woman, but not always. Sometimes you're a man and sometimes you're a man who wishes he were a woman, but that's not what's important. What's important is that a good cry can purge you of all those ugly feelings. Feelings like all men are evil (they are) and testosterone is the devil's potion (it is). So when you've been dumped and you're alone on a Saturday night and you feel like taking a handful of Valium and opening a vein into a warm bathtub while listening to Billie Holiday wail the blues, watch one of these movies instead. And go ahead, feel sorry for yourself, you deserve it.

1. Casablanca
Humphrey Bogart, Ingrid Bergman, Paul Henreid (1942, PG, 102m, DVD)
They'll always have Paris; you'll always have this video.

2. Splendor in the Grass
Warren Beatty, Natalie Wood (1961, NR, 124m)
Young love lost has never been more heartbreaking. This is the movie in which Beatty got his big break from Director Elia Kazan—which is why Beatty jumped to his feet when Kazan got his Honorary Award at the 1999 Oscar® ceremony while Nick Nolte and Ed Harris scowled with arms folded in protest against the anti-Communist informer.

3. Tess
Nastassja Kinski, Tony Church (1980, PG, 170m)
A sumptuously wrought realization of the tragic Thomas Hardy novel. In fact, this film is so gorgeous it belongs in a museum. Heartbreaking tale of poor, sweet Tess, for whom nothing goes right. It's a film that evokes classic Flemish paintings and 18th century European landscapes populated by sorrowful peasants.

4. Sophie's Choice
Meryl Streep, Kevin Kline, Peter MacNicol (1982, R, 157m, DVD)
Men are evil. Sometimes men even kill your children. Let that be a lesson to you.

5. Gone with the Wind
Vivian Leigh, Clark Gable (1939, NR, 231m, DVD)
Because, frankly you don't give a damn. Really, really, really, you don't—and you just keep telling yourself that, Sweetheart.

6. Umberto D.
Carlo Battisti, Maria-Pia Casilio (1955, NR, 89m)
There's not even a love story (unless you count the dog) but for a good cry this can't be beat—about a retired old man and his pup looking for a scrap of dignity.

7. Dark Victory
Bette Davis, George Brent, Humphrey Bogart (1939, NR, 106m, DVD)
An old-fashioned weepy—served with generous helpings of corn.

8. A Place in the Sun
Elizabeth Taylor, Montgomery Clift, Shelley Winters (1951, NR, 120m)
Based on the novel, *An American Tragedy*, it covers the familiar theme of a poor guy falling for a rich girl with tragic results. Moving performances from Taylor, Clift and Winters make this film especially memorable.

9. The Man in the Moon
Reese Witherspoon, Jason London (1991, PG-13, 100m)
A beautiful rural coming of age story about unrequited love and all those other teenage things that hurt so much before you learn you can stuff all those emotions way deep inside and make yourself feel better by buying a new outfit.

10. Love Story
Ali MacGraw, Ryan O'Neal (1970, PG, 100m)
"Love means never having to say you're sorry." What does that mean? I'm in love with my wife and I still have to say, "I'm sorry," about twice a day.

WHEN TO WATCH
Any Saturday night when you haven't got a date.

WHAT TO EAT
Ben and Jerry's Chunky Monkey® and lots of it.

GREAT LINE
from *Casablanca* by Murray Burnett and Joan Alison (play) and Julius J. Epstein, Philip G. Epstein and Howard Koch

> *"If that plane leaves the ground and you're not with him,*
> *you'll regret it. Maybe not today. Maybe not tomorrow, but*
> *soon and for the rest of your life."*
> —HUMPHREY BOGART as RICK BLAINE

Dateless and Desperate
WHEN YOU'RE FEELING LIKE YOU'LL NEVER GET LAID AGAIN

When you're on a streak of bad luck, sometimes it feels like it'll never end. So if you haven't been laid in a while—like forever—it may seem like it'll never happen. Don't get down on yourself (I know, if you could, you wouldn't ever need to leave the house) just rent one of these movies where people have love lives worse than, or at least as bad as your own. And isn't that one of the reasons we love movies? Because sometimes they make us feel like our lives aren't so bad after all? Give yourself a little ego boost and get a load of these losers. A word of warning: some of these characters do pull out of their slumps and end up getting more action than you, but just look at that as a sign of hope that, yep, it could even happen to someone like me. So spend your Saturday night with one of these stories, because I'm sure you don't have any better offers.

1. Getting it Right
Jesse Birdsall, Helena Bonham-Carter, Lynn Redgrave (1989, R, 101m)
This is a great, overlooked comedy about a thirty-one-year-old virgin. You must see it now!

2. The Last Temptation of Christ
Willem Dafoe, Harvey Keitel (1988, R, 164m)
About a thirty-three-year-old virgin.

3. Remains of the Day
Anthony Hopkins, Emma Thompson (1993, PG, 135m)
Unrequited love in English drawing rooms leads to emptiness for Hopkins, who puts service to his employer before his own yearnings.

4. Kiss of the Spider Woman
William Hurt, Raul Julia, Sonia Braga (1985, R, 119m)
An incarcerated window dresser is in love with his straight cell-mate, a political prisoner, in this intense and original character study. Hurt's character not only has bad luck choosing potential partners, but also has really bad taste in movies as he escapes into his B-movie fantasies. This captivating and ultimately tragic story is the perfect movie to escape into if you want to be reminded just how much better your love life is than some people's.

5. A Dangerous Woman
Debra Winger, Gabriel Byrne, Barbara Hershey (1993, R, 101m)
Winger, as a mentally impaired woman, finally finds love with a handyman.

6. The Fisher King
Amanda Plummer, Robin Williams, Jeff Bridges (1991, R, 138m, DVD)
Plummer has no experience with "the dating process," Bridges has plunged himself into an alcoholic stupor and Williams is a homeless madman. There are plenty of losers for everybody to relate to in this enchanting urban fairy tale for grown-ups.

7. Cat People

Nastassja Kinski, Malcolm McDowell (1982, R, 118m, DVD)

Even Kinski was a virgin once. Or at least played one in the movies. In real life, she was having sex with Roman Polanski when she was a teenager.

8. Jacknife

Ed Harris, Kathy Baker, Robert De Niro (1989, R, 102m)

A brother and sister live a quiet life of desperation until De Niro, who isn't exactly Mr. Life of the Party himself, enters their world in this play-about-post-traumatic-stress-syndrome-turned-movie.

9. The Lonely Passion of Judith Hearne

Maggie Smith, Bob Hoskins (1987, R, 116m)

Ultra-depressing movie about an ultra-repressed piano teacher.

10. The Piano

Holly Hunter, Harvey Keitel, Anna Paquin (1993, R, 120m, DVD)

At least you're not walking around pretending to be a mute while trading sexual favors for piano keys. Are you? Tell me you're not.

WHEN TO WATCH

February 8. Perpetual virgin Gary Coleman's birthday (1968).

WHAT TO EAT

Some "Soup for One."

GREAT LINE

from *Remains of the Day* by Kazuo Ishiguro (novel), Ruth Prawer Jhabvala

"Do you know what I am doing, Miss Kenton? I am placing my mind elsewhere while you chatter away."
　　　　　　　—ANTHONY HOPKINS as STEPHENS

They Just Don't Fit In

WHEN YOU'RE FEELING LIKE YOU'RE THE ONLY ONE

You were picked on as a kid, but that's all over now. Now it's time to have fun at the expense of others.

1. The World According to Garp
Robin Williams, Mary Beth Williams (1982, R, 136m)
Here's a great book that survived its translation to the screen intact. Quirky story about mother and son who live in their own world populated by eccentric characters.

2. Cool Hand Luke
Paul Newman, George Kennedy (1967, NR, 126m, DVD)
Jailed for his non-conformist ways, Newman is working on the chain gang trying to maintain his humanity in this outstanding prison movie.

3. Edward Scissorhands
Johnny Depp, Winona Ryder (1990, PG-13, 100m)
A marvelous Tim Burton creation, Depp's Edward Scissorhands is the ultimate outcast in a cookie-cutter suburban neighborhood. And, like just about all Tim Burton characters (Batman, Beetlejuice, Ed Wood, Pee Wee), he retreats into a world of his own artistic creation.

4. Sling Blade
Billy Bob Thornton, Lucas Black, Dwight Yoakam (1996, R, 134m, DVD)
A moronic psycho-killer makes new friends.

5. Marty
Ernest Borgnine, Betsy Blair (1955, NR, 91m)
Two losers find each other.

6. The Butcher Boy
Eamonn Owens, Stephen Rea (1997, R, 105m)
Neil Jordan's disturbing original comic tale of an adolescent child of useless parents who engages in increasingly delinquent behavior in a small Irish town.

7. Rushmore
Bill Murray, Jason Schwartzman (1998, R, 93m, DVD)
As you might be able to tell from reading this book, I'm a sucker for a fresh, original movie. This is the story of Max, who can't seem to get it together enough to do his school work because he's too busy running clubs, falling for a teacher and befriending a wealthy industrialist played by Murray. Some critics didn't like this movie, because they couldn't stand the characters. How can you not like someone with Max's ingenuity?

8. Carrie
Sissy Spacek, John Travolta (1976, R, 98m, DVD)
This just goes to show that if you raise a girl to be a nice Christian and someone dumps pig's blood on her at her prom, she will use her telekinetic powers to ruin your night.

9. Mask
Cher, Eric Stoltz (1985, PG-13, 120m, DVD)
A moving and true life story of motorcycle mama and her disfigured son.

10. What's Eating Gilbert Grape?
Johnny Depp, Leonardo DiCaprio (1993, PG-13, 118m)
I'll tell you what's eating Gilbert Grape. He's got a 500 pound mother who hasn't left the house in years, he's got a retarded brother who he has to baby-sit all the time and at a time in his life when he should be going off to college and drinking beer until he tips over, he lives in a nothing town and works as a grocery clerk.

SEE ALSO:
The Fisher King ("Dateless and Desperate")
The Elephant Man ("Losers")
Brazil ("The Future Looks Weird")

WHEN TO WATCH
August 25. Professional outsider and Director Tim Burton's birthday (1958).

WHAT TO EAT
You've got a choice: raw eggs from *Cool Hand Luke* or pig's blood (hot dogs will work) from *Carrie*. Or maybe just go pick something up from the corner market—but be nice to the clerk, okay? He's got enough problems.

GREAT LINE
from *Carrie* by Lawrence D. Cohen, Stephen King (novel)

> *"Please see that I'm not like you, mama. I'm funny. I mean all the kids think I'm funny. I don't want to be funny. I want to be normal. I want to start to try to be a whole person before it's too late for me."*
>
> —SISSY SPACEK as CARRIE WHITE to
> PIPER LAURIE as her mom, MARGARET WHITE

Movie Morons

WHEN YOU'RE FEELING LIKE AN IDIOT

These are all what I call "Dumb Guy Comedies." I know what you're thinking, "No, Steve, you don't call these 'Dumb Guy Comedies,' you call them 'Movie Morons,' just look at the title on top of this page." OK, impeach me. I can call them whatever I want whenever I please.

1. Duck Soup
Groucho, Harpo, Chico and Zeppo (1933, NR, 70m)
Classic Marx Brothers lowbrow brilliance. If you like this one, check out *Horse Feathers* and *A Night at the Opera*.

2. The Nutty Professor
Jerry Lewis, Stella Stevens (1963, NR, 107m)
Maybe I'm part French and I just don't know it, but I think this "Dr. Jekyll and Mr. Hyde" take by Lewis is brilliant.

3. Pee Wee's Big Adventure
Paul Reubens, Elizabeth Daily (1985, PG, 92m)
Pee Wee is looking for his bike. It's like the classic Italian film *The Bicycle Thief* but completely different.

4. There's Something About Mary
Cameron Diaz, Matt Dillon, Ben Stiller (1998, R, 188m, DVD)
Vastly overrated comedy which I decided to overrate by listing it high on this list because it is undeniably a perfectly moronic movie.

5. Kingpin
Woody Harrelson, Randy Quaid (1996, PG-13, 107m, DVD)
Dumb.

6. The Jerk
Steve Martin, Bernadette Peters (1979, R, 94m, DVD)
Dumber.

7. Dumb and Dumber
Jim Carrey, Jeff Daniels (1994, PG-13, 110m, DVD)
Dumbest.

8. Naked Gun: From the Files of Police Squad
Leslie Nielson, Priscilla Presley (1988, PG-13, 85m)
The team of Zucker, Abrahams and Zucker practically created their own comedy sub-genre with *Airplane!*, the TV series *Police Squad* and this inspired movie.

9. The Brady Bunch Movie

Shelley Long, Gary Cole, Florence Henderson (1995, PG-13, 88m)

On-target spoof of the show featuring everybody's favorite theme song that has the Bradys trapped in the '90s, blissfully ignorant of the changed world around them.

10. Stripes

Bill Murray, Harold Ramis, Warren Oates (1981, R, 105m, DVD)

Although she's not in the movie, I love the line Dolly Parton once used to describe herself: "You'd be surprised how much it costs to look this cheap." That reminds me of Murray when he plays roles like this. You'd be surprised how smart you have to be to act this stupid.

WHEN TO WATCH
January 17. Dumb-guy millionaire Jim Carrey's birthday (1962).

WHAT TO EAT
Just don't be an idiot. Make sure it's food before you eat anything.

GREAT LINE
from *Duck Soup* by Bert Kalmer, Harry Ruby, Arthur Sheekman, Nat Perrin

> *"Why, a four-year-old child could understand this report. Run out and get me a four-year-old child. I can't make head nor tails out of it."*
>
> —GROUCHO MARX

FEELING SICK AND CRAZY

There are a lot of sick and crazy people in our society. Maybe you're one of them. Don't get paranoid, I didn't say you *were* one of them, I said *maybe*. What, are you crazy?! No, I didn't say you *were* crazy. Stop it, you're bugging me. Hey, maybe I'm crazy! I'm the one who's talking to myself.

Sometimes we feel crazy for awhile and then we get better. That's why we have shrinks and Dr. Laura Schlessinger. She's not a real shrink, but she plays one on TV and on the radio. She also writes books about all the things people do wrong in their lives (*10 Stupid Things Women Do To Mess Up Their Lives*). Personally, I'd like to see her write a book called *10 Stupid Things Dr. Laura has Done To Mess Up Other Peoples' Lives*. She has an army of devotees who listen to her and call her show regularly, only to have her berate them for thirty seconds before she hangs up on them. I have to believe these people are either masochists or they just don't know the right movies to watch.

A new survey in *Consumer Reports* indicates that nine out of ten patients are helped by psychiatry. I don't know about the tenth. Maybe he prefers sugarless gum. Or maybe he's an ax-murderer because the therapy didn't quite work out. My point is, if you truly are sick and crazy, I urge you to get help—real professional help from a real doctor. Not from some radio pop-psychologist you've never met. If however, you're just a *little* sick and crazy, I offer the following movies as an outlet for your mild case of depravity.

Dysfunction Junction

WHEN YOU'RE FEELING OBSESSED

Here are some movies for "people who love too much." These people are obsessed and act inappropriately. Sound like someone you know? Is that you? Then you might relate to these crazies. If not, you may have been stalked by someone just like them—and won't that be fun to re-live?

1. Lolita

James Mason, Sue Lyons (1962, NR, 152m)

Mason and Lyons are great as the dirty old man and the precocious teenage tease he preys upon in this adaptation of one of the twentieth century's greatest novels. Excellent preformances from Shelly Winters and Peter Sellers. (I also liked, by the way, the Adrian Lyne version from 1997.)

2. American Beauty

Kevin Spacey, Annette Bening (1999, R, 212m)

This brilliantly eviscerating attack on American suburban ideals has Spacey go through a mid-life crisis that liberates him from his stale existence. Bening, as his miserably ambitious wife, gives a dazzling comic performance. (The clever among you will notice that the teenaged object of Spacey's affections has the same last name as Lolita from the above mentioned movie.)

3. The Heartbreak Kid

Charles Grodin, Cybill Shepherd (1972, PG, 106m)

Elaine May directs this hilarious Neil Simon story in which Grodin's a schlub who, while on his honeymoon, makes you wince as he woos bombshell Shepherd.

4. Star 80

Eric Roberts, Mariel Hemingway (1983, R, 104m)

Roberts gives such a scary performance in this movie you have to think that if it wasn't for such well-publicized personal problems, he'd be the big star in the family.

5. Fatal Attraction

Glenn Close, Michael Douglas, Ann Archer (1987, R, 120m)

You can't ignore this one. If you do, you might end up with a boiled pet on your stove.

6. The Sterile Cuckoo

Liza Minnelli, Wendell Burton (1969, PG, 108m)

Loopy, lonely Liza weasels her way into a romance with a young college freshman just like she's weaseled her way into our hearts all these years.

7. Play Misty for Me

Clint Eastwood, Jessica Walter, Donna Reed (1971, R, 102m)

Radio D. J. Eastwood is stalked by a fan in this entertaining thriller.

8. Death in Venice
Dirk Bogarde, Bjorn Andrésen (1971, PG, 124m)
Based on the classic novel, this is an interesting film with virtually no dialogue about a seemingly closeted gay man who stalks a teenage boy, who is on vacation with his family at a seaside resort.

9. Suddenly, Last Summer
Elizabeth Taylor, Montgomery Clift, Katharine Hepburn (1959, NR, 114m)
Classic Tennessee Williams adaptation with typical Williams' pathos and tragic decisions made by unenlightened souls. Taylor is haunted by the memory of her gay cousin's death, but his mother, Hepburn, has hired neurosurgeon Clift to make sure Taylor's memory stays buried so everyone can live happily ever after in denial.

10. She's So Lovely
Sean Pean, Robin Wright Penn, John Travolta (1997, R, 97m, DVD)
Mr. and Mrs. Penn play a mentally unstable couple in this story told in two halves. The first half features the crazy duo boozing and carousing. The second half, which seems almost as if it's from another movie, picks up after his ten years of institutionalization. Tour de force acting and a script by John Cassavetes make this an engaging exercise to watch.

SEE ALSO:
La Chienne ("Painters")
Taxi Driver ("Oscar® Whores")
Muriel's Wedding ("To Have and to Watch")

WHEN TO WATCH
If you are an obsessive type, maybe you'll be watching these movies every day.

WHAT TO EAT
As long as you're being obsessive, whatever food you're eating, make sure you count it. Jelly beans are good for that.

MEMORABLE LINE
from *Fatal Attraction* by James Dearden, Nicholas Meyer

> *"I am not going to be ignored, Dan."*
> —GLENN CLOSE as ALEX FORREST

Losers

WHEN YOU WANT TO BE REALLY DEPRESSED

Wanna be depressed? Here's how: watch one of these movies. I always enjoy a little artificial downer when things are going too well. You don't want to allow yourself to get too happy, because you'll eventually be disappointed by something or someone, so get a jump on things by watching one of these downbeat tales.

Already depressed? Well, that works, too. When you're feeling like your life is in the crapper, then for a little boost, check out these movies and watch characters whose lives are much worse than your own. Their lives are going nowhere. Hey, at least you've got a VCR. So watch one of these and you'll see that it could be much, much worse.

1. Midnight Cowboy
Jon Voight, Dustin Hoffman (1969, R, 113m, DVD)
The story of lives of two hustlers on the streets of New York is the only X-rated (an "R" by today's standards) film to garner the Best Picture Academy Award® and this classic certainly deserved it.

2. Ladybird, Ladybird
Crissy Rock, Vladimir Vega (1993, R, 102m)
Stand-up comic Crissy Rock (not to be confused with stand-up comedy genius Chris Rock) gives a gut-wrenching dramatic performance as a working class woman with no idea how to behave as an adult. Four kids by four different fathers and she is on the verge of losing all of them to the social workers.

3. Midnight Express
Brad Davis, John Hurt, Randy Quaid (1978, R, 120m, DVD)
Davis is plunged into a horrific nightmare when he's caught with a small amount of drugs and is carted off to a Turkish prison. There's a lesson for all of us: *Just Say No.*

4. The Elephant Man
Anthony Hopkins, John Hurt, Anne Bancroft (1980, PG, 125m)
This black and white masterpiece is a real downer. The horribly disfigured Elephant Man is so unloved, your life should seem great in comparison.

5. The King of Comedy
Robert De Niro, Jerry Lewis (1982, PG, 101m)
Rupert Pupkin kidnaps a talk show host in order to get his big break as a TV star. Black comedy Hall of Famer.

6. Papillon
Steve McQueen, Dustin Hoffman (1973, PG, 150m)
Prison escape adventure set on Devil's Island is the *Shawshank Redemption* of its day.

7. Save the Tiger
Jack Lemmon, Laurie Heineman (1973, R, 100m)
Middle aged Everyman Lemmon is near total-breakdown from the pressures of the garment business in his Oscar®-winning portrayal.

8. Last Exit to Brooklyn
Jennifer Jason Leigh, Burt Young (1990, R, 102m)
Gritty, downbeat, soul-sucking, why-go-on-living drama starring Leigh as a character who gets gang raped on a dirty mattress in an alley. Hey, you're the one who wants to wallow in your own depression.

9. Pixote
Fernando Ramos Da Silva, Marília Pêra (1981, NR, 127m)
Brutally realistic and tragic portrait of the criminal street life of a ten-year-old living, pimping and sniffing glue on the streets of São Paulo.

10. Mike Leigh's Naked
David Thewlis, Lesley Sharp (1993, R, 131m)
The gritty story of a homeless rapist who preys his way into the lives of several lonely characters. Compelling adult drama.

WHEN TO WATCH
Whenever you can get your hands on some electronic equipment.

WHAT TO EAT
Most of the characters in these films resort to stealing food. In *Midnight Cowboy*, Rizzo steals salami from a party, only to have a guest explain to him that food at parties is free. So, have a party and allow your guests to steal the food.

GREAT LINE
from *Ladybird, Ladybird* by Rona Munro

"He never, ever touched the kids. You gotta give him that."
—CRISSY ROCK as MAGGIE CONLAN

Middle Age Crazy

WHEN YOU'RE FEELING LIKE STARTING OVER

For some reason, men—and it is almost always men—hit middle age and suddenly feel compelled to buy sports cars and sleep with nineteen-year-old models. The truth is, men almost always, at every age, feel like buying sports cars and sleeping with nineteen-year-old models, but it's not until they reach middle age that they can afford really good ones (sports cars or models). If you want to bond with other middle-aged men without having to join some weird men's group that would have you banging drums in the middle of the woods, watch one of these movies. You can have your own little crisis in the privacy of your living room and no one ever has to know.

1. Groundhog Day
Andie MacDowell, Bill Murray, Chris Elliott (1993, PG, 103m, DVD)
The ultimate middle-aged dream: to start over and get it right this time. This movie is inspired.

2. The Seven Year Itch
Marilyn Monroe, Tom Ewell (1955, NR, 105m)
OK, so this is really the middle-aged dream: the wife is out of town and Marilyn is hitting on you.

3. 8 1/2
Marcello Mastroianni, Claudia Cardinale (1962, NR, 135m)
Fellini's contemplation of mid-life and mid-career stagnation is a description that cannot relay all the joys of this film.

4. Defending Your Life
Albert Brooks, Meryl Streep (1991, PG, 112m)
Brooks goes to purgatory where his angst about getting into heaven, as his life is put on trial, is hilarious.

5. Fearless
Jeff Bridges, Rosie Perez (1993, R, 122m)
A great movie about fear as a motivation for change. Bridges survives a plane crash, throwing his whole life for a loop.

6. 10
Bo Derek, Dudley Moore, Julie Andrews (R, 121m, DVD)
This movie made Bo the hottest thing on the planet until she gave a lot of very bad performances in a lot of very bad films.

7. 42 Up
Documentary, directed by Michael Apted (1998, NR, 139m)
Somehow forty-two doesn't sound as old as it used to. But maybe that's just me. This fascinating film is a series of interviews of British schoolkids done every seven years as they grow up, sadly, exactly as their families' social standing would dictate. Here the real life characters face the onset of middle age.

8. Mother
Albert Brooks, Debbie Reynolds (1996, PG-13, 104m)
Brooks is such a loser at love that he moves in with Mom to figure out where it all went wrong.

9. Seconds
Rock Hudson, John Randolph (1966, R, 107m)
A captivating tale about an executive who gets a new identity, inhabiting Hudson's body. He has the time of his life...for a while.

10. Starting Over
Burt Reynolds, Jill Clayburgh, Candice Bergen (1979, R, 106m)
Reynolds is a guy who just can't seem to get on with his life (or accept his evaporating hairline) in this comedy scripted by James Brooks.

SEE ALSO:
Terms of Endearment ("Mothers and Daughters")
Crimes and Misdemeanors ("Woody's Finest: The Films of Woody Allen")
American Beauty ("Dysfunction Junction")
Faces ("Splitsville Hits")

WHEN TO WATCH
On your fortieth birthday.

WHAT TO EAT
In *Groundhog Day*, Bill Murray as Phil Connors reminisces about the day he drank piña coladas and ate lobster in the Virgin Islands, so I recommend that. You're middle-aged, you can afford to treat yourself to some lobster.

GREAT LINE
from *Mother* by Albert Brooks

"Stop. No more food. It's like Fantasia."
—ALBERT BROOKS as JOHN HENDERSON

Gross Out

WHEN YOU'RE FEELING GROSS

These are so gross, they'll kill your appetite. These, then, would be excellent movies to watch when you're trying to diet. Other people will deliberately seek these out. Why will they do this?—for some deep, twisted need to watch really gross things, I suppose. For these deviants I present a list of the grossest movies committed to celluloid.

1. Re-Animator
Jeffrey Combs, Bruce Abbott, Barbara Crampton (1984, NR, 86m)
This movie is really sick and disgusting and you shouldn't laugh at its sick jokes—unless you really like sick jokes, in which case it's very funny.

2. Henry: Portrait of a Serial Killer
Michael Rooker, Tom Towles, Tracy Arnold (1990, X, 90m)
While watching this nearly unbearably gruesome serial killer story, I didn't know whether to vomit, run screaming from the theater or join Jerry Falwell's pro-censorship crusade.

3. Se7en
Brad Pitt, Morgan Freeman, Gwyneth Paltrow, Kevin Spacey (1995, R, 127m, DVD)
Even the opening titles scare me.

4. The Texas Chainsaw Massacre
Marilyn Burns, Allen Danziger (1974, R, 86m, DVD)
The Granddaddy of all slasher pics.

5. The Bad Lieutenant
Harvey Keitel, Brian McElroy (1992, NC-17, 98m, DVD)
Depraved tale of a corrupt police lieutenant investigating a nun's rape. There are many distasteful scenes...but must we see Harvey Keitel naked?

6. La Grande Bouffe
Marcello Mastrioanni, Philippe Noiret, Michel Piccoli (1973, NR, 125m)
French movie about a bunch of guys who try to gorge themselves to death.

7. Monty Python's The Meaning of Life
John Cleese, Graham Chapman, Eric Idle, Terry Gilliam (1983, R, 107m, DVD)
A series of irreverent sketches about the phases of life from womb to tomb. The world's most obese man scene is particularly...how shall I put this...memorable.

8. Pink Flamingos

Divine, David Lochary (1972, NC-17, 95m)

John Waters film about Babs Johnson who is being challenged for her title as the "Filthiest Person Alive." The pretenders to the throne make a good case for themselves as the disgusting antics abound.

9. Curly Sue

James Belushi, Kelly Lynch, Alison Porter (1991, PG, 102m)

Well, it made *me* sick.

10. Faces of Death

Michael Carr, Thomas Noguchi (1978, NR, 85m)

If you really want to be grossed out, enjoy this exploitive crap that I'm sure one day will be a Fox TV special.

WHEN TO WATCH

May 13. Frequently nude Harvey Keitel's birthday (1939).

WHAT TO EAT

Ugh, who can eat?

GREAT LINE

from *Pink Flamingos* by John Waters

> "Kill everyone now! Condone first degree murder! Advocate cannibalism! Eat shit! Filth is my politics! Filth is my life!"
> —DIVINE as BABS JOHNSON

They're Insane!

WHEN YOU'RE FEELING NUTS

Shrinks have gone through a lot of phases in the movies. In the earliest portrayals of shrinks, they were sort of mysterious Dr. Caligari-esque figures. In the Freudian heyday that was post World War II Hollywood, they were miracle workers who cured people of all kinds of terrible maladies, as in Hitchcock's *Spellbound* (see "Always a Hitch: Films of Alfred Hitchcock"). By the time Michael Caine put on a dress in *Dressed to Kill*, they had become the evil culprits, twisting minds for their own sick purposes. Today, they are no longer the distant uninvolved figures of the past. They are accessible, vulnerable, and sometimes even available for dates, as in *The Prince of Tides*.

Sometimes nothing will do but a good insane movie and here they are. I'm not saying these are the best movies to watch when you're *in* the nut house. That would be a different list altogether, but could undoubtedly include some soothing Kenny G videos. Beside, you don't want to watch movies when you're in an institution; it's hard to rewind when your hands are strapped behind your back. What you want to do in an institution is sit out on the rolling green lawn in a white chaise lounge and quietly gaze into the distance while an old love, whom you haven't seen in six months, tries to get through to you.

1. Ordinary People
Mary Tyler Moore, Timothy Hutton (1980, R, 124m)
A shattering domestic drama about the aftermath of one son's accidental death on an upscale suburban family and the surviving son's work with his therapist. I can still hear the echo of the astonishing Moore, revealing everything about her character by assessing a cracked plate and proclaiming that it would be easy to fix because, "it's a clean break."

2. One Flew over the Cuckoo's Nest
Jack Nicholson, Louise Fletcher (1975, R, 129m, DVD)
Nicholson's institutionalized social iconoclast, R. P. McMurphy, and Fletcher's hard-hearted Nurse Ratched battle for the hearts and minds of a mental ward's patients. Belongs in the rarefied company of *It Happened One Night* and *The Silence of the Lambs* as one of the only films to sweep the top Oscars®.

3. King of Hearts
Alan Bates, Pierre Brasseur (1966, NR, 101m)
The human spirit soars in this fantasy about a wartime soldier who happens upon a French village that has been abandoned except for its mental patients. A wonderful anti-war movie.

4. Dressed to Kill
Michael Caine, Angie Dickenson (1980, R, 105m)
Brian De Palma uses perennially sexy Dickenson, AKA Sergeant Pepper Anderson, as a horny housewife, and Nancy Allen as a call girl, to bait a sexually confused psychotic killer in this enjoyable film which is practically all style.

5. Frances
Jessica Lange, Sam Shepard (1982, R, 134m, DVD)
Feisty nonconformist moviestar Frances Farmer is played by feisty nonconformist moviestar Lange in the life story of a woman who would not be constrained by the world, that is, until they gave her a lobotomy and scooped out a chunk of her brain.

6. A Woman Under the Influence
Gena Rowlands, Peter Falk (1974, R, 155m, DVD)
Rowlands is brilliant as a run-away wagon missing a couple of wheels. As she goes over the edge, Falk, as her blue-collar husband, just can't deal in another free-form John Cassavetes opus.

7. The Snake Pit
Olivia de Havilland, Mark Stevens, Leo Genn (1948, NR, 108m)
The horrors of mental asylums are exposed in this, one of the first films to deal with mental health. De Havilland is enjoyably over the top as a woman having the breakdown.

8. Three Faces of Eve
Joanne Woodward, David Wayne, Lee J. Cobb (1957, NR, 91m)
Woodward got the 1957 Oscar® for Best Actress and she didn't even have to split it with her other two personalities.

9. Harvey
Jimmy Stewart, Josephine Hull (1950, NR, 104m)
Stewart's Elwood P. Dowd is a crazy alcoholic with an imaginary six foot rabbit companion, but the folks down at the asylum are okay with that in this appealing comedy classic.

10. Don Juan DeMarco
Johnny Depp, Marlon Brando, Faye Dunaway (1994, PG-13, 92m)
A winning fantasy in which Depp is institutionalized for believing he is Don Juan, the world-renowned Latin Lover. Things get a little out of control when he begins to convince his shrink (an enormous Brando) that maybe he is.

SEE ALSO:
The Prince of Tides ("Adulterous Faves")
Birdy ('Nam")
Spellbound ("Always a Hitch: Films of Alfred Hitchcock")

WHEN TO WATCH
May 6. Cocaine fiend Sigmund Freud's (1856-1939) birthday.

WHAT TO EAT
Sometimes a banana is just a banana.

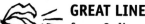 **GREAT LINE**
from *Ordinary People* by Alvin Sargent, Judith Guest (novel)

"You tell me the definition of happy, huh? But first, you better make sure that your kids are safe, that no one's fallen off a horse, or been hit by a car or drowned in that swimming pool you're so proud of and then you come and tell me how to be happy."

—MARY TYLER MOORE as BETH JERROD

FEELING HUNGRY AND THIRSTY

Scientists discover all kinds of fun things. For example, researchers have discovered that certain species of fish change sexes to suit social circumstances. (You'll see them soon in your grocer's freezer as "Mrs. Ru Paul's Fishsticks.") It seems like about once a week there's a new study done about a particular food that causes cancer or changes your life in some way. This is not a good trend. First of all, it limits the amount of fun stuff you can consume, and secondly, it puts the responsibility for death squarely in your own lap. If you get cancer, it's your fault because you consumed artificial sweeteners or not enough fiber.

There's always a silver lining to these studies. For example, a new study finds that drugs to lower cholesterol cause cancer. But the good news is cancer causes weight loss, so cheer up! I like the old days, when we either didn't know what killed us or we could sue the tobacco companies for our own indulgences. The good news is, since you can't possibly keep track of all these weekly scientific bulletins, why not just throw up your arms, say to hell with it all and eat what you want? Go ahead...have a Twinkie.

Eat, drink and be merry, and enjoy a hunger or thirst-inducing movie to set the mood.

I'll Drink to That

WHEN YOU'RE FEELING LIKE AN ALCOHOLIC

Nothing is more annoying than a recovering alcoholic who doesn't want to remain anonymous. Hey, I don't want to hear your story, even though you are on step five or seven—they have little clubs for that, don't they?

Check out these movies for recovering alcoholics. These movies feature drunks who are bottoming out in a big way. Even alcoholics can watch these and feel superior. In fact, get two of these and make it a double.

1. Barfly

Mickey Rourke, Faye Dunaway (1987, R, 100m)

That thing about the French liking Jerry Lewis is a bit passé. Rourke is the guy the French *really* take to heart. And when you see his hygiene in this film you have to wonder if that's the connection. Dunaway and a Charles Bukowski-esque Rourke give shattering performances as a couple of street-drunks.

2. Who's Afraid of Virginia Woolf?

Richard Burton, Elizabeth Taylor (1966, NR, 127m, DVD)

Burton and Taylor, as a long-married professor and his wife, play wicked, booze-induced mindgames in an effort to see who can be the most cruel the other, causing great distress for their dinner guests, George Segal and Sandy Dennis. The high point of all their careers.

3. The Lost Weekend

Ray Milland, Jane Wyman (1945, NR, 100m)

This powerful drama stars Oscar®-winner Milland as a writer, or at least he would be a writer if he would come up for air from that bender he's on.

4. The Days of Wine and Roses

Jack Lemmon, Lee Remick (1962, NR, 138m)

Based on a TV movie, this is a superb rendition of the story of a drunk who pulls his wife down into the gutter with him.

5. A Star is Born

Judy Garland, James Mason (1954, PG, 175m)

Director George Cukor, who always had a way with getting great performances out of actresses, pulls one out of Garland, who plays a star on her way to the top while her husband is a star on his way down, a trajectory accelerated by the hooch.

6. Sweet Bird of Youth

Geraldine Page, Paul Newman (1962, NR, 120m)

A big screen adaptation of the Tennessee Williams play, starring Page as a washed-up movie star who's on the sauce. When she hits rock bottom, she takes up with opportunistic Newman. Only in the movies can sleeping with Newman be a sign that a woman has bottomed-out.

7. Ironweed
Meryl Streep, Jack Nicholson (1987, R, 135m)
The two greatest actors working in films today prove that they deserve that description in this unrelentingly downbeat portrait of two homeless alcoholics in William Kennedy's adaptation of his Pulitzer Prize-winning novel. This would be the triumph of a lifetime for any actor other than one of these two, who routinely disappear into the characters they inhabit.

8. Affliction
Nick Nolte, James Coburn, Sissy Spacek (1997, R, 113m, DVD)
Some people get sweet and cuddly when they get drunk. Not Coburn—he's a nasty son of a bitch and he's got the Oscar® to prove it.

9. When a Man Loves a Woman
Meg Ryan, Andy Garcia (1994, R, 126)
When America's cupie doll has one too many cocktails, Ryan has to take the long walk to sobriety—twelve steps at a time.

10. Clean and Sober
Michael Keaton, Kathy Baker, Morgan Freeman (1988, R, 124m)
Denial. Denial. Denial. Keaton won't even admit he's an addict after he checks himself into rehab. But he'll learn.

SEE ALSO:
Leaving Las Vegas ("Oscar® Whores")
Tender Mercies ("They Sing, They Have Problems")

WHEN TO WATCH
Please, not before two in the afternoon and certainly not with those bright lights on.

WHAT TO EAT
Food? While spoil a good buzz? Stick to something out of a plain brown bag.

GREAT LINE
from *Who's Afraid of Virginia Woolf?* by Edward Albee and Ernest Lehman

> *"Martha, in my mind you're buried in cement right up to the neck. No, up to the nose, it's much quieter."*
> —RICHARD BURTON as GEORGE

Cocktail Cinema

WHEN YOU'RE FEELING LIKE A DRINK

Sure, the people in these movies may very well be alcoholics, but they're also having a great time. They don't go to meetings; they don't have to make amends to anyone. The only twelve steps they're taking lead right up to the bar. These are great movies to watch while you, yourself, are swilling a fancy cocktail—perhaps a martini or a Manhattan. As Frank Sinatra said, "I feel sorry for people who don't drink. When they wake up in the morning, that's as good as they're going to feel all day."

1. The Thin Man
Myrna Loy, William Powell (1934, NR, 90m)
I love the scene near the beginning where Nora Charles finds her husband, Nick, at a bar and asks him sternly how many drinks he's had. Just when you think she's gonna bawl him out, she looks at the waiter and orders enough martinis to catch up.

2. My Favorite Year
Peter O'Toole, Joseph Bologna (1982, PG, 92m)
O'Toole plays a swashbuckling moviestar who's making an appearance on a '50s television show if he can stay sober. Hey, that's *Titanic's* Gloria Stuart dancing with O'Toole in a nightclub.

3. The Moderns
Keith Carradine, Linda Fiorentino (1988, R, 126m)
Always-interesting and sometimes-maddening director Alan Rudolph creates another visually stylish treat. This one's about the American ex-pat artist community in Paris during the '20s.

4. Auntie Mame
Rosalind Russell, Forrest Tucker (1958, NR, 161m)
Russell is bigger than life in this story of the outlandish aunt who has enough *joie de vivre* and gin for everyone.

5. Arthur
Dudley Moore, Liza Minnelli, John Gielgud (1981, PG, 97m, DVD)
Sure, he's a lovable alcoholic, but underneath it's really a cautionary tale: alcohol might make you marry Liza.

6. Madam Satan
Kay Johnson, Reginald Denny, Lillian Roth (1930, NR, 115m)
This is one whacked-out movie. A lavish Cecil B. DeMille silent film with one of the most amazing party scenes ever filmed—a big bash aboard a blimp.

7. Mrs. Parker and the Vicious Circle
Jennifer Jason Leigh, Matthew Broderick (1994, R, 124m)
Tales from the days when the savage literary wits gathered at New York's Algonquin Hotel and slung barbs at each other across Dorothy Parker's roundtable. The only problem I have with this movie is that Leigh mumbles through the whole thing so it's hard to understand her. I think she said something like, "I write doodads because it's a doodad kind of town." Huh?

8. The Party
Peter Sellers, Claudine Longet (1968, NR, 99m)
Pure slapstick has Sellers playing an awkward guest at a Hollywood power-party. Sellers joins the comic ranks of Jacques Tati and Buster Keaton with this minimal dialogue performance.

9. Design for Living
Fredric March, Gary Cooper, Miriam Hopkins (1933, NR, 90m)
Sophisticated Noel Coward story about a love triangle among American friends in Paris. As Isaac Davis says in Woody Allen's *Manhattan,* "I feel like we're in a Noel Coward play. Someone should be making martinis."

10. Don's Party
Pat Bishop, Graham Kennedy (1976, NR, 90m)
A group of Australian friends and neighbors get together to watch election returns and the booze flows so freely that lots of people do and say things they will regret in the morning. It's funny when you're the one watching it and not the one doing it.

SEE ALSO:
The Philadelphia Story ("Delusional Cinema")
The Palm Beach Story ("Delusional Cinema")

WHEN TO WATCH
January 16. Prohibition Remembrance Day.

WHAT TO EAT
Cocktail onions, finger sandwiches and a nice dry gin martini straight up with a twist.

GREAT LINE
from *The Thin Man* by Albert Hackett, Frances Goodrich, Dashell Hammett (novel)

> *"The important thing is the rhythm. Always have rhythm in your shaking. Now a Manhattan you always shake to fox-trot time, a Bronx to two-step time, a dry martini you always shake to waltz time."*
> —WILLIAM POWELL as NICK CHARLES

Mouth-Watering Movies

WHEN YOU'RE NOT FEELING HUNGRY

Granted, rarely do you go to the video store and say to yourself, "I'm looking for a movie that will make me really hungry." On the other hand, there are those people who genuinely appreciate food. There are people who really love the taste of it, the look of it, the scent of it. For these foodies, I present the following mouth-watering movies to savor. I'd like to suggest that you eat while watching these, otherwise your salivary glands may have a melt-down.

1. Big Night

Tony Shaloub, Stanley Tucci, Isabella Rossellini, Minnie Driver (1995, R, 109m, DVD)

A pair of brothers host one last hurrah in an attempt to save their failing Italian restaurant, *a pièce de résistance* meal to end all meals, in this nostalgic comedy set in 1950s New Jersey.

2. Eat Drink Man Woman

Sihung Lung, Kuei-Mei Yang, Yu-Wen Wang, Chien-Lien Wu (1994, R, 123m)

A delicious comedy in which a Chinese chef who is losing his sense of taste tries to connect with his three very different daughters.

3. Babette's Feast

Stephane Audran, Bibi Andersson (1987, NR, 102m)

Feast your eyes on this mouth-watering adaptation of an Isak Dinesen (*Out of Africa*) story that leads up to the most sumptuous meal ever committed to celluloid.

4. Tampopo

Ken Watanabe, Tsutomu Yamazaki (1986, NR, 114m, DVD)

A funny, fresh Japanese comedy about making the perfect noodle. Trust me on this one.

5. Like Water for Chocolate

Lumi Cavazos, Marco Leonardi (1993, R, 105m)

A mystical film in which passion expressed through cooking transforms a woman's ordinary existence into a magical one.

6. My Dinner with Andre

Andre Gregory, Wallace Shawn (1981, NR, 110m, DVD)

Eavesdropping on people while they eat dinner is a passion of mine, so imagine how I enjoyed this movie which consists entirely of two old friends having an engrossing dinner conversation about the way they see life.

7. Emma

Gywneth Paltrow, Jeremy Northam, Toni Collette (1996, PG, 121m, DVD)

This pleasing adaptation of Jane Austen's comedy of manners makes the list because of its Victorian obsession with teas, luncheons, parties and picnics.

8. Tom Jones

Albert Finney, Susannah York (1963, NR, 121m)

The famous chicken-eating scene is just one of the assets of this bawdy period piece about a lovable rapscallion social-climbing his way through eighteenth century English society.

9. Soul Food

Vanessa L. Williams, Vivica A. Fox, Nia Long, Brandon Hammond (1997, R, 114m, DVD)

This heartfelt domestic drama about an African American family in Chicago gets played out over Sunday dinners of ham hocks, black-eyed peas, collard greens and sweet corn bread.

10. Eating

Nelly Alard, Frances Bergen (1990, R, 110m)

Henry Jaglom's movies are generally self-aware exercises in narcissism in which he stars, but this one focuses on women and their love/hate relationship with food and he has better luck.

WHEN TO WATCH

Any of the films (except for *Eating*—No one wants to listen to women talk about bulimia at a party) on this list would be good to organize a big Saturday night party around.

WHAT TO EAT

The perfect risotto. The perfect noodle. The perfect anything. For the truly ambitious (insane?) here is what the perfect meal consisted of in *Big Night* (as described in the Chicago Tribune): Start with some toasted crostini with herbed cream cheese. Then a clear consommé, made with lobster stock. Tri-color risotto (red seafood, white Parmesan and green pesto) is next followed by timpano (a stuffed pastry). Following that is whole-roasted red snapper with braised artichokes. Then comes roasted chicken, with roasted tomatoes and garlic heads, followed by steamed mussels. A platter of biscotti and fresh fruit for the final course. And lots of wine. Good luck to you.

GREAT LINE

from *Big Night* by Joseph Tropiano, Stanley Tucci

> *"Bite your teeth into the ass of life."*
> —IAN HOLM as PASCAL

FEELING LIKE A GUY

Since men rule the world (sorry, ladies), a lot of movies cater to us. Lots of stupid movies in which things get blown up. Lots of movies with women relegated to minor roles in which no one talks about feelings or even has any discernible feelings about anything. Interestingly, no one has a dismissive nickname for these kinds of movies. If it's a women's movie, it's a "Chick Flick." If it's a men's movie, it's just called a movie. No one goes around calling it a "Prick Flick" (though maybe you women out there might want to try that and see if it sticks). I'm not saying men don't ever want to see movies about feelings. That's a tired cliché. Men happen to feel *very* strongly about killing other men, for example, and we hold many other related topics close to our hearts.

Perhaps if you explore the following selections of films, you might learn something about your own maleness, but hopefully not too much. And, guys—the good news is you don't have to pull over and ask anyone for directions. I've included all the films right here in this book.

Some Movies Are from Mars...

WHEN YOU'RE FEELING MACHO

Slip into your dingiest boxers, open a six-pack, cut loose some gas and enjoy one of these fine films. She may not enjoy them, but let's admit it—you don't enjoy a lot, or even most, of the things she really enjoys, like a good manicure or a hot bubble bath. So treat yourself to a movie you really like. These are all classic *Guy Movies*—and don't listen to her when she calls 'em "Prick Flicks."

1. Terminator 2: Judgment Day
Arnold Schwarzenegger, Linda Hamilton, Edward Furlong (1991, R, 139m, DVD)
Ah-nold is a robot sent from the future to save the world in the ultimate special effects action movie of all time and what is surely one of film history's greatest sequels.

2. Die Hard
Bruce Willis, Bonnie Bedelia, Alan Rickman (1988, R, 114m, DVD)
This story of a Los Angeles high-rise under siege by terrorists is often imitated but seldom matched (not even by its two above-average sequels). This film is a real kick in the ass.

3. Dr. No
Sean Connery, Ursula Andress, Joseph Wiseman (1962, PG, 111m)
The first and still one of the best James Bonds. With Connery as Bond and Andress as Honey Ryder.

4. Caddyshack
Chevy Chase, Rodney Dangerfield, Bill Murray (1980, R, 99m, DVD)
Chase, Dangerfield, and Murray get involved in some moronic highjinks at an affluent country club. Don't you just want to throw it on and watch it right now?

5. The Three Stooges: Curly Classics
Moe Howard, Larry Fine, Curly Howard (1999, NR, 108m, DVD)
Includes such classic shorts from the '30s and '40s as: *A Plumbing We Will Go, Men in Black,* and *Micro-Phonics.* The Stooges—it's a gender thing.

6. The Usual Suspects
Kevin Spacey, Gabriel Byrne, Chazz Palminteri (1995, R, 105m, DVD)
Five New York criminals—introduced to one another by the police, thank you very much—plot a very elaborate heist which is elaborately constructed by writer Christopher McQuarrie.

7. Deliverance
Jon Voight, Burt Reynolds (1972, R, 109m)
Weekend canoeing get-away turns into a harrowing adventure for a group of businessmen. The "squeal like a piggy" scene holds a particularly horrific place in the hearts of men.

8. The Dirty Dozen

Lee Marvin, Ernest Borgnine, Charles Bronson (1967, PG, 149m, DVD)
Rollicking war adventure about twelve loathsome miscreants who are recruited out of prison for a secret mission where they have the opportunity for redemption.

9. Hard-Boiled

Chow Yun-Fat, Tony Leung Chiu Wai (1992, NR, 126m)
Master violence choreographer John Woo shows off with some astounding action.

10. Dirty Harry

Clint Eastwood, Harry Guardino (1971, R, 103m, DVD)
San Francisco cop Harry Callahan kicks bad guys' asses as he pursues a sniper. You have to ask yourself one question: "Do I feel lucky? Well, do ya punk?"

SEE ALSO:
The Godfather ("Gangsters")
Lawrence of Arabia ("Epics")
The Road Warrior ("The Future Looks Weird")
Braveheart ("Epics")

WHEN TO WATCH
May 26. Right-wing devotee John Wayne's birthday (1907-1979).

WHAT TO EAT
How about a Stooges pie fight? Or *Deliverance* squeal-like-a-piggy pork chops?

GREAT LINE
from *Die Hard* by Roderick Thorp (novel), Jeb Stuart and Steven E. De Souza

"Yippie-ki-yea, motherfucker."
—BRUCE WILLIS as JOHN MCCLANE

Win-Win

WHEN YOU'RE FEELING LIKE YOU WANNA COMPROMISE

He wants to watch a movie about sports. She wants to watch a love story. Well these movies have both—it's two, two, two movie treats in one! (Listen guys, if you're at the video store, I'm telling you, bring one of these movies home. You see a movie you might actually like *and* you might actually get laid.)

1. Jerry Maguire
Tom Cruise, Cuba Gooding Jr., Renée Zewelleger (1996, R, 135m, DVD)
Show me the movie! This movie completes me.

2. Field of Dreams
Kevin Costner, Amy Madigan, Ray Liotta (1989, PG, 106m, DVD)
I can't promise that if she watches it, she will come, but this is one sports movie women love.

3. The Hustler
Paul Newman, Jackie Gleason, Piper Laurie (1961, NR, 134m)
Newman's Fast Eddie Felson burns his way into our collective cinema conscience and into Laurie's heart with his riveting performance as a small time pool shark who takes a shot at the big time.

4. The Natural
Robert Redford, Glenn Close (1984, PG, 134m)
Big old-fashioned romantic baseball picture with romance between Redford and Close.

5. Bull Durham
Kevin Costner, Susan Sarandon (1988, R, 107m, DVD)
A sexy baseball romance with a sting. Sarandon is the brightest minor league baseball groupie in the game.

6. Chariots of Fire
Ben Cross, Ian Charelson (1981, PG, 123m, DVD)
A much-heralded, impeccably tasteful film about two Olympic runners in Europe in the 1920s. One is a Scottish missionary and one is Jewish. In depth portrayal of their passions for running. Romantic? To me, the whole '20s look is very romantic. High ideals are very romantic. And then there's the slow-motion Vangelis-scored running on the beach stuff.

7. Rocky
Sylvester Stallone, Talia Shire, Burgess Meredith, Carl Weathers (1976, PG, 125m, DVD)
Before Mr. T and Dolph Lungren, there was Apollo Creed vs. Rocky Balboa. This is the underdog story of a nobody who wants to be a champ and has nothing but drive. The fictional story is nicely paralleled by the real-life story of Stallone, a nobody who wrote and was able to star in this film because, like Rocky, of his sheer tenacity. Whether the "real-life" story is Hollywood PR hype or some version of the truth, it works for me.

8. *White Men Can't Jump*

Woody Harrelson, Wesley Snipes, Rosie Perez (1992, R, 115m)

From the writer and director of *Bull Durham* comes another pointed sports movie. This time the target is basketball.

9. *All the Right Moves*

Tom Cruise, Lea Thompson, Craig T. Nelson(1983, R, 90m)

An early Cruise movie in which he's trying to use his football skills as his ticket out of a working class Pennsylvania mill town.

10. *Tin Cup*

Kevin Costner, Rene Russo (1996, R, 133m, DVD)

It's writer-director Ron Shelton again. While not quite in the same league as *Bull Durham* or *White Men Can't Jump,* this story of a washed-up golf pro trying to qualify for the U.S. Open is still an enjoyable diversion.

WHEN TO WATCH
January 18. U. S. mail fan Kevin Costner's birthday (1955).

WHAT TO DRINK
A six pack for him and a nice Merlot for her.

GREAT LINE
from *Jerry Maguire* by Cameron Crowe

> *"Have you ever gotten the feeling that you aren't completely embarrassed yet, but you glimpse tomorrow's embarrassment?"*
> —TOM CRUISE as JERRY MAGUIRE

Real Sports Movies

WHEN YOU'RE FEELING LIKE A JOCK

OK, here are the sports movies about sports. No dance numbers, no slow motion walks on the beach. She may not appreciate these, so watch 'em when she's out shopping. These movies capture all the passion of sports, and let you experience it without ever moving your lard-ass off the couch. That's a beautiful thing.

1. Raging Bull

Rober De Niro, Cathy Moriarty, Joe Pesci (1980, R, 128m, DVD)
De Niro gained sixty pounds to portray retired fighter Jake La Motta. Never have hot fudge sundaes been so well used. De Niro gives one of the greatest screen portrayals of all-time in a raw and searing movie with everything going for it. A real champion. The black and white cinematography by Michael Chapman and editing by Thelma Schoonmaker are of particular note.

2. Eight Men Out

John Cusack, D.B. Sweeney, Perry Lang, David Strathairn (1988, PG, 121m)
This baseball tragedy sympathetically chronicles the unfortunate true story of the 1919 Chicago Black Sox, who threw the World Series.

3. Hoop Dreams

Documentary, directed by Steve James (1994, PG-13, 169m)
This movie reminds you that being talented and working hard can sometimes get you nowhere. One of the great documentaries of all time.

4. Body and Soul

John Garfield, Lilli Palmer (1947, NR, 104m)
This heavyweight boxing movie is in a class with *Raging Bull* and no others. Although, relationship-phobes should beware, the love of a good woman plays a pivotal role.

5. The Longest Yard

Burt Reynolds, Eddie Albert (1974, R, 121m)
Reynolds is a pro-quarterback incarcerated in a Florida prison and ordered to organize a team of prisoners to play the guards. The movie is all about the game, which is great entertainment.

6. The Endless Summer

Documentary, directed by Bruce Brown (1966, NR, 90m)
Amusing narration adds to the enjoyment of this surfing documentary about the round-the-world pursuit of a year-round, non-stop surfing safari.

7. Pride of the Yankees

Gary Cooper, Teresa Wright, Babe Ruth (1942, NR, 128m, DVD)
A biography of baseball great Lou Gehrig. What more do you need?

8. Hoosiers
Gene Hackman, Barbara Hershey, Dennis Hopper (1986, PG, 115m)
A great Cinderella story of an Indiana high school basketball team.

9. This Sporting Life
Richard Harris, Rachel Roberts (1962, 134m, DVD)
Intense game action in this impactful film about coal miner who dreams of being a professional rugby player.

10. Slap Shot
Paul Newman, Michael Ontkean (1977, R, 123m, DVD)
Newman leads second rate hockey team to success when they decide what they need to do is play dirty. As a result many big laughs are scored.

WHEN TO WATCH
There are only two days in the year when there are no professional sports (MLB, NBA, NHL, or NFL) games in the United States. Either of these days would be a great day to watch one of these movies. (By the way, the only two days of the year in which there are no professional sports games are the day before and the day after the Major League Baseball All-Star Game.)

WHAT TO EAT
Whatever you can dig out from the couch cushions. And beer. Always lots of beer. And if you're a real jock or just want to eat like one, grab some of those high-energy protein bars.

GREAT LINE
from *Raging Bull* by Jake LaMotta (novel) and Joseph Carter

"I coulda been a contender."
—ROBERT DE NIRO as JAKE LAMOTTA
quoting *On the Waterfront*

# FEELING LIKE A GIRL

Hollywood has long relegated women to object status. This is particularly damaging to the careers of actresses over forty. It's interesting to note that when there's a love story like *Harold and Maude*, between a woman who's a senior citizen (Ruth Gordon was in her seventies) and a very young man (Bud Cort was in his twenties), Hollywood treats it like an implausibly hilarious black comedy. However, in a movie like *Entrapment,* where the love story involves a man who's a senior citizen (Sean Connery was seventy) and a very young woman (Catherine Zeta-Jones was twenty-eight), we're supposed to believe it's true love.

In the movie *Punchline*, Sally Field played Tom Hanks' love interest. A few years later, in *Forrest Gump*, she played his mother. That's what happens to actresses over forty. One minute they're in bed with the leading man...the next minute they're tucking him in.

Hollywood puts other pressures on women that men never have to suffer (or at least not to the same extent). In all fairness, I think women can be excused for wanting to occasionally escape into what is derisively called a "Chick Flick." In the movies listed on the following pages, there are all different kinds of women who get to do all different kinds of things, and no woman gets mangled by a chainsaw or any other power tool. A couple of men bite it in the "Kick-Ass Bitches" section, but I thought a nice role reversal like that would be a welcomed change of pace.

P.S. My wife made me write this.

Some Movies Are from Venus...

WHEN YOU'RE FEELING LIKE A GIRLIE-GIRL

I know, I know, he's a jerk. When you go to the video store, he won't let you rent what he mockingly calls "Chick Flicks." Well, all I can say is, ladies, I hope you can pick out movies better than you can pick out guys. But I can only help you with one of those and it's the videos. I know there are certain movies that strike a chord with women and guys just don't get. So watch these when he's not around cause he may not appreciate these movies the way that they deserve to be appreciated—and you know how that feels.

1. Sense and Sensibility
Emma Thompson, Kate Winslet, Hugh Grant (1995, PG, 135m, DVD)
A beautifully done rendition of Jane Austen's novel. It's a jaunty (you can only use that word when you're talking about an Austen piece) period film that'll make you laugh and cry.

2. The Earrings of Madame de...
Charles Boyer, Danielle Darrieux (1954, NR, 105m)
A tragic French love story following a pair of diamond earrings as they slip in and out of the hands of a self-absorbed Countess.

3. The Age of Innocence
Michelle Pfeiffer, Winona Ryder, Daniel Day-Lewis (1993, PG, 138m)
This lavish turn-of-the-century New York drama is so detailed that every china pattern and nuance in a gesture is imbued with great meaning.

4. Thelma & Louise
Susan Sarandon, Geena Davis (1991, R, 130m, DVD)
If this were a song, it would be the Feminist National Anthem.

5. Roman Holiday
Audrey Hepburn, Gregory Peck (1953, NR, 118m)
Hepburn is a princess flitting about Rome to escape her ivory tower life until she falls for American Peck.

6. Working Girl
Melanie Griffith, Sigourney Weaver, Harrison Ford (1988, R, 115m)
Underrated actress and funny sidekick Joan Cusack has the great line, "Sometimes I dance around my apartment in my underwear. Doesn't make me Madonna, never will." But the star attraction is Griffith's Tess, who really gives you someone to root for. Go girl!

7. Sleepless in Seattle
Meg Ryan, Tom Hanks (1993, PG, 105m, DVD)
A Nora Ephron romantic movie about widowed Hanks and engaged Ryan who meet through a computer, wait, no, I mean a radio show.

8. Enchanted April

Joan Plowright, Miranda Richardson, Polly Walker, Josie Lawrence (1992, PG, 93m)

Four English women escape their rainy, dreary lives and rainy, dreary husbands to spend a month in an Italian seaside villa.

9. Pride and Prejudice

Jennifer Ehle, Colin Firth (1996, NR, 300m, DVD)

You owe it to yourself, so sit down put your feet up and watch all five hours of this miniseries that is a delight with great sets, costumes and that overly polite, deliciously accented Jane Austen dialogue.

10. Steel Magnolias

Sally Field, Julia Roberts, Shirley MacLaine, Dolly Parton (1989, PG, 118m)

Six moviestars pretend they're down home Southern pals in this tear-jerker.

SEE ALSO:
The Women ("Splitsville Hits")
The Joy Luck Club ("Mothers and Daughters")
Little Women ("Girl Power")
Postcards from the Edge ("Mothers and Daughters")

WHEN TO WATCH
August 26. Susan B. Anthony Day. Or how about on the last Sunday in January—Superbowl Sunday. You just slip away into another room with one of these.

WHAT TO EAT
High tea includes things like crumpets, scones, and ladyfingers.

GREAT LINE
from *Thelma and Louise* by Callie Khouri

> *"You better be sweet to them, especially your wife. I had a husband that wasn't sweet to me and look how I turned out."*
> —GEENA DAVIS as THELMA

Femme Fatales

WHEN YOU'RE FEELING JUST A LITTLE MEAN AND MANIPULATIVE

The Femme Fatale character is a great cinematic archetype that emerged after World War II when soldiers came home and discovered that their gals, who had been running things while they were away, got a little uppity when asked to resume their previous subservient roles. The type was realized on the screen to perfection by Barbara Stanwyck in *Double Indemnity*, but all these gals do a hell of a job playing the sneaky, scheming, out-for-themselves vilified women. Now, I won't promise that all of these have cat fights, but some of them do and that is something, at least, most men enjoy. Scratch someone's eyes out if you must, but get these movies.

1. All About Eve
Bette Davis, Anne Baxter (1950, NR, 138m)
Put on your seat belts, it's going to be a bitchy night.

2. The Manchurian Candidate
Angela Lansbury, Frank Sinatra, Janet Leigh (1962, NR, 126m, DVD)
Lansbury (that's right, sweet Mrs. Potts), is the manipulative beast behind a paranoid Cold War brainwashing conspiracy in this wicked comedy/thriller.

3. The Postman Always Rings Twice
Lana Turner, John Garfield (1946, NR, 113m)
Turner ropes Garfield into a plot to murder her husband. She's very sexy—admit it, you'd kill for her, too.

4. Jezebel
Bette Davis, George Brent, Henry Fonda (1938, NR, 105m, DVD)
When Davis lost the Scarlett O'Hara gig on *Gone with the Wind*, Warner Bros. tossed her this bone where she could play a manipulative Southern belle. And how 'bout that—she won an Oscar®. That must've helped to soften the blow.

5. Mildred Pierce
Joan Crawford, Jack Carson (1945, NR, 113m)
In this movie Crawford played a sweet, loving mother who has a bitch for a daughter. That's just make-believe, because in real life, apparently, it was the other way around. (see *Mommie Dearest* under "Are You Queer?")

6. The Little Foxes
Bette Davis, Herbert Marshall (1941, NR, 116m, DVD)
Davis again. This time she is at perhaps the zenith of her bitchy powers as the matriarch of a 19th century Southern family.

7. The Bad and the Beautiful
Kirk Douglas, Lana Turner (1952, NR, 118m)
A big screen soap opera about Hollywood, featuring the turbulent relationship between producer Douglas and ambitious actress Turner.

8. I Want to Live!
Susan Hayward, Simon Oakland (1958, NR, 120m)
By the time Hayward walks off to the electric chair in her pumps, you're rooting for the cold blooded killer.

9. Red Rock West
Lara Flynn Boyle, Nicolas Cage (1993, R, 98m)
The skinniest woman in the world, Boyle, lures Cage from his skeevy existence as the lowlife hired to kill her, into an even slimier series of adventures in this stylish film noir set in the desert.

10. Dick Tracy
Warren Beatty, Madonna, Al Pacino, Dustin Hoffman (1990, PG, 105m)
Madonna, a femme fatale? Now there's a stretch.

SEE ALSO:
Double Indemnity ("Los Angeles Noir")

WHEN TO WATCH
April 5. Scenery-chewer Bette Davis' (1908-1989) birthday.

WHAT TO EAT
Whatever it is, be prepared to hurl it across the room in a fit of rage. I suggest some greasy diner food. (á la *The Postman Always Rings Twice*).

GREAT LINE
from *All About Eve* by Joseph L. Mankiewicz, Mary Orr (story)

> *"Nice speech, Eve, but I wouldn't worry too much about your heart. You can always put that award where your heart ought to be."*
>
> —BETTE DAVIS as MARGO CHANNING

Kick-Ass Bitches

WHEN YOU'RE FEELING LIKE YOU HAVE PMS

These are good movies to watch when you need to release some tension to keep from actually killing anyone. Live vicariously through these hellcats as they kick some serious ass.

Now is a good time to go over the finer distinction between "Femme Fatales" and "Kick-Ass Bitches." Femme Fatales manipulate, lie, go behind your back and use people to get what they want. Usually what they want is what the good girl already has: a good man or a good job. "Kick-Ass Bitches," on the other hand, don't want your job *or* your boyfriend—they just want to kick your ass.

1. The Last Seduction
Linda Fiorentino, Peter Berg, Bill Pullman (1994, R, 110m)
Fiorentino is one tough chick you don't want to mess with. If you do, I promise you, she will not just kick your ass, she will also steal your money.

2. Aliens
Sigourney Weaver, Tom Skerritt (1986, R, 138m)
Weaver earns her way onto this list when she straps herself into that power loader and spits at the alien, "Get away from her, you bitch!"

3. Bound
Gina Gershon, Jennifer Tilly (1996, R, 107m, DVD)
Lesbians on the lam!

4. From Russia with Love
Sean Connery, Daniela Bianchi, Lotte Lenya (1963, PG, 125m)
This is the second James Bond movie. What are there, like eighty-seven of them now? Sixty-three-year-old Lotte Lenya (that's right, the one from that "Mac the Knife" song) as Rosa Klebb makes one sinister spy.

5. Romeo is Bleeding
Lena Olin, Gary Oldman (1993, R, 110m)
In this, Olin would just as soon as kick you in the balls as say hello. She's a sick, sick woman who needs serious professional help. Gotta see it to believe it.

6. Ms. 45
Zoe Tamerlis, Steve Singer (1981, R, 84m)
A mute woman is raped a couple of times and goes on an estrogen-fueled revenge rampage. All I can say is, watch the hell out for Ms. 45.

7. La Femme Nikita
Anne Parilaud, Jean-Hugues Anglade (1991, R, 117m)
Kinda like *My Fair Lady* except it's the violent story of a junkie made over into an amoral assassin.

8. *Basic Instinct*
Sharon Stone, Michael Douglas (1992, R, 123m, DVD)
A lot of sex and violence and Stone in her star-making (finally! this was her twenty-fourth movie) role as the bisexual suspect in an ice pick murder.

9. *Tomorrow Never Dies*
Pierce Brosnan, Michelle Yeoh, Jonathan Pryce (1997, PG-13, 119m, DVD)
It's Brosnan's turn to play James Bond (be patient, your turn is coming) in this entry into the series where the media is the villain. Bond teams up with martial arts star Yeoh, who is quite a match for the super spy.

10. *Jackie Brown*
Pam Grier, Robert Forster, Samuel L. Jackson (1997, R, 155m)
I hesitate to call Grier's Jackie Brown a kick-ass bitch, because she's really just trying to do what she has to, just to stay afloat. But she is not gonna be played by anyone in this longish but well-acted look at Los Angeles lowlifes.

SEE ALSO:
Thelma and Louise ("Some Movies Are from Venus")

WHEN TO WATCH
March 28. Occasionally pantyless Sharon Stone's birthday (1958).

WHAT TO EAT
These women don't cook. If they're hungry, they'll just take a piece of you.

GREAT DIALOGUE
from *Romeo is Bleeding* by Hilary Henkin

GARY OLDMAN as JACK GRIMALDI
So, you're the big hoodlum? Personally, I don't see it.

LENA OLIN as MONA DEMARKOV
Keep lookin'.

FEELING KINDA GAY

Millions of dollars have been spent on scientific studies trying to isolate the "gay" gene. Who cares? What I want to know is, what's the connection between gay men and Judy Garland? That's something science will never be able to answer. Or in the movie *In and Out,* one of the factors used to determine if Kevin Kline's character was gay was his affinity for Barbra Streisand. So what does that make James Brolin? *He* loves Barbra Streisand, and I'm sure he owns all her movies and CD's now, and *he's* not gay. See how tricky all this is?

It used to be Hollywood didn't really make a lot of movies about gay people, and any that were made were mostly about straight people reacting to gay people. That's all changing now, with movies like *In and Out, The Opposite of Sex* and *Billy's Hollywood Screen Kiss.*

The following pages offer a few other examples. You'll find some offbeat arty films, some old Hollywood classics, and a few mainstream blockbusters. Also, be sure and check out the list in the "Feeling Romantic" chapter entitled "The Love that Dare Not Speak Its Name." Whichever movie you choose, like the Flintstones in Bedrock, you'll have a gay old time.

What a Drag

WHEN YOU FEEL LIKE DRESSING UP IN WOMEN'S CLOTHING

Actors have a great tradition of dressing up in women's clothing. Sometimes, they even do it while they are acting, as they do in these cross-dressing pictures.

1. Some Like it Hot

Tony Curtis, Jack Lemmon (1959, NR, 120m)
A brilliant Billy Wilder comedy in which Lemmon and Curtis dress in drag to hide out in an all-girl band in order to evade mobsters.

2. Tootsie

Dustin Hoffman, Jessica Lange (1982, PG, 110m)
Go, Tootsie, go!

3. Shakespeare in Love

Gwyneth Paltrow, Joseph Fiennes, Colin Firth (1998, R, 122m, DVD)
Paltrow poses as a man in order to pursue her dream of acting in a Shakespearean play in this rich period comedy that was the "David" that beat out the "Goliath" of *Saving Private Ryan* at the Oscars®.

4. The Adventures of Priscilla, Queen of the Desert

Terrence Stamp, Hugo Weaving, Guy Pierce (1994, R, 102m)
Never have three men enjoyed being girls more than in this energetic cross-Australia, cross-dressing road picture. Its outrageousness was topped only by Lizzy Gardiner, the film's costume designer, who wore a dress made entirely of American Express gold cards to accept her much-deserved Academy Award®.

5. Paris Is Burning

Dorian Corey, Pepper Labeija (1991, R, 71m)
This well-made documentary offers an interesting look at the New York drag scene.

6. The Year of Living Dangerously

Mel Gibson, Sigourney Weaver (1982, PG, 114m, DVD)
That's Linda Hunt as a guy. Freaky, no?

7. La Cage aux Folles

Ugo Tognazzi, Michel Serrault (1978, R, 91m)
This ebullient French farce set in a drag show nightclub was remade in the U. S. as the hit comedy *The Birdcage* and as a Broadway show.

8. Victor/Victoria

Julie Andrews, James Garner, Lesley Ann Warren (1982, PG, 133m)

This woman-pretending-to-be-a-man-pretending-to-be-a-woman farce was also made into a Broadway show (and, by the way, so was *Some Like it Hot* which was made into a show called *Sugar*).

9. Ma Vie en Rose

Georges DuFresne, Jean-Philippe Ecoffey (1997, R, 90m)

A stylish Belgian comedy about a boy who believes he is a girl which, though not every parent's dream, is tolerated—until he starts hitting on the boss's son, which is problematic to say the least.

10. The Birdcage

Robin Williams, Nathan Lane (1995, R, 120m, DVD)

This is faithful to the original French film, *La Cage aux Folles*, upon which it is based. This is a madcap Lane-Williams comedy.

SEE ALSO:
Glen or Glenda ("They Suck")

WHEN TO WATCH

April 7. No Housework Day. You can't be expected to do housework in pearls and high heels.

WHAT TO EAT

Here are some food ideas from Dustin Hoffman as Michael Dorsey in *Tootsie*: "That's what I said, George, if he can't move, how's he gonna sit down? I was a stand-up tomato, George. A juicy, sexy, beefsteak tomato! Nobody does vegetables like me! I did a whole evening of vegetables off-Broadway! I did the best tomato, the best cucumber. I did an endive salad that knocked the critics on their ass!"

GREAT LINE

from *Tootsie* by Larry Gelbart, Elaine May, Don McGuire (story)

DORIS BELACK as TV DIRECTOR, RITA MARSHALL
I'd like to make her look a little more attractive. How far can you pull back?

CAMERAMAN
How do you feel about Cleveland?

Are You Queer?

WHEN YOU'RE FEELING GAY

This is a queer aptitude test. These are movies with a gay sub-text rather than an explicitly gay theme (for that, see "The Love that Dare Not Speak Its Name"). For whatever reason, these movies appeal to gay men. Although none of these movies even has any major gay characters, if you love these movies, you might be gay. Count how many of these are among your favorites—if you score between 8-10, you might want to order your pink triangle bumper sticker right away.

1. What Ever Happened to Baby Jane?

Joan Crawford, Bette Davis (1962, NR, 132m, DVD)
When Crawford's Blanche pitifully whines to Davis' Jane that Jane wouldn't be able to do all the awful things she's doing to her if Blanche weren't wheelchair bound, Davis wickedly retorts: "But you are Blanche, you are in that chair!" If you can repeat dialogue from this film as you watch it, or if you said it aloud as you just read it: you're gay.

2. Giant

Elizabeth Taylor, Rock Hudson, James Dean (1956, NR, 202m)
Taylor, Hudson and Dean—the gay icon trifecta.

3. Women on the Verge of a Nervous Breakdown

Carmen Maura, Fernando Guillen (1988, R, 88m)
The ever-so-gay Pedro Almodóvar's wacky Spanish farce has so much flair and visual wit that it could be a guest on MTV's House of Style.

4. Spartacus

Tony Curtis, Laurence Olivier (1960, PG-13, 196m, DVD)
Homoerotic undertones are barely beneath the surface of this gladiator movie, especially in scene where slave Curtis gives a bath to Olivier.

5. Funny Girl

Barbra Streisand, Omar Sharif (1968, G, 151m)
This Streisand classic is a must for inclusion on this list.

6. Meet Me in St. Louis

Judy Garland, Margaret O'Brien (1944, NR, 113m)
As is this Garland musical about the 1903 World's Fair. Clang clang clang goes the trolley!

7. Pillow Talk

Doris Day, Rock Hudson (1959, NR, 102m, DVD)
Remember—one foot on the floor at all times, campers!

8. Beaches
Bette Midler, Barbara Hershey (1988, PG-13, 123m)
If you're a guy and this is your favorite movie, you're probably already way out of the closet.

9. Mommie Dearest
Faye Dunaway, Mara Hobel (1981, PG, 129m)
The ultimate camp classic. Everyone, say it along with me: "No wire hangers!"

10. George of the Jungle
Brendan Fraser, Leslie Mann (1997, PG, 91m, DVD)
Fraser in a loin cloth. Enough said.

WHEN TO WATCH
October 11. National Coming Out Day.

WHAT TO DRINK
In honor of former board member Joan Crawford, open a bottle of Pepsi.

GREAT LINE
from *Mommie Dearest* by Frank Yablans, Frank Perry, Trafy Hotchner, Robert Getchell, Christina Crawford (book)

"Don't fuck with me, fellas. This ain't my first time at the rodeo."
—FAYE DUNAWAY as JOAN CRAWFORD

Feel-Good Lesbian Favorites

WHEN YOU FEEL LIKE WEARING SENSIBLE SHOES

While not overtly lesbian (for that, see "The Love that Dare Not Speak Its Name"), these films do have a women-who-love-women sensibility. Finally, someone has made a list of movies using only the criterion: "movies Eleanor Roosevelt would have loved."

1. Heavenly Creatures

Melanie Lynskey, Kate Winslet (1994, R, 110m)

Great movie! Based on a true story, this isn't a feel-good movie, but rather a really great, wicked little movie about two girls who plot a murder in New Zealand to destroy parental criticism of their intense relationship. One of the girls grew up to be the best-selling mystery writer Anne Perry.

2. Celine and Julie Go Boating

Juliet Berto, Dominique Labourier (1974, NR, 193m)

An allegorical, trippy story of two women who begin to fuse into one as they develop a deep friendship that involves sharing the same bed and eventually, thoughts. They take hallucinogenic wafers before making regular pilgrimages to a mysterious house where they become involved in lives of the other-wordly characters who live there. Its surrealism must be experienced.

3. The Blue Angel

Marlene Dietrich, Emil Jannings (1930, NR, 90m)

Tuxedo-sporting Dietrich's famed "Falling in Love Again" number makes this film a lock for this list.

4. Pat and Mike

Spencer Tracy, Katharine Hepburn (1952, NR, 95m)

Hepburn as a pro golfer and Tracy as her manager in this sports themed movie filled with cameos by famous athletes.

5. Goldfinger

Sean Connery, Honor Blackman (1964, PG, 117m)

One of the best James Bond movies with one of the best Bond babes, Pussy Galore.

6. A League of Their Own

Geena Davis, Rosie O'Donnell, Madonna, Tom Hanks (1992, PG, 127m, DVD)

Just a bunch of gals getting together to play softball and one of them is O'Donnell and another one is Madonna and not a hint of lesbian undertones—I buy that.

7. Stage Door

Katharine Hepburn, Ginger Rogers, Lucille Ball, Eve Arden (1937, NR, 92m)

This terrific comedy, chockfull of young starlets is about a boarding school for young actresses in New York City.

8. Fried Green Tomatoes

Kathy Bates, Jessica Tandy, Mary Stuart Masterson, Mary Louise Parker (1991, PG-13, 130m, DVD)

Bates listens to Tandy tell the story of a very close friendship between two women during the 1920s and '30s. A very, very close friendship. Though nothing is explicitly discussed, we're talking really close.

9. G. I. Jane

Demi Moore, Viggo Mortensen, Anne Bancroft (1997, R, 124m, DVD)

Before there was *Xena: Warrior Princess*, there was *Red Sonja*. But, I'm afraid that I can not recommend that sword-and-sorcery adventure from the writer of *Conan the Barbarian* even for its camp value. I *can* suggest *G. I. Jane,* starring a buffed-out Moore as a modern day warrior (who is not at all a bad substitute for Xena, might I add).

10. Caged

Eleanor Parker, Agnes Moorehead (1950, NR, 96m)

Classic women in prison movie.

SEE ALSO:
Thelma and Louise ("Some Movies Are from Venus")
The Women ("Splitsville Hits")

WHEN TO WATCH
August 8. Sisters' Day.

WHAT TO EAT
Something simple yet hearty, like a good juicy steak and a crisp salad with a cold can of beer.

GREAT LINE
from *A League of Their Own* by Kelly Candaele (story), Kim Wilson (story), Lowell Ganz and Babaloo Mandel

"Are you crying? There's no crying in baseball."
—TOM HANKS as JIMMY DUGAN

FEELING ARTISTIC

What is it with those crazy artists and their bohemian black clothes and sandals? Their lofts and those crazy felt hats? Their breezy attitude about life? Their rejection of all the social standards held near and dear to our parents and to most Republicans? No, they can't be constrained by a 9-to-5 job, man. Their souls cannot be caged! Their spirits need to fly; they can't be bothered with details like having to earn money to eat. They'd rather just sponge off of you. Don't you understand? They're artists! Don't hassle them just because you've sold out to The Man!

Secretly, you envy the artist. Come on, admit it. Remember when you were little and you used to color? Wasn't that fun? You used to make up stories. You used to play and dance and sing and laugh. Life used to be *fun*, right? So when was it that you cashed in all your artistic instincts, convinced they'd be no use to you in the real world? When did it happen? Was it when you decided to go to college? Get an education? Buy a suit? Do you remember the exact moment in time when every vital spark and artistic impulse ceased to fire away?

Yes, while most of us are worried about the morning's commute and making the mortgage, the artist spends his time dreaming things up all day long and occasionally lopping off an earlobe. Usually his mind just wanders and ponders things like, "Where do clouds go when they're sad?" or, "What if peacocks had birthday parties?" But these meaningless meanderings sometimes hit on something brilliant (I'm still waiting for my lightning to strike) and an artist becomes inspired, enlightened or paid, whichever comes first (but rarely all three at one time).

So get back in touch with your inner bohemian, put on a beret and plunk down in front of the TV. And don't worry, you don't have to do anything crazy like actually create something yourself—it's only a movie.

Writers

WHEN YOU'RE FEELING LITERARY

Writers, of course, write movies. This, despite the fact that actors (and audiences) think actors make up the stuff they say and do as they go along. Directors would have you believe, on the other hand, that their on-the-spot inspiration is responsible for every line of dialogue. Sometimes writers even write movies about other writers. Isn't that an interesting phenomenon? It's like painters painting a painting of a painter. When the screenwriter pens a starring role for a character who is a writer, true to form, however, the miserable, self-loathing writer generally portrays the writer as some kind of a creep.

1. Sunset Boulevard

William Holden, Gloria Swanson (1950, NR, 100m)
You wait here—I'm going to grab my thesaurus because I don't know enough adjectives to tell you how great this movie is. Holden and Swanson star as an out-of-work screenwriter and a washed-up Hollywood star who feed on each other. Love him, love her, love the movie.

2. Barton Fink

John Turturro, John Goodman (1991, R, 116m)
The Coen Brothers' loopy sensibilities are funneled into this surreal movie about writers' block. The movie deals with artistic conviction, intellectual affectation, selling-out and strangers who lurk in the corridors of a run-down Hollywood hotel in the 1930s. Though Barton Fink, the fictional writer, is stumped, the Coens have plenty of ideas.

3. My Left Foot

Daniel Day-Lewis, Brenda Fricker, Cyril Cusack, Fiona Shaw (1989, R, 103m, DVD)
Astonishing portrait of Irish writer Christy Brown who was born with cerebral palsy. Based on Brown's autobiography, the film features an extraordinary performance by Day-Lewis.

4. Reds

Warren Beatty, Diane Keaton (1981, PG, 195m)
Beatty, as American journalist and commie hero John Reed, leads a passionate life as he lives through the Russian revolution and a turbulent affair with Keaton (on and off screen, I might add) in the early twentieth century. This sweeping three and a half hour epic is a rich, beautifully textured film which earned Beatty an Oscar® for his direction.

5. An Angel at My Table

Kerry Fox, Alexia Keogh (1989, R, 157m)
Jane Campion's (*The Piano*) remarkable biography of Janet Frame, who emerges from eight years in a mental institution to become one of New Zealand's greatest writers.

6. The Life of Émile Zola

Paul Muni, Gale Sondergaard (1937, NR, 117m)
Substantial old movie about...well, I'll let you ponder the title and see if you can figure out what this film is about.

7. Deconstructing Harry

Woody Allen, Billy Crystal, Judy Davis, Elizabeth Shue (1997, R, 96m, DVD)

A lot of people started to hate Woody Allen when he married his girlfriend's daughter and that "personal journey" spills out into this movie about a writer surrounded by people who hate him for the way he conducts his personal life. Maybe Woody took up with Soon-Yi because he needed some new material. Seems to have done the trick.

8. Reuben, Reuben

Tom Conti, Kelly McGillis (1983, R, 100m)

This clever script, about a rascally drunken Scottish poet who trades on his name to take advantage of women in a small college town, is lit up by Conti's marvelous performance.

9. The Accidental Tourist

William Hurt, Geena Davis, Kathleen Turner (1988, PG, 121m)

Pensive (read: slow) examination of a travel writer's recovery from his son's death.

10. The Shining

Jack Nicholson, Shelley Duvall (1980, R, 143m)

Stylish Stanley Kubrick film based on Stephen King book about a writer's descent into madness as he and his family spend the winter holed up in vacated resort hotel.

SEE ALSO:
Shakespeare in Love ("What a Drag")
Sophie's Choice ("Pity Party: The Tear-jerkers")
Naked Lunch ("Hip Flicks")
Cross Creek ("Rural Reminiscences")
The Player ("Movies about Movies")

WHEN TO WATCH
April 23. William Shakespeare's birthday (1564-1616).

WHAT TO EAT
How about a *Reuben, Reuben* sandwich?

GREAT LINE
from *Sunset Boulevard* by Billy Wilder, Charles Brackett, D. M. Marshman, Jr.

"We didn't need talking. We had faces."
—GLORIA SWANSON as NORMA DESMOND

Painters

WHEN YOU'RE FEELING ARTISTIC

To a lot of people, painters are a mysterious bunch. They think of painters as being crazy geniuses. I'm here to help you get over that misconception. Being crazy doesn't help you become a better painter any more than it helps you be a better accountant. Granted, that's just my opinion, and it seems that there is a different point-of-view expressed in many of the films listed here, since many of the painters are portrayed here are "a wee bit mad" (as they say in England).

1. La Chienne
Michel Simon, Janie Mareze (1931, NR, 93m)
A brilliant masterpiece, this French film by Jean Renoir, who obviously knows something about painting (being the son of famed Impressionist Pierre Auguste Renoir and all), is the story of a mild-mannered banker who paints as a hobby. The painter is taken advantage of by a prostitute (title translates to "The Bitch") and her pimp. Remade in the U. S. half a century ago in a just OK version called *Scarlet Street*. Attention all producers: this film is ripe for a remake!

2. The Mystery of Picasso
Documentary, directed by Henri-Georges Clauzot (1956, NR, 78m)
This documentary shows Pablo Picasso at work. He paints on glass so the camera can come in close on the back of the "canvas." For much of the film, the entire screen is filled with these paintings coming to life—no painter, no brush, just the paint moving around. It's a privilege to watch. Upon completion of film, all the paintings were destroyed, per Picasso's contract.

3. Vincent & Theo
Tim Roth, Paul Rhys (1990, PG-13, 138m)
Robert Altman's renegade style works well in this deep look into the relationship of Vincent Van Gogh and his brother/manager.

4. Life Lessons from New York Stories
Nick Nolte, Rosanna Arquette (1989, PG, 124m)
Three short stories by three different directors is the concept for this hit and miss film. A definite hit is the first sequence—Martin Scorsese's "Life Lessons," featuring Nolte as a passionate painter involved with Arquette as his assistant.

5. Lust for Life
Kirk Douglas, Anthony Quinn (1956, NR, 122m)
Based on the Irving Stone biography of tortured painter Vincent Van Gogh, this film effectively gets under the painter's skin (and behind his ear).

6. Crumb
Documentary, directed by Terry Zwigoff (1994, R, 119m, DVD)
Comic book creator R. Crumb is one sick bastard. The revelation in this fascinating documentary is that, as we meet the other people in his life, he is the sanest of the bunch. When you're done, you'll want to take a shower to wash away the creepiness.

7. The Agony and the Ecstasy
Charlton Heston, Rex Harrison (1965, NR, 136m)
Another Irving Stone biography. This time it's a portrait of Michaelangelo in this sprawling tableau of the painter's run-ins with the Pope.

8. A Sunday in the Country
Louis Ducreux, Sabine Azema (1984, G, 94m)
Impressionistic visuals reflect the movies nostalgic look at an aging painter reflecting on his life and how things didn't quite turn out as he planned. By the way, is it an actual law that every French film contain a picnic?

9. Sirens
Hugh Grant, Sam Neill, Elle Macpherson (1994, R, 98)
Uptight minister is plunged into a den of iniquity when he and his wife bunk at a bohemian artists colony. This film is a lot of fun.

10. Basquiat
Jeffrey Wright, David Bowie, Dennis Hopper, Gary Oldman, Christopher Walken, Benicio Del Toro (1996, R, 108m)
New York graffiti sensation and spoiled bad boy, Basquiat fancies himself above the rules that govern polite behavior. At least in this film portrayal, he just comes off as a marginally talented asshole. What's interesting is the hype that builds around him.

WHEN TO WATCH
September 15. Inheritor of artistic genes Jean Renoir's birthday (1894-1979).

WHAT TO EAT
Why don't you make yourself a nice picnic? Have some fresh fruit, a jug of wine, a baguette and a wedge of cheese. Spread it all over your living room floor and pretend you live in an impressionistic painting.

GREAT LINE
from *Life Lessons* by Martin Scorsese

> *"It's art. You give it up, you were never an artist in the first place."*
> —NICK NOLTE as LIONEL DOBIE

Dancers

WHEN YOU FEEL AS IF YOU COULD DANCE ALL NIGHT

So, you wanna be the Lord of the Dance. Hey, I'm OK with that. In fact, let me offer you some inspiration.

1. Strictly Ballroom
Paul Mercurio, Tara Mortice (1992, PG, 94m)
Baz Luhrmann directed this wonderfully infectious quirky Australian comedy about a competitive ballroom dancer who dances to the beat of his own drummer.

2. Saturday Night Fever
John Travolta, Karen Lynn Gorney (1977, R, 118m)
How deep is your love? This disco classic has been made into a big Broadway musical. And, having seen it, I can tell you—it's way better than *Cats*.

3. The Turning Point
Anne Bancroft, Shirley MacLaine (1977, PG, 119m)
Loser of twelve Oscars®, this is a wonderful peek into the world of ballet. Bancroft and MacLaine play off of each other beautifully as a diva, who gave up her life for dance, and a mother, who gave up dance for her life.

4. All That Jazz
Roy Scheider, Jessica Lange (1979, R, 120m)
Fellini has *8 1/2*, Woody Allen has *Stardust Memories* and choreographer Bob Fosse has his biographical opus, *All That Jazz*.

5. Flashdance
Jennifer Beales, Michael Nouri (1983, R, 95m)
Welder by day, dancer by night. This is a preposterous fantasy with a peppy pop music score. I say what the hell, rip up your sweatshirts and enjoy it, everyone else did.

6. The Full Monty
Robert Carlyle, Tom Wilkinson, Mark Addy, Steve Huison, William Snape, Paul Barber, Hugo Speer (1996, R, 90m)
The little film that could. This film about a group of out-of-work steel workers who conjure up the notion to generate some cash by performing a male strip show, revealing "The Full Monty," as apparently they say in the U. K., is jolly good fun.

7. Top Hat
Fred Astaire, Ginger Rogers (1935, NR, 97m)
Quintessential Fred and Ginger.

8. Shall We Dance?

Koji Yakusho, Tamiyo Kusakari (1996, NR, 118m)

A sweet Japanese movie about an uptight business man who is, in his heart, a free spirited ballroom dancer.

9. The Red Shoes

Anton Walbrook, Moira Shearer (1948, NR, 136m)

Not to be confused with Showtime's *The Red Shoe Diaries,* this is Michael Powell and Emeric Pressburger's classic backstage ballet tragedy about a woman forced by an impresario to choose dance over love.

10. Waiting for Guffman

Christopher Guest, Eugene Levy (1996, R, 84m)

Hilarious mockumentary about the making of a small town pageant featuring well done improvised performances—especially from Guest, starring as Broadway wannabe Corky St. Clair.

SEE ALSO:
Footloose ("Six Degrees of Kevin Bacon")
Dirty Dancin' ("Romantic Movies for Jews")

WHEN TO WATCH
February 18. Former Sweathog John Travolta's birthday (1954).

WHAT TO EAT
Celery sticks and carrots—those dance clothes are tight.

GREAT LINE
from *Saturday Night Fever* by Norman Wexler, Nik Cohn (article)

> *"When you make it with some of these chicks, they think you gotta dance with 'em."*
>
> —JOHN TRAVOLTA as TONY MANERO

They Sing, They Have Problems

WHEN YOU'RE FEELING LIKE A SAD SONG

There seems to be a thread running through musicians stories: they love the smack or the hooch or the snuff or whatever their addiction of choice is. It's either that or the fame just wrecks them, but in any event, "No one gets out of here alive."

1. Coal Miner's Daughter

Sissy Spacek, Tommy Lee Jones (1980, PG, 125m)

Spacek is a revelation. She goes from scared little teenager to full-blown country star Loretta Lynn over the course of this biopic. She even sings all the songs. This is a one-of-a-kind achievement.

2. What's Love Got to Do with It?

Laurence Fishburne, Angela Bassett (1993, R, 118m, DVD)

This is the story of how Ike Turner used Tina not only to make him a big singing star but also as a punching bag. The only thing I didn't buy about this movie—which earned lead actors Bassett and Fishburne Academy Award® nominations—is how anyone could mess with someone as buff as Bassett.

3. Sid & Nancy

Gary Oldman, Chloe Webb (1986, R, 111m, DVD)

Nancy is the role Courtney Love was born to play. Unfortunately for Courtney, Webb beat her to it and does a good job of capturing punk star Sid Vicious' obnoxious girlfriend in this tale of serious downward mobility. Interestingly enough, do look for Courtney in a smaller role.

4. The Rose

Bette Midler, Alan Bates (1979, R, 134m)

Will they never learn? Controlled substances don't seem to enhance anyone's singing career. This is Midler's sizzling big screen debut as Janis Joplin, except it's not *really* Janis Joplin (wink wink).

5. The Fabulous Baker Boys

Michelle Pfeiffer, Jeff Bridges, Beau Bridges (1989, R, 116m)

Pfeiffer teams up with two mediocre talents to form a lounge act. Things fall apart when she causes tension between the two brothers, played by real-life brothers Jeff and Beau Bridges who are both very good at playing the mediocre talents.

6. The Doors

Val Kilmer, Meg Ryan (1991, R, 138m, DVD)

Break on through to the other side...

7. Sweet Dreams

Jessica Lange, Ed Harris (1985, PG-13, 115m)

It's no *Coal Miner's Daughter*, but this story of Patsy Cline is very good. Lange lip-synchs as the country star and juke box hero.

8. Purple Rain

Prince, Apollonia, Morris Day (1984, R, 113m, DVD)

The mega-platinum Artist's music is the greatest asset of this fictional story of an ascending rock star.

9. Lady Sings the Blues

Diana Ross, Billy Dee Williams (1972, R, 144m)

Queen of cool, Billie Holiday, was a strung-out junkie way before heroin chic. Diana, er, excuse me, Miss Ross, does a great job in the lead role in her first film.

10. Georgia

Jennifer Jason Leigh, Mare Winningham (1995, R, 117m)

Leigh has a truly irritating singing voice. And she's either a really great actress or a truly irritating person as well. In this film, there is no question that she is the former.

WHEN TO WATCH
June 7. The Artist-Formerly-Known-as-Prince's birthday (unless he's changed it, too) (1958).

WHAT TO EAT
A raspberry frappé, the kind they sell in the ice-y cream store.

GREAT LINE
from *Sid & Nancy* by Alex Cox, Abbe Wool

"Never trust a junkie."

—CHLOE WEBB as NANCY SPUNGEN

FEELING LIKE GETTING OUTTA TOWN

Teen crime is still out of control in this country. Instead of dreaming about becoming President, they're dreaming about how they can rip the CD player out of your dashboard. They don't care what you have to say, they'd rather listen to KoЯn. Hey, did I miss a meeting here—when did the Lord of the Flies take over? Somebody fax me the memo.

People living in cities in this country are more paranoid than Don Knotts after a bong bender. We've gone from Main Street to Crack Street. The vision of city life used to be an archetype of gentility. People wanted to move on up to the East side, to a deluxe apartment in the sky! Now we'll settle for making it through an intersection without getting shot in the head.

When did our cities become some sort of drug-induced Salvador Dali nightmare? It's tough to be an urbanite when the urban landscape looks like Tim Burton's Gotham. There's simply nothing very urbane about it. You used to dream about picking out a dream home—now you've got real estate agents trying to convince you that the constant whirring of police choppers overhead sounds "just like the ocean." City dwellers have been forced to become urban guerrillas. Through our tortuously warped, post-modern turn-of-millennium prism, *Blade Runner* looks as quaint as Lake Woebegone.

With increasing regularity, it seems we're reminded that we're living in a tinder box doused in flammable prejudices, just waiting for a jury to strike the match of rage. Maybe we're a little tense because we're wedged into housing like B. F. Skinner's rats. It's like watching a movie at one of these crackerbox multi-plexes where you pay for one movie but get to hear three. They're just going to scoop us all up when things get too crowded and put the Cuisinart on frappé. Soylent Green is people!

Cities are supposed to be cultural centers. What do we find? The intellectual heft of a Fabio novel. If you call an asphalt island with a Sav-On, 59 Minute Photo, California Pizza Kitchen, and a Frame 'n' Lens an urban amenity, then you're in luck, because strip malls cover more corners than most hookers will see in a lifetime.

Move to a nice small town? Good luck. Small town shops run by Mom and Pop are being driven out of business as fast as you can say "Wal-Mart." The only small town American streets left are in Disneyland, and who wants to listen to "Zip-A-Dee-Doo-Dah" day and night?

The problem is we don't know our neighbors. We spend more time with the cast of *Friends* than at neighborhood barbecues. When you've blurred the line between fact and fiction so much you list David Schwimmer as a reference on your resumé, it's time to come up for air, Mr. Limpet. Really, how hard is it to say "hello"? I'm convinced that a neighborhood progressive dinner party would do more to prevent crime than the NRA wet dream of an Uzi in every house. This, of course, is purely speculative, because I couldn't pick my neighbors out of a crowd of one. But do as I write, not as I do. You know why the neighbors always think that the guy who was picking state troopers off with his rifle from atop the water tower is such a nice guy? Because they haven't got a clue! Would you trust your neighbors to psychoanalyze you? They'd have better luck interpreting the Dead Sea Scrolls.

If we couldn't get that Hands Across America thing together, maybe we can at least accomplish Hands Across the Street. Excuse me for waxing a little like Mary Richards here, but let's try the Buddy System, America. I want everyone, right now, to go next door and borrow a cup of sugar. Even if you don't need sugar, just do it. Odds are you won't get your head blown off and you might even make a new friend.

Of course, if you're too fed up with city life to even make an attempt at being neighborly, pack the bags and get out of town. Or better still, how about taking a little two-hour vacation called a movie? That is, if some crackhead hasn't stolen your TV.

Los Angeles Noir

WHEN YOU'RE FEELING LIKE SEEING THE DARK SIDE OF SUNNY SOUTHERN CALIFORNIA

L. A., she's my lady. But she can be as wicked as the afternoon sun is hot, as she proves in these film noir classics. These stories play themselves out from the sprawling San Fernando Valley to the twisting roads of the Hollywood Hills to the oil wells of San Pedro. Just be careful, you might get burned.

1. Chinatown
Faye Dunaway, Jack Nicholson (1974, R, 131m)
Robert Towne didn't have to write another word after finishing this screenplay to seal his reputation as one of the greatest screenwriters ever. Unfortunately, he did go on to write the convoluted sequel, *The Two Jakes,* but that's not what we're here to talk about. Everything about this 1930s faux history of the underbelly of Los Angeles is perfectly executed. A masterpiece.

2. Devil in a Blue Dress
Denzel Washington, Jennifer Beals, Tom Sizemore (1995, R, 102m, DVD)
This Carl Franklin film is in a league with *L.A. Confidential,* which is pretty damn good. Film noir with beautiful evocation of mid-century Los Angeles. This under-appreciated African-American film has the style and plot twists to stack against the best in the genre.

3. Double Indemnity
Barbara Stanwyck, Fred MacMurray (1944, NR, 107m, DVD)
Stanwyck is the ultimate femme fatale and MacMurray is her ideal stool pigeon in this enduring film noir thriller set into motion in that house in the Hollywood hills.

4. Farewell, My Lovely
Robert Mitchum, Charlotte Rampling (1975, R, 95m)
Hard-boiled detective Phillip Marlow is brought to life in the third version of Raymond Chandler's novel. This is a classic film noir that stylishly recreates a mythic Los Angeles reminiscent of the era between World Wars.

5. Kiss Me Deadly
Ralph Meeker, Albert Dekter (1955, NR, 105m)
Director Robert Aldrich effectively brings Mickey Spillane's Mike Hammer to the screen in this movie that was big inspiration to the French New Wave. (See *Breathless* under "Gangsters.")

6. The Long Goodbye
Elliott Gould, Nina Van Palandt (1973, R, 112m)
Robert Altman's take on the film noir genre is a bit quirky, but this is an interesting journey through the world of Raymond Chandler's Los Angeles.

7. One False Move

Bill Paxton, Cynda Williams (1991, R, 105m, DVD)

Carl Franklin again. This film opens with a brutal blood bath in L. A. and then hits the road in what turns out to be an effective modern day twist on the film noir genre.

8. The Grifters

Annette Bening, John Cusack, Anjelica Huston (1990, R, 114m, DVD)

Karma catches up with small-time crooks in one of several films on this list with an incest theme.

9. Dead Again

Kenneth Branagh, Emma Thompson (1991, R, 107m)

This is an interesting hybrid of a film noir thriller and a reincarnation romance. Branagh and Thompson's love has endured through two lifetimes in the movie (but lasted only a few years in Hollywood).

10. D.O.A.

Edmund O'Brien, Pamela Brittan (1950, NR, 83m)

This is a movie about a guy who wakes up to discover he's been poisoned by radiation and he has a matter of days to find out the who and why of his murder.

SEE ALSO:

L.A. Confidential ("Oscar® Whores")

Blade Runner ("Worst Oscar® Oversights")

WHEN TO WATCH

August 18. Banished Roman Polanski's birthday.

WHAT TO EAT

Order out for Chinese.

GREAT DIALOGUE

from *Chinatown* by Robert Towne

> JACK NICHOLSON as J. J. GITTES
> *I said the truth!*

> FAYE DUNAWAY as EVELYN MULWRAY
> *She's my sister.*

Gittes slaps her again.

(cont.)

(cont.)

> EVELYN
> *She's my daughter.*

Gittes slaps her again.

> EVELYN
> *My sister.*

He hits her again.

> EVELYN
> *My daughter, my sister...*

He belts her finally, knocking her into a cheap Chinese vase which shatters and she collapses on the sofa, sobbing.

> GITTES
> *I said I want the truth.*

> EVELYN
> *She's my sister and my daughter!*

Kyo comes running down the stairs.

> EVELYN
> *(in Chinese) For God's sake, Kyo, keep her upstairs, go back!*

Kyo turns after staring at Gittes for a moment then goes back upstairs.

> EVELYN
> *My father and I, understand, or is it too tough for you?*

We'll Always Have Paris

WHEN YOU'RE FEELING LIKE A LITTLE *JOIE DE VIVRE*

Everyone loves Paris. It's so romantic. But do you know why it's romantic? Because there's nothing to do there except make goo-goo eyes at each other. You've got museums and restaurants...after that, what? Try to find a basketball game or a Broadway play, I dare you. The longer you stay there, the more clear it becomes that people don't hang out at sidewalk cafés because they are discussing Proust. They hang out there because they have no where else to go. They are either unemployed and on the government dole, on strike, or they're tourists from Des Moines. But you hang on to your romantic fantasies about Paris and enjoy these movies that keep the dream alive. But enough with the fromage. Oh, and by the way, cheese is not a dessert, it's part of a sandwich. Got that, Croque Monsieur?

1. *Dangerous Liaisons*
Glenn Close, Michelle Pfeiffer, John Malkovich (1988, R, 120m)
It's a sumptuous recreation of 18th century France. Close, as the manipulative Marquise De Merteuil, with help of Malkovich, is out to shatter a few lives for her own amusement. But who'll be sorry in the end?

2. *An American in Paris*
Gene Kelly, Leslie Caron (1951, NR, 113m)
One of the great Hollywood musicals has Kelly starring as a painter gallivanting around Paris to some great Gershwin tunes.

3. *Children of Paradise (Les Enfants du Paradis)*
Jean-Louis Barrault, Arletty (1944, NR, 188m)
Classic French film romance that has the place in the hearts of the French that *Gone with the Wind* does in the hearts of Americans.

4. *Les Misérables*
Jean-Paul Belmondo, Michel Boujenah (1995, R, 174m)
This beloved (the French are so passionate) French story has been retold many times, but this is one of the most interesting versions. And it was not a hit in France, so you might actually like it.

5. *'Round Midnight*
Dexter Gordon, Lonette McKee (1986, R, 132m)
A valentine to American jazz from the French filmmaker Bertrand Tavernier. A boozy Gordon gives a nice, boozy rendition of himself.

6. *Funny Face*
Fred Astaire, Audrey Hepburn (1957, NR, 103m)
Astaire is the photographer, Hepburn is the model and Paris is the background in this stylish musical.

7. Le Million
Annabella, Rene Lefevre (1931, NR, 83m)
Entertaining classic French film about a mad search for a lost lottery ticket.

8. Everyone Says I Love You
Woody Allen, Drew Barrymore, Goldie Hawn, Edward Norton (1996, R, 105m)
Woody takes his angst on the road as he makes a foray out of New York and visits romantic European locations, Venice and Paris. If you can avoid throwing up while he makes out with Julia Roberts you might find this musical—that's right, a musical!—very appealing.

9. Discreet Charm of the Bourgeoisie
Milena Vukotic, Fernando Rey (1972, R, 100m)
Scathing satire of the French middle class is very funny in an artsy kinda way.

10. L'Atalante
Dita Parlo, Jean Daste (1934, NR, 89m)
This film's director, Jean Vigo, didn't have such a great life. He was raised in boarding schools and died in obscurity at the age of twenty-nine. Today, he is recognized as the master of "poetic realism." This is the romantic story of a couple who begin their life together sailing down the Seine on a barge.

SEE ALSO:
Breathless ("Gangsters")
Mon Oncle ("Foreign Faves")
The Red Shoes ("Dancers")
An Angel at My Table ("Writers")
Diva ("So Five Minutes Ago: Movies of the '90s")
Belle de Jour ("Dirty Movies for the Art House Crowd")

WHEN TO WATCH
July 14. Bastille Day.

WHAT TO EAT
Champagne, pâté de foie gras, crepes and lots of cheese.

GREAT LINE
from *An American in Paris* by Alan J. Lerner

"Back home, everyone said I didn't have any talent. They might be saying that here, but it sounds better in French."
—GENE KELLY as JERRY MULLIGAN

It's a Hell of a Town

WHEN YOU'RE FEELING LIKE A SLICE OF THE BIG APPLE

If I can make it there,
I'll make it anywhere.
It's up to you,
New York, New York!

1. Manhattan
Woody Allen, Diane Keaton, Mariel Hemingway, Meryl Streep (1979, R, 96m)
Woody's masterpiece in the eyes of many critics. This is when Woody first really fully demonstrated his pedophilia streak by dating, on screen, high schooler Mariel Hemingway. It also has the added bonus of Streep as Woody's lesbian ex-wife.

2. The French Connection
Gene Hackman, Roy Scheider (1971, R, 102m)
They just don't make good ol' fashioned sleazy smack movies like this anymore.

3. After Hours
Griffin Dunne, Rosanna Arquette, John Heard, Teri Garr (1985, R, 97m)
If it's not one thing it's another in this hilarious Martin Scorsese comedy, where nothing can go right for Dunne. He just wants to go out for a cup of coffee and maybe meet a nice girl—which turns out to be a tall order in New York.

4. On the Town
Gene Kelly, Frank Sinatra, Vera-Ellen (1949, NR, 98m)
Three sailors on leave do up the town in a colorful musical celebration of New York's zesty spirit.

5. New York, New York
Robert De Niro, Liza Minelli (1977, PG, 163m)
Another departure for Scorsese. This time he tries his hand at a musical, with somewhat messy results. But it is an interesting experiment and Liza and De Niro are very engaging.

6. The Apartment
Jack Lemmon, Shirley MacLaine (1960, NR, 125m)
Comedy/drama about the things we are capable of doing to compromise ourselves in the name of upward mobility.

7. The Out-of-Towners
Jack Lemmon, Sandy Dennis (1970, G, 98m)
Forget the tepid, tries-too-hard remake. All the good stuff is in this version. Lemmon and Dennis battle every obstacle New York serves up as everything that can go wrong does for this Ohio couple.

FEELING LIKE GETTING OUTTA TOWN | 171

8. Sabrina
Humphrey Bogart, Audrey Hepburn, William Holden (1954, NR, 113m)
A love triangle finds wealthy brothers Bogart and Holden fighting for poor Hepburn's attentions in this romantic classic.

9. Washington Square
Jennifer Jason Leigh, Ben Chaplin (1997, PG, 115m)
Mid-nineteenth century New York makes an interesting setting for story of ugly duckling Leigh, pursued by a gold-digger. Previously made as *The Heiress*.

10. Six Degrees of Separation
Stockard Channing, Will Smith, Donald Sutherland (1993, R, 112)
About duplicity, wealth and the stratified class system in New York. The Big Apple locations look great.

WHEN TO WATCH
Last week in September through the first week in October. This is generally when the New York Film Festival takes place.

WHAT TO EAT
Deli take-out food. If there isn't a good deli in your neighborhood—somewhere you can order delicious cheese blintzes to go—all the better. Order some lame fast food and complain about how much better the food is in New York (this works for pizza, too).

GREAT LINE
from *The Out-of-Towners* by Neil Simon

"I'm not giving up. I'm just saying, 'I'll never make it.' Giving up is when you can still make it, but you give up."
—JACK LEMMON as GEORGE KELLERMAN

On the Road

WHEN YOU FEEL LIKE RUNNING AWAY FROM EVERYTHING

Sometimes you just want to chuck it all, pack it in, hit the road and run from everything. I'm not going to tell you your troubles will follow you, that you can't hide from yourself or anything remotely that sage. I will give you ten pieces of advice, however. These movies might allow you a vicarious release and may be enough to alleviate some of that burning desire to give up on everything and maybe even give you the perspective you need. A good road picture will give you a couple of hours of inertia and that's all you need to allow lethargy to set in so you just won't have the energy to hit the road.

1. Badlands
Martin Sheen, Sissy Spacek (1974, PG, 94m)
If *Natural Born Killers* had been done in good taste, it would have been this movie.

2. Stranger than Paradise
Richard Edson, Eszter Balint (1984, R, 90m)
Indie darling Jim Jarmusch made this funny film about three quirky traveling companions who drive all over the country and almost nothing happens.

3. Harry and Tonto
Art Carney, Ellen Burstyn (1974, NR, 115m)
A man and a cat go for a very long ride. Carney beat out Jack Nicholson in *Chinatown*, Al Pacino in the *Godfather II*, Dustin Hoffman in *Lenny* and Albert Finney in *Murder on the Orient Express* to win the Oscar®. He *must* be good.

4. Lost in America
Albert Brooks, Julie Hagerty (1985, R, 91m)
Yuppie couple chucks it all and for what? To work as a chef and a crossing guard. Hilarious.

5. Paper Moon
Ryan O'Neal, Tatum O'Neal (1973, PG, 102m)
See, the depression wasn't so depressing. It's funny in this stylish period comedy by ex-film critic Peter Bogdanovich. Who says critics don't know anything about making movies?

6. The Fugitive
Harrison Ford, Tommy Lee Jones (1993, PG-13, 127m, DVD)
How hard can it be to find a guy with only one arm?

7. My Own Private Idaho
River Phoenix, Keanu Reeves (1991, R, 105m)
Phoenix is a prostitute who suffers from narcolepsy (that's narcolepsy, not necrophilia—get your mind out of the gutter) and Reeves is his Shakespeare-spouting "co-worker" in Gus Van Sant's (*Good Will Hunting*) original road picture.

8. Vanishing Point

Barry Newman, Cleavon Little (1971, R, 98m)
Chase across the American Southwest is aided and abetted by radio D.J. who helps driver evade the police as the driver races to an uncertain future.

9. Paris, Texas

Harry Dean Stanton, Nastassja Kinski (1983, R, 98m)
Wim Wenders weaves a thematic tapestry in this tale of a man trying to win back his son after a four-year absence.

10. Love Field

Michelle Pfeiffer, Dennis Haysbert, Stephanie McFadden (1991, PG-13, 104m)
Pfeiffer is obsessed with Jackie Kennedy. She's basically stalking Jackie and John Kennedy's corpse as a woman who makes the journey to Washington from Dallas on a bus so she can attend the President's funeral.

SEE ALSO:
Thelma and Louise ("Some Movies Are from Venus")
Pierrot le Fou ("Gangsters")

WHEN TO WATCH
Labor Day. The day of the ultimate annual road movie that goes nowhere—The Indianapolis 500.

WHAT TO EAT
In *The Fugitive*, Tommy Lee Jones as Marshal Samuel Gerard requests "a cup of coffee and a chocolate doughnut...with some of those little sprinkles on top."

OPENING LINE
from *My Own Private Idaho* by Gus Van Sant

"Always know where I am by the way the road looks."
—RIVER PHOENIX as MIKE WATERS

Desert Island Movies

WHEN YOU'RE FEELING LIKE YOU WANT TO GET AS FAR AWAY AS POSSIBLE

When people talk about their "Desert Island Movies" and some people do (they're usually at those cocktail parties you have to attend to make your spouse/boss/parents happy), they mean that if you were stranded on a desert island what movies would you want to have with you. Now, why you can have a DVD player to watch movies but not have a way to get off the island is not their point. Their point is what are your ten essential movies worth repeated viewings. When *I* say desert island movies, I mean movies set on a desert island. I'm a little literal. These are probably the last movies you'd want on a desert island because you probably wouldn't be swayed by the romance of a stranded-on-a-tropical-island theme if, in order to have enough water to survive, you had to filter your own urine.

1. Swept Away
Giancarlo Giannini, Mariangela Melato (1975, R, 116m)
AKA *Swept Away by an Unusual Destiny in the Blue Sea in August*. Italian director Lina Wertmüller's stranded on a desert island love story. Wertmüller would become the very first woman ever nominated for a Best Director Oscar® for *Seven Beauties*, the film she made after *Swept Away*.

2. Male and Female
Gloria Swanson, Thomas Meighan (1919, NR, 110m)
Cecil B. De Mille's sexy sea story about a wealthy couple stranded on a desert isle with their butler and maid. All class distinctions dissolve when society's shackles are removed.

3. Tabu: A Story of the South Seas
Matahi, Anne Chevalier (1931, NR, 81m)
You say Tabu, I say Taboo, let's call the whole thing a masterpiece. Actually, no one says anything in this classic silent film. It's an ethnographic (look it up) film with a superimposed narrative about two Tahitian lovers trying to flea their island customs. Directed, written and produced by two early film masters, F. W. Murnau and Robert Flaherty.

4. Mutiny on the Bounty
Charles Laughton, Clark Gable (1935, NR, 132m)
Laughton and Gable appear in the greatest version of this oft-told tale about a rebellion against a tyrannical Captain Bligh while on a voyage to the South Seas.

5. Blue Lagoon
Brooke Shields, Christopher Atkins (1980, R, 105m)
I know you're too high-brow for this: beautiful teenagers in loin cloths swimming around a deserted island—yeah, I'm the only one who enjoys this. So watch it for its camp value.

6. *Tarzan*
Minnie Driver, Tony Goldwyn, Rosie O'Donnell (1999, G, 88m, DVD)
Disney's winning formula and gorgeous animation make this extreme sports Tarzan the best of the fifty or so Tarzan movies out there. So it's more of a remote jungle than an island, it's still a stranded-by-a-shipwreck story.

7. *Swiss Family Robinson*
John Mills, Dorothy McGuire (1960, NR, 126m)
No sex, but all the other fun of being stranded on a desert island (like the Gilligan-esque gadgets) in this Disney adaptation of classic children's book.

8. *Joe vs. the Volcano*
Tom Hanks, Meg Ryan (1990, PG, 106m)
Kinda bizarre, but an interesting comedy about being stranded on a desert island with a lot of natives. Ryan does a Peter Sellers thing where she takes on multiple roles.

9. *The Seventh Voyage of Sinbad*
Kerwin Matthews, Kathryn Grant (1958, G, 94m)
Classic Ray Harryhausen stop motion animation brings to life this family-friendly adventure.

10. *South Pacific*
Mitzi Gaynor, Rossano Brazzi (1958, NR, 167m, DVD)
Not really a deserted island, just one filled with colorful characters—but let's not quibble. This tedious and overlong musical will make you feel as if you have been stranded in front of the TV—just fast forward to the musical numbers, some of which are classic.

WHEN TO WATCH
August 21. The day Hawaii became the 50th state (1959).

WHAT TO EAT
Poi and a roast pig with an apple in its mouth. And you'll need a great big rum drink with flowers and fruit coming out of it, to wash it down.

GREAT LINE
from *Joe vs. the Volcano* by John Patrick Shanley

> *"My father says that almost the whole world is asleep.*
> *Everybody you know. Everybody you see. Everybody you talk*
> *to. He says that only a few people are awake and they live in*
> *a state of constant total amazement."*
> —MEG RYAN as PATRICIA

Rural Reminiscences

WHEN YOU'RE FEELING A LITTLE BIT COUNTRY

Sometimes you want to think back wistfully on those languid summer days when you would sit on the back porch, until, when your mom wasn't looking, you and your friends would run off down to the creek and swing on that rope she always told you you'd break your neck on. And then you snap out of it and say to yourself, "I grew up in a concrete building in New Jersey." But it was nice to get away for a few seconds, even if it was only in your head—wasn't it? These movies will make you long for a simpler time—a time that probably never existed because as we all know, life has never been simple.

1. The Last Picture Show
Cybill Shepherd, Jeff Bridges (1971, R, 118m)
Peter Bogdanovich's 1971 study of small town Texas life in the '50s is a black and white American masterpiece. Okay, fine. So we'll let *some* critics make movies.

2. Melvin and Howard
Mary Steenbergen, Paul LeMat, Jason Robards, Jr. (1980, R, 95m)
A brilliant chronicle of the American dream. Based on the true tale of country bumpkin Melvin Dumar who showed up with a will proclaiming himself heir to the massive Howard Hughes fortune claiming that he once picked up the hitchhiking recluse. Steenbergen has more funny moments here than in the entire run of her sitcom "Ink."

3. The Stone Boy
Glenn Close, Robert Duvall, Wilford Brimley (1984, PG, 93m)
A real find. This poignant rural family drama features an all-star cast doing really good work. Don't ask me why this movie isn't better known. It's your fault—you've never seen it.

4. Places in the Heart
Sally Field, John Malkovich, Danny Glover (1984, PG, 113m)
A farm fresh country-fried gem. This is the movie that earned Field her second Oscar®, and gave her the chance to make that speech she lies awake at night wishing she could do over.

5. Cross Creek
Mary Steenbergen, Rip Torn (1982, PG, 115m)
Beautiful script by Dalene Young adapted from writer Marjorie Kinnan Rawlings autobiographical book about life in a remote Florida backwater.

6. Bagdad Café
Marianne Saegebrecht, Jack Palance (1988, PG, 91m)
Irresistible, eccentric slice-of-life about a remote highway café populated by colorful characters.

7. Passion Fish

Mary MacDonnell, Alfre Woodard (1992, R, 136m, DVD)

A slow-paced but engrossing character study. A spoiled soap opera star, played effectively by MacDonnell, is hit by a cab and paralyzed. She goes back home to recuperate in Louisiana swamp country and finally meets her match in Woodard, as the live-in nurse who manages to thaw her out a bit.

8. Square Dance

Winona Ryder, Rob Lowe (1987, PG-13, 118m)

Gemma is a thirteen-year-old who begins to grow up fast when she moves in with her fast-living mom in this Texas tale. Lowe acts retarded, but this time on purpose.

9. The River

Sissy Spacek, Mel Gibson (1994, PG, 124m, DVD)

Family struggles with nature as a river encroaches on their farm. Hey, I have an idea—move!

10. Gas Food Lodging

Brooke Adams, Ione Skye, Fairuza Balk (1992, R, 100m)

The coming-of-age novel of three young women growing up and bored in a New Mexico small town is brought to life by MacArthur Grant Genius Award winner and Director Allison Anders.

SEE ALSO:

Grapes of Wrath ("Working Class Heroes")
Paris, Texas ("On the Road")
Country ("Marital Bliss")
Once Upon a Time...When We Were Colored ("African American Movies to Watch on Kwanzaa")

WHEN TO WATCH

July 30. Cybill Shepherd's ex-husband Peter Bogdanovich's birthday (1939).

WHAT TO EAT

Chicken fried steak, like they ate in *The Last Picture Show*.

GREAT LINE

from *Cross Creek* by Dalene Young, Marjorie Rawlings (book)

"Cross Creek belongs to the wind and the rain, to the sun and the seasons, to the cosmic secrecy of seed, and beyond all to time."

—MARY STEENBURGEN as MARJORIE KINNAN RAWLINGS

FEELING LIKE A GENRE MOVIE

In case you don't know the differences between your movie genres, I'll tell you how a typical "boy-meets-girl" love story would be told differently in each genre. This hypothetical movie stars a boy named Jack, a girl named Jane and a villain named Mr. Big.

MUSICAL

Jack, an usher at a Broadway theater, sees Jane dancing in the chorus of a Broadway show and is instantly smitten with her. But, of course, she's dating the theater owner, Mr. Big, a heartless man who cares only about money. Our usher scrapes together all his resources to produce a show and offers her the lead. "There's something about this kid," thinks Jane, and she leaves the big show to appear in Jack's low-budget, off-Broadway show, which becomes a huge sensation and drives Mr. Big out of the business.

WESTERN

Jack, the sheriff of the dusty one-saloon town, falls for Jane, the new school teacher. He's an ex-gunfighter who has fled from the East Coast to run away from his mysterious past. However, when Mr. Big and a gang of black-hatted bank robbers rides into town, he's forced to defend Jane. Jack takes on all the robbers in a slow-motion, twenty-minute gunfight sequence in which all the bad guys end up killing each other.

GANGSTER

Jane is a saloon girl in a speakeasy accessed through a secret panel in the back of a pawn shop. Mr. Big is the cold-hearted gangster who has just mowed down six men with his tommy gun and talks out of the side of his mouth. He's pursuing Jane romantically and she takes her life in her hands by defying him. Jack is the naive young delivery boy who works for his father in the pawn shop upstairs. He ends up getting cozy with the good girl with the tawdry reputation and a heart of gold and guns down Mr. Big to defend her honor.

EPIC

It's sometime during the Roman Empire. Jack rides off into battle on the back of a horse while wearing a lot of things made out of metal. Jane is the Queen who wants to reward the soldier for his bravery. The King (Mr. Big) is in Thebes on a diplomatic mission (but he's really there to see his mistress). The King orders Jack into the gladiator ring to uphold the honor of the empire, but really it's because he wants Jack dead. Jack becomes a huge gladiator star and eventually the King poisons himself with hemlock because he's been shamed. Jane and Jack free all the peasants and live happily ever after.

SCREWBALL COMEDY

Jack and Jane decide to get a divorce because they just aren't right for each other. Jane decides to take a train trip to Florida to forget about everything and maybe meet a millionaire who will take care of her. Jack decides to disguise himself as a wealthy millionaire, Mr. Big, and boards the train. He's mistaken for the head of the railroad and ends up having to steer the train due to a series of mishaps involving an all-girl marching band and a yak being transported to the zoo. Jane falls for who she thinks is the railroad tycoon, but tells him she's discovered she really loves her husband. Jack then pulls off his disguise, and the train goes into a dark tunnel.

BLACK COMEDY

Disguised as a plumber, Jane is a hit woman for mob boss, Mr. Big. Her assignment is to kill Jack. Jack, disguised as an electrician, is a hitman for a rival gang and has been assigned to electrocute her. They meet at a hardware store and fall in love. Jack impregnates Jane and then has misgivings about killing her because he always wanted to have a son. Jack and Jane then go in together to off Mr. Big and put his remains down a garbage disposal and start their own family and home improvement business.

FILM NOIR

Jane dupes her boyfriend into an insurance scam designed to inherit the huge fortune of her industrialist father, Mr. Big. Jack is the private eye hired by Jane's father to investigate his daughter. When he visits their Hollywood Hills solarium, she brings him an iced tea which sets into motion a plot so convoluted, not even Jack and Jane know what's going on. But they do know they'll smoke several cigarettes, look meaningfully into each other's eyes and share a passionate kiss, even though they're no good for each other.

COURTROOM DRAMA

Jane is accused of murdering her husband, Mr. Big. Jack is her attorney. They know it's wrong, but they just can't help it and they have an affair. As the trial nears the end, all looks lost as even Jack begins wondering if maybe Jane didn't kill her husband. A stunning revelation reveals that, in fact, it was the judge who was the real killer. Jane is acquitted and she and Jack go off on their honeymoon where Jack discovers that maybe Jane planted the evidence against the judge and is the real killer after all.

WAR MOVIE

Jack has been in the rainy 'Nam jungle for seventeen straight days and has witnessed almost every one of his buddies get blown away by the enemy. He finally gets two days of much-deserved R 'n' R (loud Jimi Hendrix plays here). In town, he meets a young prostitute who calls herself Jane. She works for a heartless pimp who only cares about money and calls himself Mr. Big. We learn Jane was forced into prostitution to help support her four brothers. Jack decides to rescue her. They marry and he puts her on a plane back to America, but the plane is shot down. War is hell.

HORROR

Jack and an enormously-breasted teenage Jane go off to summer camp where seventeen of their friends are hacked to pieces by an ax-wielding lumberjack named Mr. Big who has been misfigured by a horrible logging accident and has escaped from Jane's nightmares. Jack goes into Jane's nightmares and disembowels the lumberjack. But is he really dead?

ARTSY INDEPENDENT FILM

Grainy low-budget black and white film in which dreadlocked black Jack and performance artist white Jane meet while both throwing up in an alley from shooting too much heroin. Jack sleeps with Jane's boyfriend, Mr. Big; then the three of them get a loft in Soho.

Musicals

WHEN YOU FEEL LIKE BREAKING INTO SONG IN THE MOST UNLIKELY PLACES

Gotta dance!

1. *Little Shop of Horrors*
Steve Martin, James Belushi, Rick Moranis, Bill Murray, John Candy (1986, PG-13, 94m)
This black comedy is the greatest musical to grace the silver screen in years. Never mind that the genre was dead when this hit the big screen in 1986 and there hadn't been any musicals in years.

2. *West Side Story*
Natalie Wood, Richard Beymer (1961, NR, 151m, DVD)
Sizzling gangland adaptation of Shakespeare's *Romeo and Juliet* is a classic loaded with memorable Steven Sondheim tunes.

Hollywood loves Shakespeare. First and foremost, the guy has no agent, so you save money right there. Second, the scripts are already written. And the scripts are so adaptable that you can change them around and people won't even recognize that you've ripped them off. For example, did you know that the beer-swilling movie *Strange Brew* is a remake of *Hamlet*? Or that the Jessica Lange film *A Thousand Acres* is a reworking of *King Lear*? And the teen comedy *10 Things I Hate About You* is based on *The Taming of the Shrew*?

3. *Guys and Dolls*
Marlon Brando, Frank Sinatra, Vivian Blaine (1955, NR, 150m)
Big splashy musical rendition of hit Broadway play marks Brando's foray into the genre.

4. *Seven Brides for Seven Brothers*
Howard Keel, Jane Powell, Julie Newmar (1954, NR, 103m)
Matrimonial fever breaks out in the woods when eldest brother decides to get married and his six brothers follow suit when they decide to kidnap women to be their brides. What's a little misogyny amongst friends? The explosive Michael Kidd choreography is incredible.

5. *The Band Wagon*
Fred Astaire, Cyd Charisse (1953, NR, 112m)
"That's Entertainment!" is the rousing number from this backstage musical that best describes it.

6. *Absolute Beginners*
David Bowie, Patsy Kensit (1986, PG, 107m)
Musical from the early MTV era shows the influence of director Julien Temple's work on music videos. This stylish British musical is a high energy romp through the summer of 1958 as teenagers deal with racial and hormonal issues.

7. The Music Man
Robert Preston, Shirley Jones (1962, G, 151m, DVD)
Preston's lovable con man hoodwinks town into living their dreams in this turn-of-the-century American treat.

8. Grease
Olivia Newton-John, John Travolta (1978, PG, 110m, DVD)
Won't go to bed til she's legally wed...! Ah, I can still hear the tunes rattling around my big vacant head.

9. Damn Yankees
Gwen Verdon, Ray Welston (1958, NR, 110m)
Manager sells his soul to the devil for a star player in this entertaining Faustian baseball tale.

10. Pal Joey
Frank Sinatra, Rita Hayworth (1957, NR, 109m)
Hep cat seeks to get cool club happening in 'Frisco. Jammed with Sinatra tunes. You'll be "Bewitched, Bothered, and Bewildered."

SEE ALSO:
Singin' in the Rain ("Movies about Movies")
An American in Paris ("We'll Always Have Paris")
Oliver! ("Stories for Boys")
The Sound of Music ("Girl Power")
The Court Jester ("Good, Wholesome Family Adventures")
Pennies from Heaven ("Beautiful Bombs")
Umbrellas of Cherbourg ("Cult Classics")
Top Hat ("Dancers")
Jailhouse Rock ("It Rocks!")
On the Town ("It's a Hell of a Town")

 WHEN TO WATCH
August 23. Film musical synonym Gene Kelly's birthday (1912-1996).

 WHAT TO EAT
Have some fast food, because *"Grease is the word, is the word that you heard..."* And, go ahead, have seconds. As Oliver would say, "Please sir, I want some more."

 GREAT LINE
from *The Band Wagon* by Betty Comden, Adolph Green

"I can stand anything but pain."
—OSCAR LEVANT as LESTER MARTON

Westerns

WHEN YOU'RE FEELING LIKE THIS TOWN AIN'T BIG ENOUGH FOR THE BOTH OF US

Like jazz and infomercials, the western is a uniquely American art form. Once regarded as a merely commercial exercise, the western has had its station elevated by European cinephiles. Isn't that just like us to not trust the merits of our own work until French intellectuals take up the cause? We've got to get over that. Well now, who knows, maybe one day the AbRoller infomercial will be considered great art.

1. Unforgiven
Gene Hackman, Clint Eastwood, Morgan Freeman (1992, R, 131m, DVD)
This Eastwood anti-Western Western is so stupendous that it makes me dizzy just to think about it.

2. The Searchers
John Wayne, Natalie Wood (1956, NR, 119m, DVD)
This film is arguably among the very best Westerns ever made. The Duke, as a Confederate soldier veteran, is obsessed with rescuing his niece from Indian kidnappers who abducted her years earlier. But why is he so driven?

3. The Good, the Bad, and the Ugly
Clint Eastwood, Eli Wallach (1967, NR, 161m)
Classic Clint. Sergio Leone's definitive spaghetti Western starring Eastwood's no-name stranger.

4. McCabe and Mrs. Miller
Warren Beatty, Julie Christie (1971, R, 121m)
You let Robert Altman make a genre picture and he's sure to come up with something surprising— as he does here in this atmospheric story of an entrepreneurial woman who is starting up a new business, a whorehouse, in a booming frontier town.

5. Shane
Alan Ladd, Jean Arthur (1953, NR, 117m)
Ladd is Shane, the good guy who swoops in on his horse to save a defenseless prairie family from the bad guys (including a menacing Jack Palance) and becomes the hero of a young boy, in this classic.

6. The Wild Bunch
William Holden, Ernest Borgnine (1969, R, 145m, DVD)
Sam Peckinpah broke the mold when he made this Western that was, at the time, considered a controversial blood-bath of violence. We've seen a lot worse since then, so this film can be appreciated for its other qualities, which include a nice cast of aging gunslingers out for a last round-up.

7. Butch Cassidy and the Sundance Kid

Paul Newman, Robert Redford (1969, PG, 110m)

Charming in every way.

8. Once Upon a Time in the West

Henry Fonda, Jason Robards, Jr. (1968, PG, 165m)

This excellent, if longish, Western has Fonda as one of the coolest bad-asses in the movies.

9. My Darling Clementine

Henry Fonda, Victor Mature (1946, NR, 97m)

This shoot-out at the OK Corral is the very definition of the Western genre.

10. Seven Samurai

Toshiro Mifune, Takashi Shimura (1954, NR, 204m, DVD)

Seminal samurai epic is one of the most influential movies in all of film history. And although it is set in medieval Japan it has inspired many films, especially the Western remake, *The Magnificent Seven.*

SEE ALSO:

High Noon ("Films that Should Have Won the Oscar®")

Red River ("King of all Genres: Films of Howard Hawks")

WHEN TO WATCH

July 14. Owen Wister's birthday (1860-1938). Who, you ask? He's only the author of *The Virginian,* the novel which was instrumental in introducing the mythic heroism of the American cowboy into popular culture, that's all.

WHAT TO DRINK

Give me a whiskey and put it in a dirty glass.

GREAT LINE

from *Unforgiven* by David Webb Peoples

"I ain't like that anymore, kid. It's whiskey done it much as anything else, and I ain't had a drop in over ten years. My wife, she cured me of that. Cured me of drink and wickedness."

—CLINT EASTWOOD as WILLIAM MUNNY

Gangsters

WHEN YOU'RE FEELING LIKE YOU WANNA KILL SOMEONE

Many of these movies speak about our society and the levels of corruption under which it operates; others just have obscenely high body counts, with beautifully choreographed killing featuring slow motion blood splattered all over high priced Las Vegas hotel suites. Personally, I always think a little of both is nice.

1. The Godfather

Marlon Brando, Al Pacino, Robert Duvall, Diane Keaton, James Caan (1972, R, 171m)
The Sistine Chapel of movies. The pinnacle achievement of an art form with grand characters, sweeping storylines and rich themes.

2. The Godfather II

Al Pacino, Robert De Niro, Robert Duvall, Diane Keaton (1974, R, 200m)
The adulation continues...it's also got something no painting's got: amazing performances.

3. Bonnie and Clyde

Faye Dunaway, Warren Beatty (1967, NR, 111m, DVD)
You can thank this stylish winner for spawning generations of pale imitations that only superficially copy the violence and anti-hero characters without ever achieving its depth.

4. Breathless

Jean Seberg, Jean-Paul Belmondo (1959, NR, 90m)
Hip, 1959, French New Wave classic about an aimless small-time hood, who fancies himself a kind of Humphrey Bogart, and his American newspaper vendor girlfriend. Directed by Jean-Luc Godard, it was revolutionary in its day and is still a thrilling achievement today. This may be the coolest movie ever made.

5. GoodFellas

Robert De Niro, Ray Liotta, Joe Pesci, Paul Sorvino (1990, R, 146m, DVD)
Martin Scorsese's great gangster *oeuvre*. Based on real-life experiences of Henry Hill, an eager-to-please young Brooklyn thug looking to climb the Mob's corporate ladder. Hill's post-mob life was the basis for the Steve Martin comedy, *My Blue Heaven*.

6. Bugsy

Warren Beatty, Annette Bening (1991, R, 135m, DVD)
This sexy (Beatty and Bening fell in love during its production), gangster saga about the founding of Las Vegas is the only gangster film with music so lush and romantic, it has a score you can score with.

7. Married to the Mob

Michelle Pfeiffer, Matthew Modine (1988, R, 102m)
Off-center gangster comedy about mob widow Pfeiffer's inability to flee the underworld because a lecherous Mafioso wants a date with the Mrs.

8. Little Caesar
Edward G. Robinson, Glenda Farrell (1930, NR, 80m)
This is the first of all the gangster films released during the Depression. Robinson is the barely disguised (and barely palatable) Al Capone.

9. Pierrot le Fou
Jean-Paul Belmondo, Anna Karina (1965, NR, 110m, DVD)
Another teaming of Godard and Belmondo gives us this memorable film about two charismatic lovers on the lam in the South of France running from his wife and her gangster associates.

10. Scarface
Al Pacino, Michelle Pfeiffer (1982, R, 170m, DVD)
Pacino, as the foul-mouthed Miami drug lord, must break some kinda record on the Fuck-o-Meter for his colorful language in this long remake of the Howard Hawk's film.

SEE ALSO:
Chinatown ("Los Angeles Noir")
Scarface ("King of All Genres: Films of Howard Hawks")
Public Enemy ("Films that Should've Won the Best Picture Oscar®")
Pulp Fiction ("Copycat Crimes")
Mona Lisa ("Best Performances by a Male Actor")
The Long Goodbye ("Los Angeles Noir")
Blade Runner ("Worst Oscar® Oversights")
The Godfather Trilogy ("The Longest Movies in the World")

WHEN TO WATCH
April 3. Huge star Marlon Brando's birthday (1924).

WHAT TO EAT
May I recommend a big hearty Italian meal with lots of pasta, tomato sauce and red wine? Maybe even a canoli for dessert—but make sure you sit with your back to the wall.

GREAT LINE
from *The Godfather* by Mario Puzo and Francis Ford Coppola

"I'm gonna make him an offer he can't refuse."
—MARLON BRANDO as DON VITO CORLEONE

Epics

WHEN YOU'RE FEELING LARGER THAN LIFE

Livin' large on the big screen.

1. Lawrence of Arabia

Peter O'Toole, Omar Sharif, Anthony Quinn (1962, PG, 221m)

The story goes that O'Toole was so good looking in this, his film debut, that the movie was nick-named *Florence of Arabia*. But, what looks even better than the star is the beautiful widescreen cinematography and the grand storytelling of this film biography of T. E. Lawrence.

2. The Last Emperor

John Lone, Joan Chen (1987, PG-13, 140m)

The expansive story of Pu Yi, China's last emperor, who reigned from the age of three. It's got pageantry! It's got Peter O'Toole! It's got it all!

3. Amadeus

Tom Hulce, F. Murray Abraham (1984, PG, 158m, DVD)

Rock me, Amadeus. This bio-pic of Mozart portrays the 15th century composer as the world's first bad-boy rock star in this lavish canvas of a life story.

4. Braveheart

Mel Gibson, Sophie Marceau (1995, R, 178m)

Like the first three films on this list, this one also earned an Academy Award® as best film of the year. Guess the Academy likes those epics. While not entirely accurate (apparently the Scots didn't wear that blue paint on their faces during the period portrayed in the movie), this is a rich and rewarding film.

5. The Man Who Would Be King

Sean Connery, Michael Caine (1975, PG, 129m, DVD)

Among the very best big-screen-sand-and-camel adventures.

6. Ran

Tatsuya Nakadai, Akira Terao (1985, R, 160m, DVD)

A high voltage Technicolor adaptation of *King Lear*, this epic Shakespearean magnum opus is as beautiful to watch as it is to contemplate.

7. Intolerance

Lillian Gish, Mae Marsh (1916, NR, 175m, DVD)

You almost can't believe that a movie like this, with a cast of thousands and sets for days, could have been made in 1916. This film was Director D. W. Griffith's apology for the racist *Birth of a Nation*. Many people do not accept this apology to this day.

8. Barry Lyndon
Ryan O'Neal, Marisa Berenson (1975, PG, 185m)
A three-hour plus, lavish Stanley Kubrick period piece about a promising and rakish young man who fumbles his promise of success (played by O'Neal, foreshadowing his subsequent career).

9. Ben-Hur
Charlton Heston, Jack Hawkins (1959, NR, 212m)
The grand-daddy of all the big splashy Hollywood epics is famed for its awesome chariot race. Took home a record-breaking haul of eleven Oscars®.

10. Love and Death
Woody Allen, Diane Keaton (1975, PG, 89m)
Woody Allen spoofs the great sprawling Russian epics in one of his earlier, funnier works.

SEE ALSO:
The Bridge on the River Kwai ("War Movies: Movies Are Hell")
Spartacus ("Are You Queer?")

WHEN TO WATCH
March 25. Two time Academy Award® winner David Lean's birthday (1908-1991).

WHAT TO EAT
A feast fit for kings, including a lot of roasted duck and turkey legs, grapes and anything that can be ripped with your teeth, along with plenty of mead (but beer may have to do).

GREAT LINE
from *Lawrence of Arabia* by Robert Bolt, Michael Wilson, T. E. Lawrence (book)

"The trick, William Potter, is not minding that it hurts."
—PETER O'TOOLE as T. E. LAWRENCE

Classic Comedies

WHEN YOU'RE FEELING LIKE A GOOD LAUGH

These movies are damn funny. They will very likely make you laugh, which is exactly what you want in a comedy. Laughing is good for you. It relieves tension, is good for your breathing and exercises the facial muscles. Most important of all, it gives you a few seconds to think up a witty response when someone asks you a pointed question.

1. The Graduate
Dustin Hoffman, Anne Bancroft (1967, PG, 106m, DVD)
A landmark comedy that hasn't aged a day since its release. Hoffman is the young graduate seduced by an older woman, played masterfully by Bancroft.

Incidentally, Bancroft was only thirty-five when she played "older woman" Mrs. Robinson. Meanwhile, the young, naive Benjamin was played by a thirty-year-old Hoffman. Charles Grodin, at thirty-two, was originally cast in the Benjamin role but allegedly left the film over a salary dispute.

2. Airplane!
Robert Hays, Julie Hagerty (1980, PG, 88m)
The Zucker Brothers invented a genre with this one.

3. Young Frankenstein
Gene Wilder, Peter Boyle, Madeline Kahn (1974, PG, 108m, DVD)
A great spoof of the classic horror film genre that makes wonderful use of some of Hollywood's best character actors.

4. Blazing Saddles
Gene Wilder, Mel Brooks, Madeline Kahn, Cleavon Little, Harvey Korman (1974, R, 90m, DVD)
Another great genre spoof. This time, of the western. Mel Brooks put out more funny movies in one year, 1974, than he has since.

5. A Night at the Opera
Groucho, Chico, Harpo, Allan Jones (1935, NR, 92m)
Classic Marx Brothers. This is the one with the scene where everyone comes tumbling out of the hotel room.

6. The Bank Dick
W.C. Fields, Cora Witherspoon (1940, NR, 73m)
Fields at his best.

7. Monty Python and the Holy Grail
Graham Chapman, John Cleese, Terry Gilliam, Eric Idle, Michael Palin, George Harrison, Terry Jones (1975, PG, 90m)
More irreverence from the British troupe.

8. What's Up Doc?
Ryan O'Neal, Barbra Streisand (1972, G, 94m)
An updated screwball comedy with Streisand continuously getting in mild-mannered O'Neal's hair.

9. A Shot in the Dark
Peter Sellers, Elke Sommer (1964, NR, 101m, DVD)
The second Pink Panther movie is a hoot. Sellers is brilliant as bumbling Inspector Clouseau.

10. Flirting with Disaster
Téa Leoni, Ben Stiller, Patricia Arquette (1995, R, 92m)
Destined to be a comedy classic, one of the funniest movies in recent years features Stiller who goes on a quest to find his birth parents and on the way scores a lot of laughs (and just a little acid). Has a very TV sitcom feel about it. Maybe because of all the great comic moments with Mary Tyler Moore, George Segal, Alan Alda, and Lily Tomlin.

SEE ALSO:
Annie Hall ("Romantic Movies for Jews")
The Philadelphia Story ("Delusional Cinema")
His Girl Friday ("Delusional Cinema")
Bringing Up Baby ("King of All Genres: Films of Howard Hawks")
This is Spinal Tap ("It Rocks!")
Duck Soup ("Movie Morons")
The Nutty Professor ("Movie Morons")
Love and Death ("Epics")
The Thin Man ("To Have and to Watch")
The Palm Beach Story ("Delusional Cinema")
M*A*S*H ("War Movies: Movies Are Hell")
Caddyshack ("Some Movies Are from Mars...")

WHEN TO WATCH
June 28. Once-funny filmmaker Mel Brook's birthday (1926).

WHAT TO EAT
Be like Monty Python and eat "ham and jam and Spam™ a lot."

GREAT DIALOGUE
from *Airplane!* by Jim Abrahams, David Zucker, Jerry Zucker

BARBARA BILLINGSLEY as JIVE WOMAN
Oh stewardess, I speak jive.

JULIE HAGERTY as FLIGHT ATTENDANT
Oh, good.

JIVE WOMAN
He said that he's in great pain and he wants to know if you can help him.

FLIGHT ATTENDANT
Would you tell him to just relax and I'll be back as soon as I can with some medicine.

JIVE WOMAN
Jus' hang loose blood. She gonna catch up on the rebound a de medcide.

AL WHITE as SECOND JIVE DUDE
What it is big mamma? My mamma didn't raise no dummy, I dug her rap.

JIVE WOMAN
Cut me some slack, jack! Chump don' wan' no help, chump don' get no help. Jive ass dude don' got no brains anyhow.

Comedy Noir

WHEN YOU FEEL LIKE A BLACK COMEDY

Admit it, you're a dark and twisted individual. The Germans have a word for it, it's "schadenfreude." You laugh at the pain and suffering of others because it makes you feel better about your own pathetic existence. You prey on their weaknesses and find joy in their very human foibles. When someone tells you they've just been dumped by their girlfriend because she couldn't stand his cologne, you barely suppress a snicker. There's something wrong with you. Me too. I think you'll enjoy these.

1. Harold and Maude
Bud Cort, Ruth Gordon (1971, PG, 92m)
If you looked up black comedy in the dictionary, you'd see a little picture of this movie about a couple obsessed with suicide.

2. Eating Raoul
Mary Woronov, Paul Bartel (1982, R, 83m)
I guess I'd have to say a funny movie about cannibalism falls under the heading "black comedy."

3. The Ruling Class
Peter O'Toole, Alastair Sim (1972, PG, 154m)
This skewering satire of uppercrust British society stars O'Toole as an heir who believes he's Jesus Christ.

4. Toto the Hero
Michael Bouquet, Jo De Backer (1991, PG-13, 90m)
I learned a very valuable lesson from this French movie: A dark revenge fantasy entirely based on a misunderstanding could really be embarrassing unless you are completely committed to your misguided notions.

5. Prizzi's Honor
Kathleen Turner, Jack Nicholson (1985, R, 130m)
A twisted comedy in which Nicholson, as a none-too-bright hit man, falls for none-too-gentle hit woman Turner, only to discover they are each others' next assignment.

6. Trainspotting
Ewan McGregor, Ewen Bremmer, Jonny Lee Miller, Robert Carlyle, Kevin McKidd (1995, R, 94m, DVD)
Despite nearly throwing up during the "filthiest toilet in Scotland" scene, I enjoyed (if watching junkies try to kick heroin can be described as enjoyable), this comedy about life in the gutter.

7. Serial Mom
Kathleen Turner, Sam Waterston (1994, R, 93m)
How can a serial killing suburban mom not be funny? Especially when it's directed by John Waters.

8. The Trouble with Harry
John Forsythe, Shirley MacLaine (1955, PG, 90m)
Alfred Hitchcock's contribution to the genre about a corpse that won't stay put.

9. Ruthless People
Danny DeVito, Bette Midler, Judge Reinhold, Helen Slater (1986, R, 93m)
DeVito can't seem to do anything to get his wife's kidnappers to keep her. This is one of the terrific comedies to come out of the Disney Studios Touchstone division in the 1980s (*Down and Out in Beverly Hills, Splash, Who Framed Roger Rabbit*).

10. The Positively True Adventures of the Alleged Texas Cheerleader-Murdering Mom
Holly Hunter, Beau Bridges, Swoosie Kurtz (1993, R, 99m)
This HBO movie is why cable was invented. Brilliant dark comedy with the always interesting Hunter as...well, the title pretty much covers a synopsis.

SEE ALSO:
Dr. Strangelove ("War Movies: Movies Are Hell")
Kind Hearts and Coronets ("Hidden Treasures")
The Opposite of Sex ("Pregnant Cinema")
Citizen Ruth ("Pregnant Cinema")
Blue Velvet ("Peeping Toms")
After Hours ("It's a Hell of a Town")
Brazil ("Hooray for Capitalism")
Little Shop of Horrors ("Musicals")
Heathers ("Hip Flicks")
To Die For ("Vidiots")

WHEN TO WATCH
October 30. Writer (*Adam's Rib, Pat and Mike*)/actress Ruth Gordon's birthday (1896-1985).

WHAT TO EAT
In *Trainspotting* there is dialogue describing the preparations one must make to kick heroin. Why don't you play along by gathering a few of these essentials? According to Renton (Ewan McGregor), you will need: "One room which you will not leave. Soothing music. Tomato soup, ten tins of. Mushroom soup, eight tins of, for consumption cold. Ice cream, vanilla, one large tub of. Magnesia, milk of, one bottle. Paracetamol, mouthwash, vitamins. Mineral water, Lucozade, pornography. One mattress. One bucket for urine, one for feces and one for vomitus. One television and one bottle of Valium."

MEMORABLE DIALOGUE
from *Trainspotting* by John Hodge, Irvine Welsh (novel)

Renton is quizzing Sick Boy on his James Bond *trivia.*

JOHNNY LEE MILLER as SIMON DAVID "SICK BOY" WILLIAMSON
You Only Live Twice?

EWAN MCGREGOR as MARK "RENT BOY" RENTON
Nineteen-sixty-seven.

SICK BOY
Running time?

RENTON
One hundred and sixteen minutes.

SICK BOY
Director?

RENTON
Lewis Gilbert.

SICK BOY
Screenwriter?

RENTON
Eh - Ian Fleming?

SICK BOY
Fuck off! He never wrote any of them.

RENTON
OK, so who was it, then?

SICK BOY
You can look it up.

Private Dicks

WHEN YOU'RE FEELING LIKE YOUR GAMS SHOULD BE ON THE LAM FROM THE FLIM-FLAM

Hard-boiled street detectives crawling through the seamy underbelly of life, discovering the most degenerate acts people are capable of, are always fun to watch. So get hot on the trail and find these excellent mystery movies.

1. The Maltese Falcon
Humphrey Bogart, Mary Astor (1941, NR, 101m, DVD)
This is "the stuff that dreams are made of." This adaptation of Dashiell Hammett's mystery novel is *the* definition of the private eye film noir. Not bad for a beginner—this was John Huston's first film as director.

2. The Third Man
Joseph Cotten, Orson Welles (1949, NR, 104m, DVD)
Cotten plays amateur sleuth in this great film noir thriller set in WWII Vienna. A lot of people think this film was directed by Orson Welles. Why? Because 1) it's a black and white deep-focus masterpiece, 2) Welles is in it, and 3) it's the favorite film of the Kir Royale-swilling cerebral set.

3. The Big Sleep
Humphrey Bogart, Lauren Bacall (1946, NR, 114m, DVD)
It takes a lot of guts to call a movie *The Big Sleep.* I think the boys in today's studio marketing departments would be afraid of that one. But, back then, hell, it was 1946 and they had Bogie, Bacall, writer William Faulkner and a mystery novel by Raymond Chandler. America had won the war and anything was possible, except figuring out this convoluted plot.

4. Out of the Past
Robert Mitchum, Kirk Douglas (1947, NR, 97m)
This crackling gritty detective thriller is seminal film noir and way better than the remake, *Against All Odds.*

5. The Long Good Friday
Bob Hoskins, Helen Mirren (1980, NR, 109m)
It's the British *Godfather.*

6. The Killing
Sterling Hayden, Marie Windsor (1956, NR, 83m)
Early work from Stanley Kubrick demonstrates how he can elevate genre picture into masterwork.

7. Love at Large
Tom Berenger, Elizabeth Perkins (1989, R, 90m)
Funny, moody piece is iconoclastic director Alan Rudolph's twist on the private eye genre.

8. Harper

Paul Newman, Shelley Winters, Lauren Bacall (1966, NR, 121m)

William Goldman (*Butch Cassidy and the Sundance Kid, All the President's Men, The Princess Bride*) wrote what is essentially a B-movie with A-list talent. It's Raymond Chandleresque done '60s style, complete with go-go dancing. Any movie with Julie Harris as a jazz singing junkie who refers to private detective Newman as "the fuzz" has to be entertaining.

9. The Untouchables

Kevin Costner, Sean Connery, Robert De Niro, Andy Garcia (1987, R, 119m)

So sue me, the detectives in this are not really private, they are federal agents. This one proves movies recycled from old TV shows are not always crap.

10. The Day of the Jackal

Edward Fox, Alan Badel (1973, PG, 142m, DVD)

A taut suspense film in which an assassin is stalking French leader Charles de Gaulle around Europe.

SEE ALSO:
The Thin Man ("Cocktail Cinema")
Devil in a Blue Dress ("Los Angeles Noir")
Vertigo ("Always a Hitch: Films of Alfred Hitchcock")
Breathless ("Gangsters")
Blade Runner ("Worst Oscar® Oversights")
A Shot in the Dark ("Classic Comedies")
Dirty Harry ("Some Movies Are from Mars...")
Dead Again ("Los Angeles Noir")

WHEN TO WATCH
January 23. Prep school dropout Humphrey Bogart's birthday (1899-1957).

WHAT TO EAT
I'd let someone else test your food first (someone you don't much care for), it might be poisoned.

GREAT LINE
from *The Big Sleep* by William Faulkner, Jules Furthman, Raymond Chandler (novel)

> *I don't mind if you don't like my manners. I don't like them myself. They're pretty bad. I grieve over them on long winter evenings.*
>
> —HUMPHREY BOGART as PHILIP MARLOWE

Courtroom Dramas: Not-so-Guilty Pleasures

WHEN YOU'RE FEELING BRAINY

You won't see *The Naked Gun* on this list even though its star, O. J. Simpson, starred in the greatest courtroom drama, er, farce, of all time. I don't think you'll find him in any future courtroom dramas (on the screen anyway) because he's too busy looking for the real killer. Or something.

Courtroom dramas can be the most riveting of all movie genres. Just one word of warning: to enjoy courtroom dramas, you usually have to pay attention and follow closely, which is more than some juries can do.

1. Anatomy of a Murder
Jimmy Stewart, George C. Scott, Eve Arden (1959, NR, 161m)
Talk about *Celebrity Deathmatch*! We've got Stewart for the defense vs. Scott on the side of the prosecution. And you gotta love Arden as the wisecracking secretary.

2. A Man for All Seasons
Orson Welles, Paul Scofield, Robert Shaw (1966, G, 120m, DVD)
It's Sir Thomas Moore and the Catholic Church vs. King Henry VIII and the Church of England in this battle. The winner here is the audience; this 1966 film raked in awards.

3. Witness for the Prosecution
Tyrone Power, Charles Laughton, Marlene Dietrich (1957, NR, 116m)
Directed by Billy Wilder, this film has more than its star power to recommend it. If I was writing for one of those blurb services that like to see their name in newspaper adds, I'd say something inane like, "This film is packed with more twists than a bag of pretzels!"

4. Twelve Angry Men
Henry Fonda, Martin Balsam (1957, NR, 95m)
Fonda plays the lone dissenter in this version of the one-person-can-make-a-difference story that is a well-loved classic.

5. Inherit the Wind
Spencer Tracy, Fredric March (1960, 1960, NR, 128m)
Tracy and March as Clarence Darrow and William Jennings Bryant argue the merits of teaching Darwin's Theory of Evolution in the public schools. Now if they could only tackle that "school choice" issue.

6. The Caine Mutiny
Humphrey Bogart, Jose Ferrer (1954, NR, 125m, DVD)
Bogart is Captain Queeg, the mentally leaky Navy commander put on trial for mutiny.

7. Judgment at Nurenberg

Spencer Tracy, Burt Lancaster, Montgomery Clift, Judy Garland, William Shatner (1961, NR, 178m)
Nazi war crimes put on trial. All-star cast makes for great entertainment.

8. A Civil Action

John Travolta, Robert Duvall, Kathleen Quinlan (1998, PG-13, 115m)
Travolta is an at-first reluctant crusader for victims of a toxic waste dump. Thoughtful courtroom drama, not given the pat Hollywood treatment, is a rich viewing experience.

9. And Justice for All

Al Pacino, Jack Warden, Christine Lahti (1979, R, 120m)
"I'm out of order? You're out of order! This whole trial is out of order!" Let's not point fingers, let's just order out for a pizza and enjoy this satiric critique of our judicial system.

10. The Music Box

Jessica Lange, Frederic Forrest (1989, R, 126m)
More Nazis on trial. Lange defends her father when he is accused of war crimes and begins to learn more than she wants to know about Dad. Don't you hate it when that happens?

SEE ALSO:
To Kill a Mockingbird ("One Hit Wonders")
The Verdict ("Best Performances by a Male Actor")

WHEN TO WATCH
First Monday in October, when the Supreme Court starts its session.

WHAT TO EAT
If you want to end up in court to see it firsthand, get some McDonald's coffee, spill it on yourself and then you can sue for millions of dollars in damages for your suffering.

GREAT LINE
from *A Man for All Seasons* by Robert Bolt, Constance Willis

> *"You're a constant regret to me, Thomas. If you could just
> see facts flat on without that horrible moral squint."*
> —ORSON WELLES as CARDINAL WOLSEY

War Movies: Movies Are Hell

WHEN YOU'RE FEELING LIKE A HIPPIE

Like you need to rent one of these anti-war movies to tell you that war is a bad thing. But this list contains some of the best war movies ever made. (Yeah, I know the Vietnam War movies are missing. They're on another list, see: "'Nam.") By the way, if you're looking for a real movie that's gung-ho about war, I'd like to suggest the John Wayne classic *Sands of Iwo Jima* which has been copied over and over again by makers of war films from Oliver Stone to Steven Spielberg since it's release in 1949.

1. Paths of Glory
Kirk Douglas, Adolphe Menjou (1957, NR, 86m)
The best war movie ever made. Ever.

2. Bridge on the River Kwai
William Holden, Alec Guinness (1957, NR, 161m)
An epic David Lean masterpiece about the construction of a bridge by British POW's during World War II.

3. All Quiet on the Western Front
Lew Ayres, Louis Wolheim (1930, NR, 103m, DVD)
Early talkie chronicling the tragedy of war.

4. M*A*S*H
Donald Sutherland, Elliott Gould, Tom Skerritt, Sally Kellerman (1970, R, 116m)
Director Robert Altman has had his ups and downs, but he certainly hits his stride with this caustic anti-war comedy.

5. La Grande Illusion
Jean Gabin, Pierre Fesnay, Dita Parlo (1937, NR, 11m, DVD)
French filmmaker Jean Renoir (son of famed French impressionist, painter Pierre August Renoir) directed this film, which takes place in a German prisoner of war camp during World War I and eloquently illustrates the hypocrisy and falsity of war.

6. Hearts and Minds
Documentary, directed by Peter Davis (1974, NR, 112m)
Brilliant Vietnam documentary that helped stir up anti-war fervor and was banned by many institutions in the 1970s.

7. The Men
Marlon Brando, Teresa Wright (1950, NR, 85m)
Brando's film debut is a powerful film about World War II vets in rehabilitation trying to get reacclimated to society.

8. Catch-22
Alan Arkin, Martin Balsam, Art Garfunkel, Jon Voight (1970, R, 121m)
Arkin plays insane to avoid going off to battle. So, who's the crazy one, huh? See the irony?

9. Idiot's Delight
Clark Gable, Norma Shearer (1939, NR, 107m)
Gable heads an all-star cast in a dated, but heartfelt movie about people trapped in a luxury hotel as war breathes down their neck.

10. The Last Detail
Jack Nicholson, Otis Young (1973, R, 104m)
Nicholson is one of two sailors who decide to take a naive young kleptomaniac under their guard out on the town to show him what he's been missing. Vintage Jack.

SEE ALSO:
King of Hearts ("They're Insane!")
Dr. Strangelove ("Films that Should Have Won the Best Picture Oscar®")
Deer Hunter ("'Nam")
Saving Private Ryan ("Crowd Pleaser: Films of Steven Spielberg")
Full Metal Jacket ("'Nam")

WHEN TO WATCH
November 11. Veterans Day.

WHAT TO EAT
"Shit on a Shingle" (chipped beef on toast) and water from a canteen.

GREAT LINE
from *M*A*S*H* by Richard Hooker (novel), Ring Lardner Jr.

"This isn't a hospital, it's an insane asylum."
—SALLY KELLERMAN as
MAJOR MARGARET "HOT LIPS" HOULIHAN

Monster Mash

WHEN YOU FEEL LIKE A GOOD SCARE

They're creepy and gross and make you sick and no, I'm not talking about the guests of the *Jerry Springer Show*. I'm talking about the sometimes slimy creatures that crawl around on the movie screen and occasionally live on in our nightmares. And here they are...

1. Alien
Sigourney Weaver, Tom Skerritt (1979, R, 116m)
A monster thriller with brains and a great lead in Weaver—who doesn't look too bad in that underwear, either.

2. The Bride of Frankenstein
Boris Karloff, Elsa Lanchester (1935, NR, 75m)
An artistic triumph. This is a rare sequel that is better than the original.

3. The Fly
Jeff Goldblum, Geena Davis (1986, R, 96m)
How 'bout that? Now we have a remake better than the original. Kudos to everyone. Nicely twisted tale of scientist who decides to play God.

4. Planet of the Apes
Charlton Heston, Roddy McDowell (1968, G, 112m)
I live for the moment when humans first speak to the apes and Heston says through clenched teeth, "Get your stinking paws off me, you damned dirty ape!"

5. Invasion of the Body Snatchers
Kevin McCarthy, Dana Wynter (1956, NR, 80m, DVD)
Often imitated, seldom duplicated.

6. American Werewolf in London
David Naughton, Griffin Dunne (1981, R, 97m, DVD)
Horror-comedy that you can only imagine would be improved by today's special effects. Come to think of it, you don't have to imagine it at all, because we have the sequel, *An American Werewolf in Paris* with much more advanced f/x. And guess what? It's not improved at all. In fact, it's worse. So I guess it's not the effects after all, but the story that make a movie great. Whatta concept, huh?

7. Dracula
Bela Lugosi, David Manners (1931, NR, 75m)
Probably the most filmed character ever, Dracula has appeared in scores of films from silents through today. But, never has the Transylvanian Count-turned-vampire been more memorable than Lugosi operating at the peak of his powers. We can only wince at what we know was to become of him as chronicled in *Ed Wood* (see "Movies about Movies").

8. Freaks

Wallace Ford, Olga Baclanova (1932, NR, 66m)

Just a little sick, this early talkie uses real circus freaks to make it extra-creepy and putting it really low on the list of politically correct films.

9. Dawn of the Dead

David Emge, Ken Foree (1978, NR, 126m, DVD)

Sequel to *Night of the Living Dead,* about four people barricaded in a shopping mall to escape an onslaught of zombies. Once not taken seriously, this film's critical reputation grows every year.

10. The Exorcist

Linda Blair, Ellen Burstyn (1973, R, 120m, DVD)

Causing quite a stir upon its release in 1973, this devil-possession movie featured Blair as Regan, a twelve-year-old girl spitting up pea soup and screeching profanity.

Did you know that in January of 1999, for the first time since 1614, the Roman Catholic Church updated rules for its still-regularly-performed exorcisms? Exorcists still make the sign of the cross, add a dash of holy water and order the devil to leave the possessed person (presumably after first asking politely), but now they are warned to distinguish between the mentally ill and the possessed. The Vatican says anyone who doesn't believe in the Devil doesn't believe in the Catholic faith.

FOR SOME SCARY HUMAN MONSTERS, SEE ALSO:
The Shining ("Writers")
Henry: Portrait of a Serial Killer ("Gross Out")
Rosemary's Baby ("Pregnant Cinema")

WHEN TO WATCH
October 31. Halloween.

WHAT TO EAT
Halloween candy until you get sick.

GREAT LINE
from *The Fly* by Charles Edward Pogue, David Cronenberg, George Langelaan (story)

"I'm an insect who dreamt he was a man, and loved it. But,
now the dream is over, and the insect is awake."
—JEFF GOLDBLUM as SETH BRUNDLE

FEELING JUDGMENTAL

I love movies. I love renting movies. I don't particularly love video stores, however. I especially don't love BIG video stores. Sure, they have every film ever committed to videotape or DVD. But go ahead...find one. I dare you. The problem is the movies are shelved by categories, and *their* categories are not necessarily *my* categories. Recently, I wanted to rent *The Last Picture Show*, but it was missing. I don't know why the video store didn't bother to find their old copy or buy a new copy, but that's "beyond my control" to quote John Malkovich in *Dangerous Liaisons* (or as I like to say with a very thick, very bad French accent, *Les Liaisons Dangereuses*). So, I decided to rent *Blue Velvet* instead. For a lifetime supply of canola-drenched popcorn, what category does that fall under? I looked under "Drama," "Comedy," "Mystery," and "Suspense." As my search came up empty, I breathlessly darted toward "Cult" and then on to "Midnight Movies," my heart pounding with hope and anticipation. All to no avail. I even tried "Clown Movies" and "Dennis Hopper's Sober Period," but still no luck.

Teetering on the edge of sanity, I ran all over the damn video store past the endless display of *Titanics* and *Armageddons*. I felt like Charley from *Flowers for Algernon* and the rat was winning! The shelves, stacked high with copies of *A Bug's Life*, towered above me like great fortress walls, keeping me from my sought-after trophy. I began to feel as though I was "dumbest." Scenes from *The Shining* started to run through my head as I turned another corner, thinking, "Haven't I already checked this aisle? Who designed this place, M. C. Escher?" Fish were turning into birds, guys were walking upside down on stairs going nowhere. I saw Bette Davis' *Dark Victory*, which oddly enough wasn't shelved under "Bette Davis Movies" or even under "Romance" or "Love Stories" either. No, they had it in the "Tear-jerkers" section. Now, if you can find two people who separate "Love Stories" from "Tear-jerkers" in the same manner, I'll give you a lifetime supply of Raisinets.

Finally, I gave up and went up to the counter. Swallowing my pride, I asked calmly, "Where is *Blue Velvet*?" "Oh, *Blue Velvet*," responded Ned, the assistant manager, a pubescent Roger Ebert wannabe. "That would be right up here." I inquired what category would that be? "Ned's Favorites," he said proudly. Yes, Rog Jr. here had hand-picked his faves from the collection and moved them up front so he could keep an eye on them. Meanwhile, toddlers were roaming freely, unsupervised through the adults-only aisles perusing such less-than-classic titles as *Shaving Ryan's Privates* and *On Golden Blonde*. As Ned rambled on and on recounting his favorite scenes from *Madeline* to anyone who would listen, I informed him I couldn't locate *Blue Velvet*. "Oh, that's checked out," he said. I looked at him, dumbfounded. "Yeah, I checked it out last night. It's *really* one of my favorites!"

The story has a sad ending (no, I didn't kill him). I rented another movie which I never had the opportunity to see because some thug smashed my car window and stole a bag out of the back containing a pair of dirty sweat socks and a copy of *Raise the Red Lantern*. Now I owe the video store $94 for a movie I've never seen while some hoodlums sit around in some crack house exclaiming "This is a great film—visually stunning. Gong Li has never been more ravishing."

I'm just sure Ned had something to do with it. It was, after all, one of his favorites.

Overrated Hall of Fame

WHEN YOU'RE FEELING SMUG

Hyperbole is a Hollywood hallmark. The Denis Leary-Sandra Bullock film, *Two if by Sea*, was released on January 12, 1996. The movie's ad featured a critic's rave: "The best comedy caper date film of the year." Yeah, and the competition in the "comedy caper date movie" genre had been so vigorous during 1996's first eleven days. Granted, that film is easy to pick on (because it sucks) but how about some tougher targets? Let me just tell you that despite glowing reviews and the classic status of the films on this list, I'd rather scrub Senator Jesse Helms clean with a moist towlette than watch one of these again. If you'd like to pick a fight with me, I suggest you watch one of these and then tell me how great it is. And yes, *Fantasia*. Especially *Fantasia*.

1. Fantasia

Leopold Stokowski, Julietta Novis (1940, NR, 116m)

If you can stay awake through this, call your doctor—you may have a problem with insomnia. This was Walt Disney's first big box office bomb. Hurt by its failure, Walt reportedly broke into tears while accepting the Irving G. Thalberg Award at the 1941 Oscar® ceremony. If you have to sit through this in one sitting, you'll probably cry too.

2. The Dead

Anjelica Huston, Donal McCann (1987, PG, 82m)

The critics fell all over themselves to praise John Huston's final film which is like spending the evening watching paint dry—that is, if paint wouldn't stop rambling on and on and on...

3. Wings of Desire

Bruno Ganz, Peter Falk (1988, PG-13, 130m)

Art house darling Wim Wenders could use an intensive story structure class. Or maybe two.

4. Gandhi

Ben Kingsley, Candice Bergen (1982, PG, 188m)

Great guy, boring movie.

5. The Spanish Prisoner

Campbell Scott, Steve Martin (1997, PG, 112m, DVD)

David Mamet is brilliant. So they tell me. But this contrived piece of hokum doesn't ring true to human experience. It's filled with gimmicky tricks—no wonder magician Ricky J is in it.

6. Around the World in Eighty Days

David Niven, Shirley MacLaine (1956, G, 178m)

At three hours (it only *feels* like eighty days), this over-inflated balloon ride is the worst movie ever to earn an Oscar® as the best film of the year.

7. Home Alone
Macaulay Culkin, Catherine O'Hara, Joe Pesci, Daniel Stern (1990, PG, 105m)

I'm sending up a flare, because I need a clue as to why this is one of the most successful films in the history of box office record-keeping. It's stupid, it's violent, it's sappy and it isn't remotely believable. But maybe those are the secrets of its success.

8. The Magnificent Ambersons
Jospeh Cotten, Anne Baxter (1942, NR, 88m)

RKO sadly butchered Orson Welles' second film. We can imagine that what he would have made would have been great, but what we have as evidence doesn't prove it.

9. Happiness
Cynthia Stevenson, Jane Adams, Lara Flynn Boyle, Philip Seymour Hoffman (1998, NR, 139m, DVD)

A dark comedy that has a view of the world in which to reach out to another human being is to court disaster and ridicules characters whose lives are pathetic. Masturbation is the only source of happiness in this film. Not up to the standards of Todd Solondz, whose previous film was *Welcome to the Dollhouse*, and containing an unnecessarily distasteful subplot about child rape, the film has some interesting moments but is not worth jerking off about as many critics did.

10. The Blair Witch Project
Michael Williams, Heather Donahue, Joshua Leonard (1999, R, 87m, DVD)

This will always be known as the first movie to effectively use the Internet as a marketing tool. The hype is brilliant (to the tune of $140 million at the box office) especially when you consider how truly bad the movie is. Hand held 16mm and video are slapped together in this student film with a seemingly improvised storyline that is as lost in the woods as its overacting characters. I'm just *so* scared. Yeah, right.

WHEN TO WATCH
New Year's Eve. The most overrated night of the year.

WHAT TO EAT
Go on a hunger strike in honor of *Gandhi*.

ON WINNING
from *Gandhi* by John Briley

"When I despair, I remember that all through history the way
of truth and love has always won. There have been tyrants
and murderers and for a time they can all seem invincible,
but, in the end, they always fall. Think of it. Always."
—BEN KINGSLEY as MAHATMA GANDHI

Pretentious Hall of Fame

WHEN YOU'RE FEELING BETTER THAN EVERYONE ELSE

If anyone tells you that these are their favorite movies, don't invite them to your house. In fact, don't even continue the conversation. Just run for the hills. Let's admit it, these movies are boring. Steer clear of these dull, pretentious movies that people only pretend to like. These are the kinds of movies film majors have to watch, and pretend to like, so they can drop names when they're out of school in hopes of being taken seriously. However, I do recommend these as "must-see's" for the very pretentious.

1. Last Year at Marienbad

Delphine Seyrig, Giorgia Albertazzi (1961, NR, 93m, DVD)

Very stylish, this film features characters named "X" and "Y," who gracefully flit around a villa in Yves St. Laurent clothing while having fragments of conversation in a convoluted dream-like timeline. A good pretentious litmus test because it is well-loved among certain film snobs.

2. La Jetée

Hélène Chatelain, Davos Hanich, Jacques Ledoux (1962, NR, 28m)

They make you sit through this a lot in film school. Luckily, it's only twenty-eight minutes long. But that's still a long time to feign interest in a lot of still images with a droning voice-over. You'd be better off sitting thorough someone's (anyone's) vacation slideshow.

3. Meshes of the Afternoon

Maya Deren, Alexander Hammid (1943, NR, 18m)

Yeah, it's brilliant avant-garde filmmaking. She walks around a house and moves the camera upside down and shakes it around. I see this kinda the way some people react to Jackson Pollack's splatter paintings. Give your kid a camcorder and he's an artist, too.

4. The Sacrifice

Erland Jospehson, Susan Fleetwood (1986, PG, 145m)

I happen to love the films of Andrei Tarkovsky. They're poetic, philosophical, contemplative, long and very Russian. They are also on the pretentious side. Especially this one. Which gets a little obtuse as six people sit in a house and wait for the end of the world until God, through one of them, performs a miracle. At least, that's what I think happens.

5. The Spirit of the Beehive

Fernando Gomez, Teresa Gimpera (1973, NR, 95m)

About a girl obsessed with Boris Karloff's *Frankenstein*. Critics call this Spanish film "haunting." If you mean "haunting" as in "mysterious," as in "it's a mystery to me why I spent an hour and a half of my life on this one," then I wholeheartedly agree.

6. Earth

Semyon Svashenko, Mikola Nademsy (1930, NR, 57m)

Russian agitprop. This Soviet-era silent film that shows up all the time on lists of the best films ever made is about the nobility of the collective farmer. But I can't say it makes an entertaining date movie.

7. Hiroshima, Mon Amour

Emmanuelle Riva, Eiji Okada (1959, NR, 88m)

A French actress and Japanese architect have an affair that consists mostly of footage of nuclear destruction.

8. Akira Kurasawa's Dreams

Akira Terao, Mitsuko Baisho (1990, PG, 120m)

Even a master can stumble and become self-conscious and preachy when he hits eighty.

9. Poison

Edith Meeks, Larry Maxwell (1991, R, 85m)

Remember kids...just because a movie has poor production values, is disturbing and its point is unclear, that doesn't make it great filmmaking.

10. The Sheltering Sky

Debra Winger, John Malkovich (1990, R, 139m)

This blows.

WHEN TO WATCH

February 6. The birthday of François Truffaut (1932-1992), darling of the intellectual cinephile magazine *Les Cahiers du Cinema* (which has championed several of the films on this list)—and what could be more pretentious than that?

WHAT TO EAT

Something pretentious and hard to pronounce from the most expensive restaurant in town, because it's very hard to keep up with what those trendy chefs are cooking.

PRETENTIOUS LINE

from *The Sheltering Sky* by Bernardo Bertolucci, Mark Peploe, Paul Bowles (novel)

"Because we don't know when we will die, we get to think of life as an inexhaustible well, yet everything happens only a certain number of times, and a very small number, really. How many more times will you remember a certain afternoon of your childhood, some afternoon that's so deeply a part of your being that you can't even conceive of your life without it? Perhaps four or five times more, perhaps not even that. How many more times will you watch the full moon rise? Perhaps twenty. And yet it all seems limitless."
—PAUL BOWLES as THE NARRATOR

They Suck!

WHEN YOU'RE FEELING LIKE SOME TRASH

Some people believe these are the kinds of movies that fall into the "They're So Bad, They're Good" category, but I'm not so sure. Sure, these are movies that you can laugh at and not with, but do you really want to watch them all the way through? That choice, of course, is all yours. But I would like to recommend that you use these like video wallpaper; put them on in the background when you have people over and when the conversation gets slow, you can turn to the TV and make a snide comment—because nothing gets a social gathering back on its feet like a little shared cruelty. By the way, the worst film I've ever seen is *Comin' at Ya* but I wouldn't wish that 3-D gimmick on anyone, no matter how poor their conversational skills.

1. Showgirls
Gina Gershon, Elizabeth Berkeley (1995, NC-17, 131m)
This is one of the most deeply thought-provoking films ever made. It will force you to reexamine your life and ask yourself all kinds of questions. Things like: Why am I here? Why am I here watching this movie? Was I born to suffer? Am I a masochist? Am I a man who hates women? Am I a woman who hates herself? Can those tits possibly be real?

2. Glen or Glenda
Ed Wood, Bela Lugosi, Dolores Fuller (1953, NR, 67m)
A bizarre film from legendarily incompetent filmmaker Ed Wood about a transvestite coming out of the closet. This is one truly bad film that you gotta see to believe.

3. Sextette
Timothy Dalton, Mae West (1978, PG, 91m)
How can you not watch this? West, honeymooning with Dalton, flirts with a bunch of other guys young enough to be her descendants who pretend not to be embarrassed. She's eighty and slurring through false teeth while romping around to Captain and Tennille. What's not to like?

4. The Seduction
Morgan Fairchild, Michael Sarrazin (1982, R, 104m)
I can't explain it, but it did happen. I was in college. We had just gotten HBO. *The Seduction* came on. And I watched it. Over and over and over again. I knew it was bad but there I sat, watching this movie and enjoying it. Maybe it was the scene where Morgan Fairchild swims naked in the pool.

5. Butterfly
Pia Zadora, Stacy Keach (1982, R, 105m)
Zadora won a Golden Globe for this, tarnishing the "Best Newcomer" award so much that it was forever eliminated from the Globes. Ouch.

6. Can't Stop the Music
Valerie Perrine, Bruce Jenner (1980, PG, 120m)
Caftan-wearing producer Alan Carr hired Nancy Walker, better known as a paper towel pitch woman, to direct the Village People in their only starring roles. Though this could have used "a quicker-picker-upper," its camp value is unrivaled.

7. Once Is Not Enough
Kirk Douglas, Deborah Raffin (1975, R, 121m)
I wouldn't be so sure.

8. Myra Breckinridge
Raquel Welch, Rex Reed (1970, R, 94m)
Based on a Gore Vidal novel, this movie does have camp value. It features Welch as a transsexual—she's the "after." And you've got Farrah Fawcett as a lesbian and it's also got Reed, Tom Selleck and John Huston; but you know what? It still sucks.

9. Caligula
Peter O'Toole, Helen Mirren, Malcolm McDowell—and a horse (1980, NR, 143m)
As far as I know, this is the only big-budget star-name porn movie ever made, and for that it deserves a place of distinction here.

10. Reefer Madness
Dave O'Brien, Dorothy Short (1938, PG, 67m)
Deliciously dated drug diatribe.

SEE ALSO:
Plan 9 from Outer Space ("Movies in Which People Were Killed for Real")

WHEN TO WATCH
Might I suggest March 24. The anniversary of the Exxon Valdez oil spill (1989). This would be a good day to commemorate one of these disasters.

WHAT TO EAT
Anything that really sucks. How about some horse steaks from that horse in Caligula along with some Jell-O® in honor of all the jiggle in Showgirls.

GREAT LINE
from *Showgirls* by Joe Eszterhas

"I like having nice tits."

—ELIZABETH BERKELEY as NAOMI MALONE

Hidden Treasures

WHEN YOU'RE FEELING LIKE DISCOVERING A REALLY GOOD MOVIE

These could be some of the best movies you've never seen, provided two things: 1) you've never seen them and 2) when you do see them, you like them.

1. Kind Hearts and Coronets
Alec Guinness, Dennis Price(1949, NR, 104m)
A hilarious black comedy in which a guy decides to kill everyone ahead of him in line for a big, juicy inheritance. Guinness plays all eight victims.

2. Quick Change
Bill Murray, Geena Davis, Randy Quaid (1990, R, 89m)
Murray stars and co-directs this wonderful film about a bungled bank heist get-away.

3. Eve's Bayou
Samuel L. Jackson, Lynn Whitfield, Jurnee Smollett (1997, R, 109m)
One of the most impressive directorial debuts ever, Kasi Lemmons creates a wholly original story of a Southern bayou family and how it holds up under stress.

4. Vanya on 42nd Street
Wallace Shawn, Julianne Moore (1994, PG, 119m)
A group of actors sits around the dilapidated New Amsterdam theater (now beautifully restored by Disney) and rehearses a Chekhov play. Sound boring? It's not.

5. Defense of the Realm
Gabriel Byrne, Greta Scacchi (1985, PG, 96m)
I'm not sure how this smart, taut British thriller about journalists investigating government corruption escaped the audience's radar, but it shouldn't have.

6. A New Leaf
Walter Matthau, Elaine May (1971, G, 102m)
Delightful movie from May, who wrote, directed (though was re-edited) and stars with Matthau in a comedy about murder with screwball sensibilities.

7. Choose Me
Keith Carradine, Genevieve Bujold, Lesley Ann Warren (1984, R, 106m)
It's amazing who's crawling around Los Angeles at night. Sexy, stylish, original, deft, shrewd...when you get sick of adjectives, let me know.

8. The Swimmer
Burt Lancaster, Janice Rule (1968, PG, 94m)
Here's the whole plot: a guy decides to swim home from the office going from one neighbor's pool to the next. Lancaster is outstanding as the swimmer for whom each pool dredges up what might have been.

9. Salvador
James Woods, James Belushi (1986, R, 123m)
Oliver Stone made his mark with this political thriller chronicling the revolution in El Salvador as seen through the eyes of journalist Richard Boyle, played by Woods. Autobiographical script co-written by real-life journalist Boyle.

10. The Navigator: a Medieval Odyssey
Hamish McFarlane, Bruce Lyons (1988, PG, 92m)
You've never seen anything like this. A group of medieval adventurers travel from plague-riddled England through the center of the Earth and emerge in present-day New Zealand. *Back to the Future* it ain't.

SEE ALSO:
Getting it Right ("Dateless and Desperate")

WHEN TO WATCH
September 21. Iconoclastic star Bill Murray's birthday (1950).

WHAT TO EAT
To celebrate discovering a hidden treasure, treat yourself to some of those gold foil-wrapped chocolate coins.

GREAT LINE
from *Kind Hearts and Coronets* by Israel Rank (novel), John Dighton, Robert Hamer, and Roy Horniman

> *"The Reverend Lord Henry was not one of those new-fangled parsons who carry the principles of their vocation uncomfortably into private life."*
> —DENNIS PRICE as LOUIS MAZZINI

Like Poetry, These are Not For Everybody

WHEN YOU FEEL LIKE TRYING SOMETHING POETIC

I happen to love all these films. But I'm always afraid to recommend them to everybody because they might be too odd and then you'd never trust me again.

1. Rashomon
Machiko Kyo, Toshiro Mifune (1951, NR, 83m)
This fascinating early Kurasawa masterpiece is one of the greatest movies ever made, and a study of point-of-view. Four witnesses to a rape and murder relay their perspective of the incident.

2. The Stalker
Alexander Kaidanovsky, Nikolai Grinko (1979, NR, 160m)
This science fiction film is a three hour meditation on the meaning of existence (in Russian, no less) as contemplated by a poet and a scientist as they approach the inner-sanctum of an off-limits site containing possible extra-terrestrial life. It's haunting. (I warned you these films weren't for everyone.)

3. Providence
John Gielgud, Dirk Bogarde (1977, R, 104m)
A dying novelist, with an excoriating sense of humor, mixes real scenes of his seemingly decent family with imagined scenes of their evil deeds which may be part of his latest book or just a product of his intense rectal spasms, we're not sure.

4. Red Sorghum
Gong Li, Jiang Wen (1987, NR, 91m)
A peaceful Chinese peasant village is ransacked by Japanese invaders in this poetic masterpiece featuring the luminesently beautiful Li.

5. Days of Heaven
Richard Gere, Brooke Adams, Sam Shepard (1978, PG, 95m)
Without a doubt, one of the most beautifully photographed films ever made. It's the early twentieth century and bucolic life is as pretty as an impressionistic painting for a family that goes to Texas to seek the good life until things take a turn for the tragic.

6. Shadows
Hugh Hurd, Lelia Goldoni (1960, NR, 87m)
John Cassavetes-directed improv about a beat-generation inter-racial romance. It's like that hep coffee house beat poetry, daddy-o.

7. Dead Man

Johnny Depp, Gary Farmer (1995, R, 121m)

Here's an idea for a movie I bet you haven't heard: A lyrical black and white, slow, mystical western starring Depp, who may or may not be the reincarnation of poet and painter William Blake.

8. Man Facing Southeast

Lorenzo Quinteros, Hugo Soto (1986, R, 105m)

This one is really odd. It's about a patient, who just might be an alien, who spends way too much time standing in the courtyard of a mental institution facing southeast. Why would you want to see that? Maybe because you appreciate a good allegory.

9. Quest for Fire

Everett McGill, Ron Perlman (1982, R, 75m)

If you are looking for a movie to watch with a bunch of your friends from the United Nations or the United Colors of Benneton this would be good, because it has no dialogue. It is, however, a real stunner about cavemen's discovery of fire.

10. Koyaanisqatsi

Documentary, directed by Godfrey Reggio (1983, NR, 87m)

Title translates to "life out of balance." Not only does this one have no dialogue, it has no plot. But what it does have are some amazing images of contemporary urban life choreographed to a Phillip Glass score. It's very cool.

WHEN TO WATCH
December 31. Chinese babe Gong Li's birthday (1965).

WHAT TO EAT
How about some red sorghum? You might like it, but then again, it's not for everyone.

GREAT LINE
from *Dead Man* by Jim Jarmusch

"I wouldn't trust no words written on no piece of paper."
—CRISPIN GLOVER as THE FIREMAN

Foreign Faves

WHEN YOU'RE FEELING *TRÈS* SOPHISTICATED

If, when you hear the words "foreign movie," the first thing that pops into your mind is, "you mean I have to read?" then perhaps you'll want to skip to the next list. But, believe it or not, there are some foreign movies actually worth reading the subtitles for. Below are some classic foreign films that are interesting and yes, they can be challenging. These films stand out from many other foreign films because, for the most part, they actually have a story and the story has a beginning, middle and an end.

1. Jean de Florette/Manon of the Spring
Gérard Depardieu, Yves Montand (1987, PG, 122m) / Yves Montand, Emmanuelle Beart (1986, PG, 113m)
And some people say there is no such thing as a decent sequel. This a beautiful, heart-wrenching two-part adaptation of a Marcel Pagnol novel about a Provence country farmer, played by Depardieu, who falls prey to his neighbor's wicked scheme to take over Depardieu's property. The equally rewarding part two reveals the farmer's daughter's revenge.

2. Cyrano de Bergerac
Gérard Depardieu, Jacques Weber (1990, PG, 135m)
Depardieu (is the ubiquitous French actor the world's first human clone?) manages to banish all other Cyrano's from memory in this definitive interpretation of the classic bulbous-nosed romantic.

3. M
Peter Lorre, Ellen Widmann (1931, NR, 111m, DVD)
A gripping work of art about a crazed child killer who is hounded by vigilantes from the Berlin criminal element. Lorre's haunted performance as the culprit is seared into the memory.

4. Salaam Bombay!
Shafiq Syed, Hansa Vithal (1988, NR, 114m)
A powerful film of overwhelming realism about a young boy's quest for survival among the squalid gutters of Bombay, which are littered with a host of vividly drawn characters, including pimps, prostitutes and pushers.

5. Best Intentions
Samuel Froler, Pernilla August (1992, NR, 182m)
Bille August directs this enthralling epic from a script by Ingmar Bergman about the courtship and subsequent relationship of Bergman's own parents. This is a kind of prequel to *Fanny and Alexander*. It was cut down from a six hour Swedish mini-series.

6. Il Postino
Massimo Troisi, Philippe Noiret (1994, PG, 115m)
Precious film about an Italian postman who gets in touch with his inner poet, inspired by his contact with famed Chilean poet, Pablo Neruda, to whom the postman delivers mail. Troisi, who played the postman, died within hours of wrapping the film.

7. Mon Oncle

Jacques Tati, Jean-Pierre Zola (1958, NR, 110m)
Tati, as Monsieur Hulot, bumbles his way through the second installment of this four-film series. Virtually without dialogue, Tati's comic skills are comparable to the silent film greats.

8. Aguirre, the Wrath of God

Klaus Kinski, Ruy Guerra (1972, NR, 94m)
Kinski is a mad conquistador who leads an expedition away on a search through the Amazon for El Dorado, the lost city of gold.

9. Solaris

Donatas Banionis, Natalya Bondarchuk (1972, NR, 167m)
It's the Russian *2001: A Space Odyssey*.

10. The Gods Must Be Crazy

N!xau, Marius Weyers (1984, PG, 109m)
This diverting little ditty is the only film I know of that crossed-over to an American mainstream audience from Botswana.

SEE ALSO:
Life is Beautiful ("Life During World War II")
Cinema Paradiso ("Movies about Movies")
La Chienne ("Painters")
La Dolce Vita ("Hip Flicks")
Breathless ("Gangsters")
Rashomon ("Like Poetry, These Are Not for Everybody")
Belle de Jour ("Dirty Movies for the Art House Crowd")
The 400 Blows ("Growing Up Foreign")
Seven Samurai ("Westerns")
My Life as a Dog ("Growing Up Foreign")
Umberto D. ("Pity Party: The Tear-jerkers")
Les Enfants du Paradis ("We'll Always Have Paris")

WHEN TO WATCH
December 27. Star of every French film ever made, Gérard Depardieu's birthday (1950).

WHAT TO EAT
Something foreign. French croissants? French crepes? French toast? French fries?

GREAT LINE
from *The Gods Must Be Crazy* by Jamie Uys

> *"Xi was beginning to think he would never find the end of the Earth. And one day, suddenly, there it was."*
> —PADDY O'BYRNE as THE NARRATOR

FEELING LIKE A WINNER

There are so many award shows now, you can actually win an award in Hollywood for your performance on an award show. In real life, this just doesn't happen. It'd be like getting the Congressional Medal of Honor for getting the Purple Heart.

But it's great when Hollywood takes time out of its busy schedule of sycophantic glad-handing for its annual round of award shows. Award Season begins in early December when the Los Angeles and New York film critics associations announce their respective picks for the best in film and ends in late March with the grand-daddy of them all...the Oscars®. (This puts Award Season roughly between Hillside Brushfire Season and TV Pilot Season, both of which are often disastrous). You've got the People's Choice Awards...the Screen Actors Guild Awards...the MTV Movie Awards...the Blockbuster Video Awards...the Golden Globe Awards...and dozens of new ones every year, which, let's be honest, no one really cares about except that they're usually prognosticators of how the Academy Awards® will play out.

The Oscar® (not even the Nobel Prize gets an "®," and you have to go to Stockholm to pick up one of those babies) ceremony is so revered, it now unofficially has its own day. That's right..."Oscar® Sunday." *One whole day* devoted to an award show! And not just the ceremony itself, but also all the pre-ceremonial "red carpet" hoopla and post-ceremonial partying.

Of course, the length of the show itself is legendary. Along about the third hour, when your chips and dip are gone and your butt's numb, you begin to wonder when Jerry Lewis is going to come out and beg for money. The show is usually televised around the first day of Spring. March 21st is known as the Vernal Equinox, which is (and my recollection is admittedly a little rusty on this) the one day of the year when the length of the night is exactly equal to the length of the Oscar® telecast.

Not only do the Oscars® recognize great entertainment, they *are* great entertainment. Who can forget the streaker running across the stage in 1974? Or the David Letterman "Uma, Oprah...Oprah, Uma" bit? And without the Oscars®, would we even know of the journalistic skills and comedic stylings of Melissa Rivers? No, the Academy Awards® have an aura and mystique all their own, and that's why we love watching them. And it's not just about the movies...the Oscars® are too big for that. Through the years, we've learned from Richard Gere they're about freeing Tibet. And Vanessa Redgrave taught us the purpose of the award is to solve the conflicts in the Middle East (or in her case, inflame them). My personal favorite moment from Oscar® history is when Marlon Brando, *vis à vis* Sasheen Little Feather, refused his Best Actor Oscar® in 1973 because he believed it was the role of the Oscar® pageant to improve the treatment of Native Americans. Yes, the Academy Awards® telecast is one of those rare occasions when you're likely to hear the back-to-back sentences, "I think we all need to stand up against the genocide in the Sudan," and, "Spin around so we can see your gown."

Best Performances by a Male Actor

WHEN YOU FEEL LIKE WATCHING AN ARTIST AT WORK

Wouldn't it be great if I decided who the won all the awards? OK, maybe you don't think it would be so great, but it would certainly be fun for me. So play along with me and check out my favorites.

1. Mean Streets
Robert De Niro, Harvey Keitel (1973, R, 112m, DVD)
De Niro is a superb psycho street thug. What more could you want out of life than to be able to watch a movie as entertaining as this one?

2. Dog Day Afternoon
Al Pacino, John Cazale (1975, R, 124m, DVD)
Pacino gives a flashy performance as a loser who bungles a bank robbery in an attempt to raise money for his lover's sex-change operation.

3. Reversal of Fortune
Jeremy Irons, Glenn Close (1990, R, 112m)
Proving you don't have to explode to be great, Iron's fireworks are all kept tightly wrapped behind an icy facade as he recreates real-life accused wife-killer Claus Von Bulow (I'm convinced the guy is guilty based on his dastardly name alone).

4. City Lights
Charlie Chaplin, Virginia Cherrill (1931, NR, 86m)
Chaplin creates a beautiful work of art in this poignant tale of the little tramp's relationship with an innocent blind girl.

5. The Verdict
Paul Newman, James Mason (1982, R, 122m)
Newman has given many great performances in *The Hustler, Hud,* and, well, I could just go on and on—so I think I will...*Mr. and Mrs. Bridge, Nobody's Fool, Butch Cassidy and the Sundance Kid, Cool Hand Luke, Cat on a Hot Tin Roof, Sweet Bird of Youth, The Sting,* and so many more. But he is perhaps at his most amazing in *The Verdict,* where he is able to convey a whole lifetime in the simplest means as he plays a drunken lawyer with a shot at redemption.

6. The Falcon and the Snowman
Sean Penn, Timothy Hutton (1985, R, 110m)
Penn has given some of the consistently best performances (in an uneven collection of movies) in recent years. This film about two buddies who decide to sell U. S. secrets to the Russians is a great example of how Penn can get lost inside a character. Someone, please, give this man an Oscar®!

7. On the Waterfront
Marlon Brando, Rod Steiger (1954, NR, 108m)
Not only was he a contender, but Brando won the Academy Award® for his performance as someone who has given up his boxing dreams and fallen in with some seamy characters in this classic about a waterfront union that Brando made about two hundred pounds ago.

8. The Pawnbroker
Rod Steiger, Brock Peters (1965, NR, 120m)
Steiger, before he poured himself into a bottle of booze and started making low budget horror quickies like *The Kindred*, was a national treasure. See why in this story of a Jewish Holocaust survivor who finds his way to Harlem and more depression.

9. Hamlet
Lawrence Olivier, Basil Sydney (1948, NR, 153m)
Olivier, widely regarded as the greatest actor of the twentieth century, proves why as he tackles the greatest role written for an actor.

10. Mona Lisa
Bob Hoskins, Cathy Tyson (1986, R, 104m)
Hoskins is outstanding as a kind of Everyman involved in the slimy underbelly of the crime world in 1980s Britain.

SEE ALSO:
Raging Bull ("Real Sports Movies")
My Left Foot ("Writers")
Silence of the Lambs ("Book Reports Made Easy")

WHEN TO WATCH
January 26. Salad dressing king Paul Newman's birthday (1925).

WHAT TO EAT
In honor of *Mean Streets*, have some Sicilian-style pizza. Then, in honor of Brando's girth, have some more.

GREAT LINE
from *On the Waterfront* by Budd Schulberg, Malcolm Johnson (articles)

> *"You don't understand. I could've had class. I could've been a contender. I could've been somebody, instead of a bum, which is what I am."*
> —MARLON BRANDO as TERRY MALLOY

Best Performances by a Female Actor

WHEN YOU FEEL LIKE WATCHING AN ARTIST AT WORK

Most of these performances have already received many awards, which is great, if you care about that sort of thing—but you should really see these films because in them, the female leads are breathtaking.

1. A Cry in the Dark

Meryl Streep, Sam Neill (1988, PG-13, 120m)

Streep is one of the most honored actress of the twentieth century (for example, she's given sixteen performances that have been nominated for a Golden Globe Award). But you should see this particular film so you can see her amazing performance as Lindy Chamberlin and so you can hear her say, "A dingo stole my baby!"

2. The Trip to Bountiful

Geraldine Page, Rebecca De Mornay (1985, PG, 102m)

Page finally got her Oscar® for this film after seven previous nominations. It couldn't have gone to a better performance. It's the simple story of a loopy old lady who just wants to go home—and just why shouldn't she be able to?

3. A Streetcar Named Desire

Vivian Leigh, Marlon Brando, Kim Hunter (1951, PG, 122m, DVD)

"The Method" is born. It's the fifties and there's Brando and suddenly everything is different in film acting. This adaptation of the Tennessee Williams play is a five-star classic with acting as good as it gets. It's amazing to watch Leigh's Blanche DuBois crack as she can no longer live in denial.

4. Adam's Rib

Katharine Hepburn, Spencer Tracy (1950, NR, 101m)

I think we all just enjoy the hell out of Hepburn, perhaps more than any other screen actress. Let me tell you, she was never more enjoyable than in this teaming with her partner, Tracy, as a couple of lawyers on opposite sides of a case.

5. Blue Sky

Jessica Lange, Tommy Lee Jones (1991, PG-13, 101m)

No one does crazy like Lange does crazy.

6. Born Yesterday

Judy Holliday, Broderick Crawford (1950, NR, 103m)

This must be a good performance. Holliday's deft comic turn earned an Oscar® over Bette Davis in *All About Eve* and Gloria Swanson's big comeback in *Sunset Boulevard*.

7. The Prime of Miss Jean Brodie
Maggie Smith, Pamela Franklin (1969, PG, 116m)
Smith, earning an Oscar®, fully inhabits the character of the lively school teacher who inspires "her girls" to take on life. Filmed on location in photogenic Edinburgh, Scotland.

8. Come Back, Little Sheba
Shirley Booth, Burt Lancaster, Terry Moore (1952, NR, 99m)
This domestic drama about a frumpy housewife and her alcoholic hubby was the first film for Booth and right out of the gate she nabs the Oscar®. And it gets even better for her, because from here she goes on to become TV's lovable maid *Hazel*.

9. Ponette
Victoire Thivisol, Marie Trintignant (1995, NR, 92m, DVD)
This amazing film is a grim tale about a girl trying to cope with the loss of her mom. This actress is four years old. That's right, four! She gives (or, more likely, has wrenched out of her by the director) a performance so powerful that, it's, well, it's a freak show is what it is. She makes what all the Oscar®-ed Anna Paquin's and Tatum O'Neal's of this world do, look like child's play.

10. Breaking the Waves
Emily Watson, Stellan Skarsgård (1995, R, 152m)
Watson's film debut earned her an Oscar® nomination as a psychologically disturbed woman who takes the advice of her mentally unstable husband (what a pair these two are). After he has an accident that renders him paralyzed, he encourages her to start having sex with lots of guys and describe the acts to him while he's in the hospital.

SEE ALSO:
Coal Miner's Daughter ("They Sing, They Have Problems")
Three Faces of Eve ("They're Insane!")
Who's Afraid of Virginia Woolf? ("I'll Drink to That")
Whatever Happened to Baby Jane? ("Are You Queer?")

WHEN TO WATCH
May 12. Goddess (to understand fully, you must watch *The Philadelphia Story*) Katharine Hepburn's birthday (1907).

WHAT TO EAT
In honor of *A Streetcar Named Desire*, why don't you whip yourself up some good New Orleans cooking like simmering Cajun catfish?

GREAT LINE
from *The Trip to Bountiful* by Horton Foote

"I wonder why the Lord isn't with us everyday. Sure would be nice if He was. Well, maybe, then we wouldn't appreciate it so much on those days when He is with us. Or maybe He's with us always and we just don't know it."
—GERALDINE PAGE as CARY WATTS

Films that Should Have Won the Best Picture Oscar®

WHEN YOU FEEL LIKE RIGHTING A WRONG

These are the films that should have taken home the big prize. I would like to mention that, although *Singin' in the Rain* can be found on the list "Movies about Movies," it could easily be on this list. In 1952, *The Greatest Show on Earth* was selected as the best picture of the year and *Singin' in the Rain*, the best Hollywood musical ever made, was not even nominated. Is there no justice in the world? Is there no appeals process? Is there no sanity? Is there nothing more important I could spend my time worrying about?

1. Citizen Kane

Orson Welles, Joseph Cotten, Agnes Moorehead (1941, NR, 119m)

How Green Was My Valley is an excellent movie and is not a bad choice for best picture of the year—most years. But, in 1941, *Citizen Kane* was released and isn't that supposed to be the best movie ever made? As Marlene Dietrich said about the God-like director, Orson Welles, "I think you should cross yourself when you say his name." Louella Parsons, right-wing gossip columnist and William Randolph Hearst employee, was successful in campaigning against this movie because she and her boss felt it made newspaperman Hearst look bad. Boo-hoo for him.

2. High Noon

Gary Cooper, Grace Kelly (1952, NR, 85m)

The *Greatest Show on Earth* sucks! If not *Singin' in the Rain,* then surely this brilliant western should have taken home the little gold guy. Someone should be gunned down in the streets of Beverly Hills.

3. Dr. Strangelove, Or: How I Learned to Stop Worrying and Love the Bomb

Peter Sellers, George C. Scott (1964, NR, 93m, DVD)

My Fair Lady? I don't think so. Not over Stanley Kubrick's brilliant anti-war black comedy.

4. Touch of Evil

Charlton Heston, Orson Welles (1958, PG-13, 108m)

To make Welles' humiliation in Hollywood complete, they not only didn't pick his last great movie as Best Picture, they didn't even nominate it. Instead, they chose the pedestrian musical *Gigi*. If you think I'm just biased against musicals, ask me what I think of *Singin' in the Rain* not getting the Best Picture of 1952.

5. Laura

Gene Tierney, Dana Andrews (1944, NR, 85m)

Going My Way has not only failed the test of time, it has failed pretty badly. Watch the mysterious *Laura* and the goofy *Going My Way* back-to-back, then let's have another vote.

6. Dodsworth

Walter Huston, David Niven (1936, 1936, NR, 101m, DVD)

You know what the difference between *The Great Ziegfeld's* story and *Dodsworth's* story is? *Dodsworth* has one.

7. The Crowd

Eleanor Boardman, James Murray (1928, NR, 104m)

Broadway Melody is a weak and lame backstage musical. You've never seen it and you never should. You should, however, check out *The Crowd*—it's an astonishing look (still) at Jazz Age alienation.

8. Do the Right Thing

Spike Lee, Rosie Perez, John Turturro (1989, R, 120m, DVD)

The Academy compensated for failing to give *Driving Miss Daisy's* director, Bruce Beresford, a nomination by giving the film the Best Picture Award. Meanwhile, Oliver Stone earned the Best Director prize for the more-deserving *Born on the Fourth of July*. But, the real story is that *Do the Right Thing*, the best film of the year, did not even get nominated for Best Picture *or* Best Director.

9. My Man Godfrey

William Powell, Carole Lombard (1936, NR, 95m, DVD)

If you don't like *Dodsworth*, I have another selection for 1936 that's better than *The Great Ziegfeld*. Powell, the star of *The Great Ziegfeld*, made another movie in 1936 that wasn't even nominated for Best Picture. But, it's amazing what time will tell and the film of his that survives to this day is the wonderful screwball comedy, *My Man Godfrey*.

10. Public Enemy

James Cagney, Edward Woods (1931, NR, 85m)

Cimarron? Get real.

SEE ALSO:
Singin' in the Rain ("Movies about Movies")

WHEN TO WATCH
May 6. Mistreated genius Orson Welles' birthday (1915-1985).

WHAT TO EAT
I would go with a liquid diet in honor of Dr. Strangelove's paranoid Ripper's obsession with fluids: "I can no longer sit back and allow Communist infiltration, Communist indoctrination, communist subversion, and the international Communist conspiracy to sap and impurify all of our precious bodily fluids."

GREAT LINE
from *Citizen Kane* by Orson Welles, Herman J. Mankiewicz

"Dear Wheeler - You provide the prose poems - I'll provide the war."

—ORSON WELLES as CHARLES FOSTER KANE

Oscar® Whores

WHEN YOU'RE FEELING LIKE A WHORE

Hollywood has never been shy about rewarding whores. If a woman wants to make her way in Tinseltown, then being a, I mean, *playing* a whore is often her ticket to the big time. Here is a sampling of some of the women who have portrayed prostitutes in pursuit of Hollywood's greatest honor. And funny (funny odd, not funny ha-ha), I'm guessing these leggy beauties don't resemble too many of the crack whores you've ever seen walking the streets of this fair city.

1. L. A. Confidential
Kim Basinger, Kevin Spacey, Russell Crowe, Guy Pearce (1997, R, 136m, DVD)
Basinger took home the prize for her portrayal of prostitute Lynn Bracken. Not bad for the former Bond girl from *Never Say Never Again*.

2. Taxi Driver
Jodie Foster, Robert De Niro (1976, R, 112m, DVD)
Giving the name *Freaky Friday* a whole other connotation, Foster costars as a twelve-year-old streetwalker in the Martin Scorsese classic. It impressed John Hinkley so much, he tried shooting President Reagan to get Jodie's attention.

3. From Here to Eternity
Donna Reed, Montgomery Clift (1953, NR, 118m)
That's right, the beloved, pearl-adorned housewife of '50s TV, Reed was once a whore—at least in the movies. The World War II drama earned a deserved Best Picture Award.

4. Elmer Gantry
Shirley Jones, Burt Lancaster (1960, NR, 146m)
This movie is like Steve Martin's *Leap of Faith*, except that it's really good. This is about a scamming tent evangelist on tour through the heartland of this great nation of ours. When Lancaster dumps his girlfriend, Jones, what does she do? A) go home to mother, B) seek therapy, or C) become a whore. The correct answer is C, and for that Shirl-girl, AKA Mrs. Partridge, nabbed an Oscar®.

5. Leaving Las Vegas
Elizabeth Shue, Nicolas Cage (1995, R, 120m, DVD)
I don't know what she had to do to get this role, but Shue makes a huge artistic leap in her career from *oeuvre* like *Cocktail* to this real downer of a movie about an ex-movie exec who decides to drink himself to death and the hooker with whom he spends his final days.

6. Klute
Jane Fonda, Donald Sutherland (1971, R, 114m)
Sutherland plays Klute, a cop looking for a killer with a connection to hooker Bree Daniels. But no one really remembers he was in the movie; they do remember the searing Fonda in her Oscar® winning role.

7. Pretty Woman
Julia Roberts, Richard Gere (1990, R, 117m, DVD)

It's hard to remember that Roberts was not just a prostitute, but a Hollywood street-walking whore in this movie. By the time Richard Gere put her in the bubble bath, the diamonds and the Rodeo Drive couture, she was America's sweetheart. Her "My Fair Lady" transformation is enough to induce nausea, but she sure is damn cute.

8. Mighty Aphrodite
Mira Sorvino, Woody Allen, Helena Bonham-Carter (1995, R, 95m, DVD)

When Mira won the Oscar® for the role, her dad, Paul Sorvino, was crying buckets in the audience. I think that's a normal reaction—considering he had to watch his twenty-something daughter, as a hooker, have sex with the sixty-year-old Woody.

9. Casino
Sharon Stone, Robert De Niro (1995, R, 177m, DVD)

Stone, as high priced call girl Ginger McKenna, finds cash and swimming pools, if not love and stability, when she marries Mafioso Sam Rothstein. Acting opposite De Niro had to be intimidating for Stone, considering her previous greatest acting notoriety came from not wearing panties.

10. Butterfield Eight
Elizabeth Taylor, Laurence Harvey (1960, NR, 108m)

La Liz swiped the Oscar® for this call girl role boosted by the sympathy vote when she landed in the hospital on the verge of death (yet again!).

WHEN TO WATCH

December 8. Former town owner Kim Basinger's birthday (1953).

WHAT TO EAT

To get yourself in a whorish mood, may I recommend some aphrodisiacs? Polenta is a dish that contains tryptophan, which allegedly has sexy qualities—but it also produces gas, which is less than sexy. Instead, try sexy fruits like avocados, apricots and peaches.

GREAT LINE

from *Leaving Las Vegas* by John O'Brien (novel), Mike Figgis

"I am a drunk, and you're a hooker. I want you to know I am a person who is totally at ease with this."
—NICOLAS CAGE as BEN SANDERSON

The Worst Oscar® Oversights
WHEN YOU FEEL LIKE YOU KNOW MORE THAN THEY DO

Singin' in the Rain, Psycho, 2001, Do the Right Thing, Some Like it Hot, The African Queen, The Third Man, Double Indemnity, The Maltese Falcon, Bringing Up Baby and *Duck Soup* are all great films included in this book that not only did not win a Best Picture prize—they were not even nominated. So don't feel too badly if you've never won an Oscar®. I mean, in 1969, John Wayne received a sentimental Oscar® for his work in *True Grit,* besting nominees Dustin Hoffman and Jon Voight from *Midnight Cowboy,* Richard Burton in *Anne of the Thousand Days,* and Peter O'Toole from *Goodbye Mr. Chips.* But that's nothing, get a load of these...

1. Blade Runner
Harrison Ford, Sean Young (1982, R, 122m, DVD)
Blade Runner is one of the most, if not the most, important and influential movies when it comes to visual design. The fact that it lost the art direction Oscar® to a *Gandhi,* a movie shot almost entirely on location, adds insult to injury. *Gandhi* also beat out *Victor/Victoria* for costumes. Costumes? Nice sheets.

2. Tender Mercies
Robert Duvall, Tess Harper (1983, PG, 88m)
The Academy doesn't have a great track record when handing out the Best Song Award. In the past it has gone to such weak material as "You Light Up My Life" and "Thank God it's Friday." It's my understanding that the Best Song is one that helps further the story of the movie, not some power ballad wailed over the closing credits. Why then, did they award the trophy to "Flashdance...What a Feeling" from *Flashdance* over songs from *Yentl* and *Tender Mercies*? By the way, the *Flashdance* song also won the Golden Globe, Grammy, the British Academy Award and the People's Choice Award—so I guess I'm wrong.

3. Who Framed Roger Rabbit
Bob Hoskins, Christopher Lloyd (1988, PG, 104m, DVD)
Along comes a movie unlike anything that's ever been done. It's done brilliantly. It's got Hoskins, who's great. Does it win Best Picture? No. Does it get nominated? No. Does Hoskins get Best Actor? No. Does he get nominated? No. Does *Stand and Deliver's* Edward James Olmos get nominated? Yes.

4. Cat on a Hot Tin Roof
Elizabeth Taylor, Paul Newman (1958, NR, 108m, DVD)
This film, starring Ms. Taylor-Hilton-Wilding-Todd-Fisher-Burton-Burton-Warner-Fortensky, an adaptation by Richard Brooks and James Poe of the Tennessee Williams play, lost in the "Screenplay - Based on Material from another Medium" to the lame-ass *Gigi.*

5. Toys
Robin Williams, Joan Cusack (1992, PG-13, 121m)
Bad movies can have great set and costume design. The Academy forgets that sometimes and votes for their favorite movie in a category regardless of the craft the category is supposed to be honoring. So what chance did the superior art direction of *Toys* have against the superior film, *Howards End*?

6. Jagged Edge
Glenn Close, Jeff Bridges (1985, R, 108m)
For Best Supporting Actor of 1985, Robert Loggia in the *Jagged Edge*, William Hickey in *Prizzi's Honor*, Klaus Maria Brandauer in *Out of Africa* and Eric Roberts in *Runaway Train* all lost to Don Ameche in *Cocoon*. And they say Hollywood isn't sentimental.

7. Mr. Blandings Builds His Dream House
Myrna Loy, Cary Grant (1948, NR, 93m)
You can have your Julia Robertses and your Pamela Lee Andersons, I'll take Loy any day of the week. She was never even nominated for an Oscar®, though they did give her an Honorary Award in 1991. Check out her underrated comedy work in this classic on which *The Money Pit,* with Tom Hanks and Shelley Long, was based.

8. Baby Doll
Carroll Baker, Eli Wallach, Karl Malden (1956, NR, 115m)
It's the *Lolita* of the '50s. This script, along with the screenplays for *Giant, Lust for Life* and *Friendly Persuasion* unjustifiably lost to the tepid star-vehicle *Around the World in Eighty Days.*

9. Anna Christie
Greta Garbo, Charles Bickford (1930, NR, 90m)
You think Harvey and Bob Weinstein of Miramax invented the Oscar® campaign? Guess again. Norma Shearer can't act. The fact that she won an Oscar® for her stilted, maudlin work in *The Divorcée* is a tribute to her powerful husband, movie mogul Irving Thalberg. I would say, if she's on a ballot to receive an acting award, pick anyone else—but especially if you can choose Garbo in *Anna Christie.*

10. The Sweet Hereafter
Ian Holm, Sarah Polley (1996, R, 110m, DVD)
A movie about a bunch of school kids who drown on a bus. OK, so it's not for everyone's taste; but this is a damn fine movie. In a year when the Academy was passing out wheelbarrows of awards to the mediocre *As Good as it Gets,* you have to wonder how they could have passed up nominating this picture with a shattering performance by Holm.

WHEN TO WATCH
The Oscars® are generally held sometime in mid-March.

WHAT TO EAT
Throw your own big Oscar® party with champagne and those little bite-sized quiches. You can have someone dress up in a white tuxedo and pass them around on a tray.

GREAT LINE
from *Cat on a Hot Tin Roof* by Richard Brooks, James Poe, Tennessee Williams (play)

"I'm not living with you. We occupy the same cage. That's all."
—ELIZABETH TAYLOR as MAGGIE to
PAUL NEWMAN as BRICK

Discovered at Sundance

WHEN YOU'RE FEELING INDEPENDENT

Films like *Welcome to the Dollhouse, Big Night* and *Hoop Dreams* all made a big splash at Sundance and helped to boost the reputation of what has become America's most prestigious film festival. Here are ten more films, each interesting in its own way, that were brought to the public's attention through Robert Redford's Sundance Film Festival.

1. sex, lies, and videotape
Andie MacDowell, James Spader, Laura San Giacomo (1989, R, 101m, DVD)
The title that launched a million catch phrases and newspaper play-on-words headlines. Spader, as Gallagher's old college chum, drops by for a visit and really rocks his world, turning everything upside down.

2. Blood Simple
Frances McDormand, John Getz, Emmet Walsh (1985, R, 96m)
A stylish, inventive murder-thriller from the always interesting Coen brothers.

3. When We Were Kings
Documentary, directed by Leon Gast (1996, PG, 94m, DVD)
An Oscar®-winning documentary about the "Rumble in the Jungle" bout between heavyweight champs George Forman and Mohammed Ali.

4. Smooth Talk
Laura Dern, Treat Williams (1985, PG-13, 92m)
This original coming-of-age tale is just one more reason to love Dern.

5. Living in Oblivion
Steve Buscemi, Catherine Keener, Dermot Mulroney (1994, R, 92m)
A low budget film about the making of a low budget film. It has a winning cast and script (the movie, not the movie within the movie).

6. Happy, Texas
Jeremy Northam, Steve Zahn (1999, PG-13, 98m)
Comedy about a couple of escaped cons who pass themselves off as a gay couple slated to judge a small town beauty pageant.

7. Ruby in Paradise
Ashley Judd, Todd Field, Bentley Mitchum (1993, R, 115m)
Judd caught up with, and in many minds surpassed, the artistic reputations of her mama and sister, the singing Judds, in this earnest screen debut. It's a slice-of-life drama about a working class woman striking out on her own in Florida.

8. Brother's Keeper
Documentary, directed by Joe Berlinger and Bruce Sinofsky (1992, NR, 104m)
Widely-lauded documentary about three seriously country-fried brothers who all share the same one room shack, who are all accused of killing the fourth brother.

9. The Waterdance
Eric Stoltz, Wesley Snipes, Helen Hunt (1991, R, 106m)
Writer/co-director Neal Jimenez's semi-autobiographical account of his recovery from a debilitating accident gives us this fine drama.

10. Sherman's March
Documentary, directed by Ross McElwee (1986, NR, 155m)
Another documentary. Filmmaker McElwee, on his way to using a grant to make a boring movie about civil war history, took a turn and decided to focus on what really interests most people a lot more: one's own personal quest to get laid.

SEE ALSO:
Big Night ("Mouth-Watering Faves")
Welcome to the Dollhouse ("Zit Flicks")
Hoop Dreams ("Real Sports Movies")
The Blair Witch Project ("Overrated Hall of Fame")

WHEN TO WATCH
The Sundance Film Festival is usually held the third week in January.

WHAT TO EAT
If you are in Park City for Sundance, you ought to try some aprés ski s'mores.

GREAT OPENING LINE
from *sex, lies, and videotape* by Steven Soderbergh

> *"Garbage. All I've been thinking about is garbage. I mean I*
> *just can't stop thinking about it."*
> —ANDIE MACDOWELL as ANN MILLANEY

FEELING COOL

The essence of being cool is disdaining everything everyone else likes and liking what most everyone else hates. If your mom likes it, it isn't cool anymore. Of course, the tricky part is what's cool often becomes un-cool very fast, depending on how fast it becomes popular. So, you might like something that's cool and suddenly get caught holding the bag when you discover every other hipster on the planet has moved on to the Next Big Thing. Remember martini bars, cigars, Echinacea, *Spy* Magazine, Mazda Miatas and Ricky Martin? They were all cool once. So you see, it's a never-ending chore to stay on the cutting edge of it all. It's the same principle as buying Yahoo stock or getting sucked into a pyramid scheme (which are about due for a comeback): buy early, make a huge profit and get out FAST. *People* magazine and other similarly highbrow publications have made an industry out of their "What's Hot/What's Not" proclamations, but alas, by the time anything is in *People*, it's already uncool. See how complicated this whole business is? And by the way, there's no telling what will happen to anything in the future. The "Fifteen Year Rule" says that once something goes out of fashion, it's eligible to become cool and retro fifteen years later. For example, disco went out in 1980 and came back in 1995. So don't throw out your Vanilla Ice albums just yet.

I have a solution to all this: go classic. The 1955 Ford T-Bird roadster always was cool, always will be. Frank Sinatra is the T-Bird of music. Frederico Fellini is the T-Bird of filmmakers. And the simple black dress is the T-Bird of women's fashion. Whenever my wife asks me what she should wear, regardless of the occasion, my answer is "you can never go wrong with a simple black dress."

I'll place my bet right now that the following movies will *always* be cool. But just in case they do go out of fashion, just put 'em on the shelf and dust 'em off in fifteen years. You'll be the hippest cat on your block.

Hip Flicks

WHEN YOU'RE FEELING COOL

These movies are so hip, you can brag about just having seen them. And what's more, you will look very cool coming out of the video store with one of these under your arm.

1. La Dolce Vita
Marcello Mastroianni, Anita Ekberg, Anouk Aimée (1960, NR, 174m)
When people say something is Fellini-esque, this is what they mean.

2. Magnolia
Tom Cruise, Julianne Moore (1999, R, 179m, DVD)
A constantly surprising and interesting collection of interwoven stories about judgement and forgiveness as told through these flawed characters living in Los Angeles' San Fernando Valley.

3. Run Lola Run
Franka Potente, Moritz Bleibtreu (1999, R, 79m, DVD)
This adrenaline shot of a German movie about Lola, who has twenty minutes to raise 100,000 German marks in order to keep her drug dealer boyfriend alive, is constantly inventive and exciting and totally cool.

4. Dead Ringers
Jeremy Irons, Genevieve Bujold (1988, R, 117m, DVD)
This could only have come from the sick mind of David Cronenberg. It's the story of identical twins (so identical, in fact, that both are played by Irons), both gynecologists, who share lovers without bothering to tell the poor women. Then it gets more depraved. Irons is amazing.

5. Heathers
Winona Ryder, Christian Slater (1998, R, 102m)
A mean spirited (and I mean that as a compliment) high school black comedy in which no one is safe.

6. Faster Pussycat! Kill! Kill!
Tura Satana, Haji, Lori Williams (1965, NR, 83m)
Once shocking, now campy, this is a Russ Meyer classic with one of the all-time great titles.

7. Naked Lunch
Peter Weller, Judy Davis (1991, R, 117m)
The king of bad taste and moral depravity David Cronenberg, again. They said this William S. Burrough's novel was unfilmable and Cronenberg proves it. Though, I gotta tell you, it is an interesting sight to behold.

8. *The Bad Seed*
Patty McCormack, Nancy Kelly (1956, NR, 129m)
Ten-year-old McCormack is a total bitch, but you better be nice to her or she might kill you. One of the only films I can think of that has a curtain call. In a bizarre end title sequence, McCormack is spanked for her evil deeds.

9. *Rosencrantz and Guildenstern Are Dead*
Gary Oldman, Tim Roth, Richard Dreyfuss (1990, PG, 118m)
The wordplay is fast and furious in this literate look at what two minor players in Shakespeare's Hamlet were doing while everyone else was murdering each other.

10. *Ocean's 11*
Frank Sinatra, Dean Martin, Sammy Davis, Jr., Angie Dickinson (1960, NR, 148m)
Hip Vegas crime caper starring the Rat Pack. It's the *St. Elmo's Fire* of the '60s.

SEE ALSO:
Breathless ("Gangsters")
Heavenly Creatures ("Feel Good Lesbian Favorites")

WHEN TO WATCH
December 12. Perennial hipster Francis Albert Sinatra's birthday (1915-1998).

WHAT TO EAT
Nothing goes better with *Heathers* than corn nuts.

GREAT LINE
from *Heathers* by Daniel Waters

> *"Look, Heather left behind one of her Swatches. She'd want you to have it, Veronica. She always said you couldn't accessorize worth shit."*
>
> —LISANNE FALK as HEATHER MCNAMARA
> to WINONA RYDER as VERONICA SAWYER
> in reference to the deceased Heather Chandler

Cult Classics

WHEN YOU FEEL LIKE A MIDNIGHT MOVIE

They often play cult movies like *Liquid Sky, Evil Dead,* and *Atomic Café* at midnight at your local theater. You know why? Because you really don't want the people attracted to these movies to darken any doorways in the daylight, it might scare off customers. Here are some other offbeat movies that have attracted small, but loyal, followings. Who knows, you may really love one of them and then you just may become part of a cult—and won't that make your parents be proud?

1. Rocky Horror Picture Show
Tim Curry, Susan Sarandon, Barry Boswick (1975, R, 105m)
Do me a favor and see this at the movie theater. You don't want toast all over your living room.

2. Eraserhead
Jack Nance, Charlotte Stewart (1978, NR, 90m)
A truly tweaked nightmare.

3. Umbrellas of Cherbourg
Catherine Deneuve, Nino Castelnuovo (1964, NR, 90m, DVD)
This is a star-crossed lovers story set in a sherbet-colored world where no one talks, they only sing. That's right, every single line of dialogue in this charmingly quirky French classic is sung, including the famous "I Will Wait for You" (or however you say that in French).

4. One From the Heart
Frederic Forrest, Teri Garr, Raul Julia, Nastassja Kinski (1982, R, 100m)
This film's artifice is its greatest strength. This is production designer Dean Tavoularis' masterpiece. It's all about the visuals, which are jaw-dropping. In fact, you'd want to watch this with the sound off if it weren't for the moody Tom Waits music. (Warning: it seems that a lot of people hate this movie just because it has a lame plot and weak characters. Picky, picky, picky.)

5. The Dogwalker
Will Stewart, Stepfanie Kramer, John Randolph, Tony Todd (1999, NR, 105m)
Paul Duran, director of film fest fave *Flesh Suitcase,* in his sophomore outing, again delves into the world of heroin and the disenfranchised.

6. Trouble in Mind
Kris Kristofferson, Keith Carradine, Lori Singer (1986, R, 111m)
An odd little movie. It's a stylish detective mystery with a rainy noir feel, but the surrealistic setting is more like a collection of artificial movie sets rather than any real place. It works for me, but then I always have been a sucker for style over substance.

7. The Adventures of Buckaroo Bonzai Across the 8th Dimension
Peter Weller, Ellen Barkin (1984, PG, 100m)

A sci-fi adventure about a Renaissance Man/neurosurgeon turned rock star and intergalactic crime fighter. If you can tell me what this is about, drop me a note.

8. O Lucky Man!
Malcolm McDowell, Helen Mirren (1973, R, 178m)

Metaphoric and surreal, this offbeat comedy about how to succeed in business features McDowell as a salesman and tackles some elephantine themes. This is the second film in Lindsay Anderson's loosely-connected trilogy that also includes *If...*and *Britannia Hospital*.

9. Two Lane Blacktop
James Taylor, Dennis Wilson (1971, R, 102m, DVD)

'70s pop music icons Taylor and Wilson, in their only starring roles, appear in this Monty Hellman cult favorite about iconoclasts wandering the southwest drag racing. It's *Easy Rider* for poets.

10. Repo Man
Emilio Estevez, Harry Dean Stanton (1983, R, 93m)

An entertaining cross-genre film by Alex Cox. Punker Estevez gets job repossessing cars and has inexplicable encounters with something in the trunk.

WHEN TO WATCH
September 29. The anniversary of the release of *The Rocky Horror Picture Show* (1975).

WHAT TO EAT
In honor of *Repo Man*, may I suggest whatever you eat, it must be a generic plain-wrap brand.

GREAT LINE
from *The Adventures of Buckaroo Bonzai across the Eight Dimension* by

"Remember, no matter where you go, there you are."
—PETER WELLER as BUCKAROO BONZAI

The Future Looks Weird

WHEN YOU FEEL LIKE BEING DEPRESSED ABOUT HOW BLEAK THE FUTURE IS

These movies are great works of art. They are also largely pessimistic about the future of human-kind on this planet. Those artists are so negative. Why can't they be more happier—like The Backstreet Boys?

1. Brazil

Jonathan Pryce, Robert De Niro, Bob Hoskins (1985, R, 131m, DVD)
A visually stunning picture of futuristic urban alienation. According to the Los Angeles Film Critics Association, this was the best film of 1985. According to Universal Studios, it lost a lot of money.

2. 2001: A Space Odyssey

Keir Dullea, Gary Cockwood, William Sylvester (1968, G, 139m, DVD)
The sweeping and stunning imagery of this poetic and complex movie, which tells a story that spans the history of mankind and the vastness of space, is singularly suited to be experienced in a movie theater.

3. The Road Warrior

Mel Gibson, Bruce Spence (1982, R, 95m, DVD)
Jimmy Carter's ultimate nightmare is played out as a post-apocalyptic energy crisis fuels the pulsating action of this testosterone masterpiece.

4. Dark City

Rufus Sewell, Jennifer Connelly, Keifer Sutherland (1997, R, 103m)
Dark science fiction fantasy about aliens who steal humans' memories for their own illicit purposes features absolutely striking production design.

5. Delicatessen

Marie-Laure Dougnac, Dominique Pinon (1992, R, 95m)
A bleak comedy that is a lot of fun, if you can have fun watching a post-apocalyptic movie about cannibalism.

6. City of Lost Children

Daniel Emilfork, Ron Perlman (1995, R, 114m)
A triumph of style over substance from the creators of *Delicatessen*. This is visually stunning but the story of a mad scientist kidnapping children is pretty pointless. In fact, you might want to watch this dark vision of a dank city in the future with the sound off—it's in French so it's not like you're gonna miss anything.

7. Darkman

Liam Neeson, Frances McDormand (1990, R, 96m, DVD)

Neeson plays the cartoon anti-hero in this souped-up violent movie that is pretty amazing to watch thanks to the inventive director, Sam Raimi.

8. Batman

Michael Keaton, Jack Nicholson, Kim Basinger (1989, PG-13, 126m, DVD)

Tim Burton, former Disney animator, is driven by his creation of other worlds. This is Burton with a lot of money and it shows. Beautiful sets that overpower both superhumans and big moviestars, and are very nice to look at. Like most of the futures presented in these movies, this is a Gotham City that is much nicer to look at on the screen than it would be to live in.

9. What Dreams May Come

Robin Williams, Annabella Sciorra (1998, PG-13, 113m, DVD)

Admittedly, not the greatest movie in the world. In fact, some who have seen it would rather drive spikes through their eyes than see it again. I confess, I was charmed by the rare display of an unabashedly romantic view of marriage (though it did elicit in me an occasional gag reflex). The look of the movie is indisputably great, however. And although a fantasy, as opposed to a futuristic film, the worlds created in this movie can compete with the other visionary designs on this list.

10. Kafka

Jeremy Irons, Theresa Russell (1991, PG-13, 100m)

Not really the future, but a surrealistic nightmare of contemporary urban society set in Prague in 1919. Prague may be the most photogenic city in the world.

SEE ALSO:
Blade Runner ("Worst Oscar® Oversights")
Metropolis ("Movies Even Older Than Your Grandparents")
The Matrix ("Copycat Crimes")

WHEN TO WATCH
Sometime in the future.

WHAT TO EAT
Something futuristic, like a tube of meat and Tang.

GREAT LINE
from *2001: A Space Odyssey* by Arthur C. Clarke

> *"I honestly think you ought to sit down calmly, take a stress
> pill, and think things over."*
>
> —DOUGLAS RAIN as HAL 9000, the computer

Vidiots

WHEN YOU'RE FEELING MAD AS HELL AND YOU DON'T WANT TO TAKE IT ANYMORE

These are movies about TV and people who manipulate TV for evil purposes. These movies just reinforce what we already know: "TV is evil."

1. *A Face in the Crowd*
Andy Griffith, Patricia Neal, Walter Matthau (1957, NR, 126m)
Brilliant! A kind of *Meet John Doe* with more bite. Neal is an opportunistic television executive who turns a nobody into a national guru in this keen black comedy.

2. *Network*
Faye Dunaway, William Holden, Robert Duvall (1976, R, 121m, DVD)
"I'm mad as hell and I'm not going to take it anymore," is the attitude of this super intelligent comedy which takes shots at and strikes a bull's-eye at its TV target.

3. *To Die For*
Nicole Kidman, Matt Dillon (1995, R, 103m, DVD)
Who would have guessed Kidman would be so good at playing a manipulative, do-anything-for-fame, self-centered bitch?

4. *Quiz Show*
Ralph Fiennes, John Turturro, Rob Morrow (1994, PG-13, 133m)
Nicely detailed masterful telling of the television game show scandals of the fifties.

5. *Medium Cool*
Robert Forster, Harold Blankenship (1969, NR, 111m)
TV news cameraman tries to remain detached as the turbulent 1968 Democratic convention erupts around him. Many scenes shot during the actual riots. Great historical document.

6. *Broadcast News*
William Hurt, Albert Brooks, Holly Hunter (1987, R, 132m)
James L. Brooks writes the hell out of this smart comedy about TV news. The cast is outstanding.

7. *Capricorn One*
Elliot Gould, James Brolin, Brenda Vaccaro (1978, R, 123m, DVD)
Fascinating fantasy about a supposed first manned mission to Mars which turns out to be a totally fabricated TV hoax.

8. *Ginger & Fred*
Marcello Mastroianni, Giulietta Masina (1986, PG-13, 126m)
Federico Fellini's TV satire, about a reunion of a pair of Fred Astaire-Ginger Rogers imitators.

9. *The Truman Show*
Jim Carrey, Ed Harris (1998, PG, 102m, DVD)
This allegedly original movie about an unwitting TV star, is virtually identical in concept to Paul Bartel's short film *The Secret Cinema,* which Bartel also made into an episode of Steven Spielberg's anthology TV series *Amazing Stories.*

10. *Pleasantville*
Reese Witherspoon, Tobey Maguire (1998, PG-13, 124m, DVD)
Artistically and emotionally rewarding look at the contrast between a '50s TV family and 1990s mores.

SEE ALSO:
Annie Hall ("Romantic Movies for Jews")
Tootsie ("What a Drag")
King of Comedy ("Losers")
Natural Born Killers ("Copycat Crimes")

WHEN TO WATCH
Anytime is a good time to watch TV.

WHAT TO EAT
TV dinner.

GREAT LINE
from *Network* by Paddy Chayefsky

"All I want out of life is a 30 share and a 20 rating."
—FAYE DUNAWAY as DIANA CHRISTENSEN

Movies about Movies

WHEN YOU'RE FEELING LIKE A MOVIE GEEK

These are some really great movies about movies. If you're a real movie freak, however, you've probably seen them all already.

1. Cinema Paradiso
Philippe Noiret, Jacque Perrin (1988, NR, 123m)
I love this valentine to the movies so much, it's probably illegal in at least eight states.

2. Singin' in the Rain
Gene Kelly, Debbie Reynolds, Jean Hagen (1952, NR, 103m, DVD)
Some will tell you this is the greatest musical Hollywood has ever made.

3. The Purple Rose of Cairo
Mia Farrow, Jeff Daniels, Dianne Wiest (1985, PG, 82)
Movie fan Farrow walks into a movie screen—where I'm sure she wishes she stayed instead of coming back and hanging out with Woody Allen for another decade.

4. The Player
Celebrity ensemble cast, directed by Robert Altman (1992, R, 123m, DVD)
Robert Altman bites the hand that feeds him.

5. The Day of the Locust
Donald Sutherland, Karen Black, Burgess Meredith (1975, R, 140m)
Scabrous (good word to know if you plan on taking a SAT test soon) look at Los Angeles during the Depression and the people on the fringes of show business just aching to get in.

6. Ed Wood
Johnny Depp, Sarah Jessica Parker(1994, R, 127m)
Tim Burton's off-beat biopic is far and away the best movie to ever have Ed Wood's name on it. The real life story of the director with all of the ambition and none of the talent to make movies. Martin Landau's Oscar®-winning portrayal of Bela Lugosi is to be cherished.

7. The Stunt Man
Peter O'Toole, Steve Railsback, Barbara Hershey (1980, R, 129m)
A brainy, funny action movie which is always as much of a pleasure as it is rare. This movie delves behind the scenes of movie production in which O'Toole wants to replace the film's top stunt man with the man responsible for his death.

8. The Front
Woody Allen, Zero Mostel, Danny Aiello (1976, PG, 95m)
Allen stars in, but did not write or direct, this story of a schlep who is recruited to put his name on scripts written by blacklisted writers to allow them to continue working. Brilliant comedy is all the more gratifying when you realize how many talented blacklisted people were able to have their say by working on it.

9. Day for Night
François Truffant, Jean-Pierre Leand, Jacqueline Bisset (1973, PG, 116m)
Truffaut's behind-the-cameras classic.

10. Mistress
Robert Wuhl, Martin Landau (1991, R, 100m, DVD)
This is an hilarious, low-budget version of *The Player*.

SEE ALSO:
Sunset Boulevard ("Writers")
Sullivan's Travels ("Satire in Style: Preston Sturges Movies")
The Big Picture ("Six Degrees of Kevin Bacon")
The French Lieutenant's Woman ("Adulterous Faves")

WHEN TO WATCH
February 11. Inventor of the movies Thomas Edison's birthday (1847-1931). Unless, of course, you're French, in which case, you might subscribe to the theory that the movies were invented by the Lumière Brothers. The brothers shared the same birthday, October 19 (Louis, 1864-1948 and Auguste, 1862-1954).

WHAT TO EAT
Movies about movies? What else: popcorn, soft drinks, licorice, Gummi™ bears, Raisinets™, chocolate bon-bons and those huge candy bars.

GREAT LINE
from *Ed Wood* by Scott Alexander, Rudolph Grey (book)

"The worst movie you ever saw? Well, my next one will be even better!"
> —JOHNNY DEPP as ED WOOD

FEELING GREATNESS: THE GREAT FILMMAKERS

Greatness isn't always easy to spot. All you have to do is take a look at some of the examples below. It's amazing how many success stories were originally deemed failures by critics and those "in the know." Which, if nothing else, should inspire all you creative geniuses out there to hang in there! I mean, look at Susan Lucci. It took her nineteen years of rejection, disappointment and embarrassment, but she finally came up a winner.

1. The *New York Daily News* said in its original 1967 review of *The Graduate* about Dustin Hoffman, "He is rather plain looking, resembling both Sonny and Cher. In addition, he'll never threaten Rock Hudson's image."

2. *The Wizard of Oz* lost a million dollars for MGM in 1939, the year it was released (which, adjusted for inflation, would probably be thirty times that amount today, if not more).

3. Andrew Sarris wrote a negative review of *2001: A Space Odyssey* in the *Village Voice* upon its 1968 release (but took it back a week later).

4. In 1975, the *New York Times* said that *Jaws* was "nothing more than a creaky, old-fashioned monster picture."

5. *Time* magazine said of 1973's Oscar®-winner for best picture, *The Sting*, "this isn't a movie, it's a recipe."

6. In 1952, *Singin' in the Rain* failed to get Oscar® nominations for either Best Picture, Director, Actor, Actress or Song.

7. The *New York World Telegram* said of *Casablanca* in 1942, "it is not the best of the recent Bogarts."

8. In 1941, gossip columnist Louella Parsons used everything in her journalistic power to thwart the success of *Citizen Kane,* which she considered a hatchet job on her boss, publisher William Randolph Hearst. Twenty years later, she held firm, remarking, "I am still horrified by the picture."

No accounting for taste, I guess. As they say, that's what makes horseracing. If you're interested in my definition of greatness, check out this chapter.

Woody's Finest:
The Films of Woody Allen

WHEN YOU'RE FEELING NEUROTIC

Some people like his earlier, funnier stuff. Some people like his later, serious stuff. Either way you slice it, there is no other voice in the history of movies like the Wood Man. His style is so distinctive that when you're in the mood to watch a Woody Allen movie nothing else will do, not even *When Harry Met Sally...*

1. Crimes and Misdemeanors
Woody Allen, Martin Landau, Alan Alda (1989, PG-13, 104m, DVD)
A masterpiece. Don't get me started.

2. Hannah and Her Sisters
Mia Farrow, Barbara Hershey, Dianne Wiest (1986, PG, 103m)
I remember in 1986, the Pulitzer Prize committee wanted to give this film the award for drama but the rules prevented it. Pulitzer? This thing is better than any play. Hell, I say give Woody the Nobel.

3. Sleeper
Woody Allen, Diane Keaton (1973, PG, 88m)
Sci-Fi comedy featuring the Orgasmatron and the nose on life support. One of his earlier, funnier movies.

4. Manhattan Murder Mystery
Woody Allen, Diane Keaton, Anjelica Huston (1993, PG, 105m, DVD)
How can anyone say that Woody Allen doesn't make out-and-out hilarious comedies anymore when he puts out this welcome Diane Keaton-Woody Allen-screenwriter Marshall Brickman reunion?

5. Bullets over Broadway
John Cusack, Chazz Palminteri (1994, R, 106m)
Cusack is a one-hit wonder playwright suffering from writers block who gets help from an unlikely source. In addition to diva Dianne Wiest's brilliant "don't speak" turn, another of the highlights is Jennifer Tilly. I guess, technically, her character isn't a prostitute. She's a no-talent mistress who's sleeping with a wealthy gangster to advance her acting career. In Hollywood we don't want to call a woman like that a hooker, we call her "ambitious."

6. Bananas
Woody Allen, Louise Lasser, Carlos Montelban (1971, PG-13, 82m)
Revolution in a Latin American "banana republic" is the setting for this hilarious gag-filled "early, funny" movie.

7. Zelig
Woody Allen, Mia Farrow (1983, PG, 79m)
Who says a good gag can't sustain a whole movie? Human chameleon Leonard Zelig changes his appearance depending on who he's with and becomes a world-wide sensation in the 1920s. Lots of manufactured fun footage of Zelig showing up in faux historical newsreels.

8. Broadway Danny Rose
Woody Allen, Mia Farrow, Milton Berle (1984, PG, 85m)
Woody's hilarious look at eccentric small time showbiz characters of a bygone era.

9. Stardust Memories
Woody Allen, Charlotte Rampling, Jessica Harpe (1980, PG, 88m)
Allen's homage to Fellini's *8 1/2*.

10. Radio Days
Mia Farrow, Dianne Wiest, Julie Kavner (1987, PG, 96m)
A lovely valentine to the golden age of the wireless.

SEE ALSO:
Annie Hall ("Romantic Movies for Jews")
Manhattan ("It's a Hell of a Town")
Love and Death ("Epics")
Purple Rose of Cairo ("Movies about Movies")
Husbands and Wives ("Delusional Cinema")
Deconstructing Harry ("Writers")
Interiors ("Splitsville Hits")
Mighty Aphrodite ("Oscar® Whores")

WHEN TO WATCH
December 1. Loving family man Woody Allen's birthday (1935).

WHAT TO EAT
In honor of *Annie Hall*, boil yourself a lobster.

GREAT LINE
from *Love and Death* by Woody Allen

> *"You know, if it turns out there is a God, I don't think that he's evil. I think that, the worst you could say about him, is that, basically, he's an underachiever."*
> —WOODY ALLEN as BORIS

Crowd Pleaser:
The Films of Steven Spielberg
WHEN YOU'RE FEELING FULL OF AWE AND WONDER

The most commercially successful director in the first century of movie-making has had his share of critical success as well. He has matured from the tales of wide-eyed suburban kids to deeply satisfying adult stories. In fact, just about the only thing about Steven Spielberg that you *can* hate is his success.

1. Schindler's List

Liam Neeson, Ralph Fiennes (1993, R, 195m)

I'd say this is Spielberg's masterpiece, but he always seems to have a way of outdoing himself. It's hard, though, to imagine a more masterful film than this story of a reluctant hero emerging from the horror of the Holocaust.

2. Jaws

Roy Scheider, Robert Shaw, Richard Dreyfuss (1975, PG, 124m)

This film demonstrates just how great a craftsman Spielberg is as he takes what could have been a very ordinary film and elevates it to a work of art.

3. Saving Private Ryan

Tom Hanks, Tom Sizemore, Adam Goldberg, Ed Burns (1998, R, 175m)

War is gross.

4. Close Encounters of the Third Kind

Richard Dreyfuss, Melinda Dillon, François Truffant (1977, PG, 152m)

I saw Spielberg on the Bravo show *Inside the Actors' Studio,* with the world's most affected man, James Lipton, who did make an interesting observation about this film. Spielberg's father was a mathematician and his mother was a musician. This film's pivotal scene has aliens and humans speaking to each other using only math and music—now, isn't that a beautiful thing? Now if I could only remember what Spielberg's favorite curse word was.

5. Empire of the Sun

Christian Bale, John Malkovich, Miranda Richardson (1987, PG, 153m)

Spielberg's first World War II epic, this combines his early "awe and wonderment through the eyes of a childhood" sensibility with his later serious tone.

6. Raiders of the Lost Ark

Harrison Ford, Karen Allen (1981, PG, 115m)

This non-stop action film revived the adventure-yarn genre once thought to be a relic of the Saturday matinee serials.

7. *The Color Purple*

Whoopi Goldberg, Oprah Winfrey, Danny Glover (1985, PG-13, 154m, DVD)
A big, splashy Hollywood rendition of Alice Walker's novel about an African-American girl living in rural Georgia, who survives indignities and pain to triumph in spirit. This expansive story covers the first half of the twentieth century. It features a number of fine performances including Oprah Winfrey's Oscar®-nominated film debut. (Nominated for twelve Oscars®, it came up with none to tie it with *The Turning Point* as the biggest Oscar® loser of all time.)

8. *Duel*

Dennis Weaver, Lucille Benson, Eddie Firestone (1971, PG, 90m)
This TV movie, released theatrically in Europe, is an effective cat-and-mouse thriller about a driver on highway being pursued by unseen trucker.

9. *Amistad*

Djimon Hounsou, Matthew McConaughey, Morgan Freeman (1997, R, 152m)
A powerful, grim tale of a slave revolt aboard a Spanish galleon that morphs into a fairly engrossing courtroom drama. Much of the film is in an African language with English subtitles, so be prepared to read.

10. *E.T. the Extra Terrestrial*

(1982, PG, 115m)
The cuddliest sci-fi film of all time.

SEE ALSO:
Jurassic Park ("Good, Wholesome Family Adventure Films")

WHEN TO WATCH
December 18. Father of seven Steven Spielberg's birthday (1947).

WHAT TO EAT
Some World War II rations. Or Reese's Pieces™. Or both.

GREAT LINE
from *Schindler's List* by Steve Zallian, Thomas Keneally (novel)

> *"It's Hebrew from the Talmud. It says 'Whoever saves one life, saves the world entire.'"*
>
> —BEN KINGSLEY as ITZHAK STERN
> reading an inscription given to Oskar Schindler

Satire in Style: Preston Sturges Movies

WHEN YOU'RE FEELING WITTY

Steve Martin, playing a film producer in *Grand Canyon* (see "Me Movies: Movies of the '80s"), derives his inspiration from the Preston Sturges film *Sullivan's Travels*. Martin's character, Davis, says, "It's a story about a guy, he's a filmmaker like me, who loses his way, and forgets what it was he set on earth to do. Fortunately, he finds his way back. It can happen, Mack. Check it out." Martin has come to the conclusion that all of life's great questions are answered in the movies. So, here in these Preston Sturges films may be the answers to all your troubles.

1. Sullivan's Travels
Joel McCrea, Veronica Lake (1941, NR, 90m)
A wonderfully insightful comedy about a big time film director who tries to get in touch with the real world. Good luck.

2. The Miracle of Morgan's Creek
Eddie Bracken, Betty Hutton (1944, NR, 94m)
A girl wakes up hung over and knocked-up. She has no idea who the father is. Pretty racy stuff for 1944. And happily, it's funny too.

3. The Lady Eve
Barbara Stanwyck, Henry Fonda (1941, NR, 93m)
Stanwyck stars in this droll tale of gold-digging con woman on the make to snare dim-witted Fonda's millions.

4. Easy Living
Jean Arthur, Edward Arnold, Ray Milland (1937, NR, 91m)
Sturges wrote, but did not direct, this uppercrust comedy about working class girl who gets mixed up in high society.

5. Unfaithfully Yours
Rex Harrison, Linda Darnell, Rudy Vallee (1948, NR, 105m)
A screwball comedy about a suspicious symphony conductor who suspects his wife of infidelity.

6. Hail the Conquering Hero
Eddie Bracken, Ella Raines (1944, NR, 101m)
Wimpy Bracken is mistaken for a war hero and his hometown goes nuts in this top-flight Sturges satire.

7. Christmas in July
Dick Powell, Ellen Drew (1940, NR, 67m)
A testament to the power of positive thinking, Powell thinks he's won a huge prize and things start to click for him.

8. The Great McGinty
Brian Donlevy, Muriel Angeles, Akim Tamiroff (1949, NR, 82m)
Remember when homeless people were called bums? Before that, they were called hobos. This is the story of a hobo who is manipulated into the governors mansion by a crooked political machine that needs a stoolie. (You know, a sucker.) This was Sturges first film as a director. He won an Oscar® for his sharp script.

9. Imitation of Life
Claudette Colbert, Louise Beavers (1934, NR, 106m)
Douglas Sirk directed this melodramatic tearjerker which I was surprised to discover Sturges wrote. It's a pretty campy story of a black girl who turns on her mother by passing for white.

10. Love Before Breakfast
Carole Lombard, Preston Foster, Cesar Romero (1936, NR, 70m)
Walter Lang directed and Lombard starred in this comedy for which Sturges' work was uncredited.

SEE ALSO:
The Palm Beach Story ("Delusional Cinema")

WHEN TO WATCH
August 29. Inventor and filmmaker Preston Sturges' birthday (1898-1959).

WHAT TO EAT
Breakfast (and make love first).

GREAT LINE
from *The Miracle of Morgan's Creek* by Preston Sturges

"Nobody believes good unless they have to, if they've got a chance to believe something bad."
—DIANA LYNN as EMMY

Six Degrees of Kevin Bacon

WHEN YOU FEEL LIKE A SLAB OF KEVIN

If you've ever played "Six Degrees of Kevin Bacon," you know some of your greatest assets are *JFK* (which gets you Kevin Costner, Sissy Spacek, Jack Lemmon, Joe Pesci, Tommy Lee Jones, Walter Matthau, Donald Sutherland and John Candy) and *Sleepers* (which gets you Robert De Niro, Minnie Driver, Brad Pitt, Dustin Hoffman, Jason Patric and Bruno Kirby). But what about sitting down and watching some of these other Bacon movies? Check 'em out:

1. Apollo 13
Tom Hanks, Gary Sinise, Bill Paxton (1995, PG, 140m, DVD)
Houston, we have a classic.

2. JFK
Kevin Costner, Tommy Lee Jones, Gary Oldman, Joe Pesci (1991, R, 189m, DVD)
Oliver Stone is way out of control in this paranoid conspiracy theory take on the Kennedy assassination, but it is dazzling filmmaking.

3. Diner
Steve Guttenberg, Daniel Stern, Mickey Rourke, Timothy Daly (1982, R, 110m)
This movie about growing into adulthood during the 1950s was a star factory, turning many in its relatively unknown-at-the-time cast to household names. This was the first film for Ellen Barkin, Paul Reiser and director Barry Levinson.

4. National Lampoon's Animal House
John Belushi, Tom Hulce, Stephen Furst (1978, R, 109m, DVD)
This movie unleashed upon us, the poor movie-going public, a rash of woefully unfunny imitations of this raucous comedy about college life in the '60s. Put on your toga and enjoy it.

5. The Big Picture
Martin Short, Michael McKeon, Jennifer Jason Leigh, Teri Hatcher (1989, PG-13, 95m)
A dead-on spoof of the film industry starring Bacon as a young filmmaker courted by various studio types. Short is hilarious as the agent.

6. A Few Good Men
Tom Cruise, Demi Moore, Jack Nicholson (1992, R, 138m, DVD)
You can't handle the truth!

7. The River Wild
Meryl Streep, David Strathairn (1994, PG-13, 111m, DVD)
Streep stars in this action movie, and Bacon is the villain. Both give top-notch performances in roles we don't usually expect from them.

8. He Said, She Said

Elizabeth Perkins, Nathan Lane, Anthony LaPaglia, Sharon Stone (1991, R, 115m)

Ever try to recall a story and then hear your significant other's version? Doesn't quite synch up, does it? Here's a simple story about how men and women remember everything completely differently.

9. Footloose

Lori Singer, Dianne Wiest, John Lithgow (1984, PG, 107m)

I suppose there may be towns with evil preachers who won't let anyone in the city limits dance, but those towns are usually only found in hackneyed movies. Bacon has charisma-plus as the city boy who takes up the cause of dancing in this immensely popular and exuberant musical.

10. She's Having a Baby

Elizabeth McGovern, Alec Baldwin (1988, PG-13, 106m)

Bacon is a young husband who is getting dragged reluctantly through the increasingly demanding levels of commitment and responsibility, from matrimony to paternity, kicking and screaming like a little baby the whole way.

SEE ALSO:

Planes, Trains and Automobiles ("Movies to Watch on Thanksgiving")

WHEN TO WATCH
July 8. Former soap opera actor Kevin Bacon's birthday (1958).

WHAT TO EAT
Bacon. (Too obvious?)

GREAT LINE
from *Diner* by Barry Levinson

> *"You know what word I'm not comfortable with?* Nuance. *It's not a real word. Like* gesture's *a good word. At least you know where you stand with* gesture. *But,* nuance...*I don't know, maybe I'm wrong."*
> —KEVIN BACON as FENWICK

King of All Genres: Howard Hawks

WHEN YOU'RE FEELING LIKE A CLASSIC

It usually takes a director a lifetime to master a single genre. Howard Hawks tackled just about all of them, with apparently effortless success. He created the definitive screwball comedy in *Bringing Up Baby*, the definitive gangster film in *Scarface* and the classic western *Red River*. To quote Wayne and Garth: "We're not worthy!"

1. Bringing Up Baby
Cary Grant, Katharine Hepburn (1938, NR, 103m)
The pinnacle of achievement in screwball comedy filmmaking.

2. Scarface
Paul Muni, Osgood Perkins, Ann Dvorak (1932, NR, 93m)
This Al Capone chronicle is one of a small handful of the truly great gangster classics.

3. Red River
John Wayne, Montgomery Clift, Walter Brennan (1948, NR, 133m, DVD)
Hawks takes on the Western and the result is one of the all-time great Westerns. It features one of Wayne's best performances.

4. To Have & Have Not
Lauren Bacall, Humphrey Bogart (1944, NR, 100m)
Leave it to Hawks, who consistently demonstrates such a gift for working with actors and agility with creating memorable scenes, to take Hemingway's worst novel and model Bacall, who had never appeared in a movie before, and create something on a par with *Casablanca*.

5. Gentlemen Prefer Blondes
Marilyn Monroe, Jane Russell (1953, NR, 91m)
Name a genre and Hawks has tackled it. Here he takes on the musical and draws effecting performances out of both Monroe and Russell in this pleasing popcorn movie.

6. Monkey Business
Cary Grant, Marilyn Monroe (1952, NR, 97m)
Cute (and I mean that sincerely and not in the condescending way that I would usually mean it) Grant-Monroe farce.

7. Rio Bravo
John Wayne, Walter Brennan, Ricky Nelson, Angie Dickenson, Dean Martin (1959, NR, 140m)
This Western, with its all-star cast, is a good example of a film that was once seen as inconsequential fluff, but has now been elevated to the stature of high art in the eyes of most critics.

8. Sergeant York

Gary Cooper, Walter Brennan, Joan Leslie (1941, NR, 134m)

Cooper shines as he goes from pacifist to World War I hero in this war-boosterism piece made during World War II.

9. I was a Male War Bride

Cary Grant, Ann Sheridan (1949, NR, 105m)

Based on a true story, this Grant comedy about a Frenchman who marries American servicewoman features many fine comic moments—including Grant in drag.

10. Come and Get It

Frances Farmer, Joel McCrea, Edward Arnold, Walter Brennan (1936, NR, 99m, DVD)

In the film biopic *Frances*, Jessica Lange's searing portrayal of rebellious iconoclastic actress Frances Farmer made Farmer more famous among late twentieth century movie-goers than Farmer's own films. If you want to see Farmer in her greatest screen role, this multi-generational Edna Ferber story is it.

SEE ALSO:
His Girl Friday ("Delusional Cinema")
The Big Sleep ("Private Dicks")

WHEN TO WATCH
May 30. Screen legend Mary Astor's brother-in-law, Howard Hawks' birthday (1896-1977).

WHAT TO EAT
Ribs, to commemorate the search for the missing dinosaur bone in *Bringing Up Baby*.

GREAT LINE
from *To Have and Have Not* by Jules Furthman, William Faulkner, Ernest Hemingway (novel)

> *"You know, you don't have to act with me, Steve. You don't have to say anything. Not a thing. Oh, maybe just a whistle. You know how to whistle, don't you, Steve? You just put your lips together and blow."*
> —LAUREN BACALL as SLIM

Always a Hitch:
The Films of Alfred Hitchcock

WHEN YOU'RE FEELING FRIGHTENED...
AND WANT TO FEEL MORE SO

You know François Truffaut wrote the definitive book on Alfred Hitchcock, and who am I to cover—in one pithy paragraph—what he did so well in an entire book? And maybe the brilliance of Hitchcock is that he is equally enjoyed by intellectuals and regular-joe movie fans alike.

1. North by Northwest
Cary Grant, Eva Marie Saint (1959, NR, 136m)
One of filmdom's enduring images, Grant being mowed down by a crop duster, is just one of the great scenes in this Hitchcock suspense thriller for the ages.

2. Strangers on a Train
Farley Granger, Robert Walker, Ruth Roman (1951, NR, 101m, DVD)
Odd that a guy you meet on a train who offers to kill someone for you in exchange for you committing murder for him would turn out to be a psychopath.

3. Shadow of a Doubt
Teresa Wright, Joseph Cotten (1943, NR, 108m)
Reportedly Hitchcock's favorite of his own films, this has Wright slowly suspecting her adored uncle of a string serial murders.

4. Rebecca
Judith Anderson, Joan Fontaine, Laurence Olivier (1940, NR, 130m)
Winner of the Best Picture Academy Award®, Hitchcock's first Hollywood picture is the account of a woman who marries into a wealthy family where everyone seems a little hooked on the old wife, Rebecca, especially the menacing housekeeper played memorably by Miss Anderson (she wasn't Dame Judith for another twenty years).

5. Notorious
Cary Grant, Ingrid Bergman (1946, NR, 101m)
Grant and Bergman hook up to hunt down Nazis in Rio. What could be more romantic?

6. To Catch a Thief
Cary Grant, Grace Kelly (1955, NR, 103m)
Kelly and Grant at their most glamorous, helped by a sexy script about a jewel thief and a French Riviera location.

7. The Birds
Tippi Hedren, Rod Taylor, Jessica Tandy (1963, PG-13, 120m)
Like *Rebecca*, this is based on a Daphne Du Maurier story (this a short story, that a novel). Hedren (Melanie Griffith's real-life mom) is the archetypal Hitchcock "cool blonde" until she starts to lose her cool when she gets pecked to pieces by a flock of crazed birds in this scenic Bodega Bay, California location.

8. Spellbound
Ingrid Bergman, Gregory Peck (1945, NR, 111)
Bergman is a psychiatrist delving into Peck's "issues"—and his pants—in this involving Hitchcock film that features surrealistic Salvador Dali dream sequences.

9. Lifeboat
Tallulah Bankhead, William Bendix, Hume Cronyn (1944, NR, 96m)
Characters adrift in a lifeboat during World War II are forced to get to know each other as they await rescue. Bankhead, as the throaty pampered journalist, gives the performance of her career. The challenge for Hitchcock was how to insert his trademark cameo. He figures it out as you will see when he floats by pictured in a newspaper ad for a weightloss product.

10. Suspicion
Joan Fontaine, Cary Grant (1941, NR, 99m)
A sweet wife suspects (hence, the title) that her husband is trying to kill her. But, don't we all suspect that of our significant others at one time or another?

SEE ALSO:
Vertigo ("Peeping Toms")
Rear Window ("Peeping Toms")
Psycho ("Book Reports Made Easy")
The Trouble with Harry ("Comedy Noir")
Mr. and Mrs. Smith ("To Have and to Watch")

WHEN TO WATCH
August 13. British Knight Alfred Hitchcock's birthday (1899-1980).

WHAT TO EAT
Birds, of course. Try turkey or chicken, unless you want to get really involved and find one of those little bitty Cornish game hen thingies.

GREAT LINE
from *North by Northwest* by Ernest Lehman

"I never discuss love on an empty stomach."
—EVA MARIE SAINT as EVE KENDALL

Independent Spirit: Films of Steve Buscemi

WHEN YOU'RE FEELING OUT OF THE MAINSTREAM

Steve Buscemi has already made an indelible mark on film history with a colorful and varied collection of characters who all seem to inhabit the outer edges of society and aren't all that anxious to get any closer. A fruitful collaboration with the quirky Coen brothers filmmaking team has lead to *The Big Lebowski, Fargo, Miller's Crossing* and *Barton Fink*.

1. Fargo
Frances McDormand, William H. Macy, Peter Stormare (1996, R, 97m, DVD)
A completely original Minnesota mass murder comedy with plenty of standout performances.

2. Reservoir Dogs
Harvey Keitel, Tim Roth, Michael Madsen, Chris Penn (1992, R, 100m, DVD)
Mr. Pink is a standout comic persona in this brilliant heist-gone-wrong caper which was Quentin Tarantino's blazing directorial debut.

3. The Big Lebowski
John Goodman, Jeff Bridges, Julianne Moore (1997, R, 117m)
Finally, a movie about bowling.

4. Miller's Crossing
Gabriel Byrne, Marcia Gay Harden, John Turturro (1990, R, 115m)
A 1929 mob war is given trademark kinks by the Coen brothers.

5. Parting Glances
Richard Ganoung, John Bolger, Adam Nathan, Kathy Kinney (1986, R, 90m)
Buscemi provides all of the highlights in this gay-themed talker.

6. In the Soup
Seymour Cassel, Jennifer Beals (1992, R, 93m)
Odd comedy about a screenwriter, played by Buscemi, and his drive to get his five hundred page screenplay made into a movie. 500 pages? After writing this book, I don't know how anyone could stand to spend that much time alone with himself.

7. The Impostors
Oliver Platt, Stanley Tucci, Lili Taylor (1998, R, 101m, DVD)
Buscemi teams up with Platt for an old-fashioned farce set aboard a luxury ocean liner with surprisingly rewarding results.

8. Twenty Bucks

Lind Hunt, Brendan Fraser, Christopher Lloyd (1993, R, 91m)
Conceptually interesting premise where the only character appearing throughout the entire film is a twenty dollar bill that gets passed from person to person, traveling through the hands of some interesting characters.

9. Trees Lounge

Carol Kane, Anthony LaPaglia, Debi Mazur (1996, R, 94m, DVD)
Ah, here we have Buscemi, the auteur! He tries his hand at writing and directing in addition to starring as a barfly in this character study of a middle-aged lay-about going nowhere slowly.

10. Armageddon

Bruce Willis, Liv Tyler, Ben Affleck (1998, PG-13, 150m, DVD)
Buscemi goes Hollywood in a big, loud, ridiculous movie about a meteor hurtling toward Earth.

SEE ALSO:
Pulp Fiction ("Copycat Crimes")
Barton Fink ("Writers")

WHEN TO WATCH
December 13. Would-be fireman Steve Buscemi's birthday (1957).

WHAT TO EAT
Steve Buscemi as Carl Showalter from *Fargo*: "I don't want more fuckin' pancakes, man. I want to go somewhere I can get a shot and a beer, and a steak, maybe."

GREAT LINE
from *Reservoir Dogs* by Quentin Tarantino

"Why can't we pick our own colors?"
—STEVE BUSCEMI as MR. PINK

Who? Films of Donald Ogden Stewart
WHEN YOU'RE FEELING LIKE A COMMUNIST SYMPATHIZER

Maybe the reason that you've never heard of Donald Ogden Stewart is because he was a victim of Senator Joseph McCarthy's witchhunt, in the form of "The House Un-American Activities Committee." He joined an anti-Nazi group during World War II and found himself blacklisted, along with dozens of other talented writers, directors and actors, who were under the impression that the United States Constitution's provisions for things like freedom of speech, assembly and religion meant that they had things like freedom of speech, assembly and religion. They were sadly mistaken.

Of course, there's another theory why you've never heard of Donald Ogden Stewart: he was just a writer. Starting out as a novelist and playwright, Stewart went on to a successful screenwriting career. But, why should you know that? Writers are rarely known outside of Hollywood studios and often not even known within them. Actors and directors get the credit for creating great movies. But, actors and directors don't just make this stuff up, somebody makes it up for them. Just look at this impressive list of scripts written and co-written by Donald Ogden Stewart.

While we're at it, how about another name for you: Bess Meredyth, a female screenwriter who started in the silent era and had a writing career for many decades. She was nominated for the Oscar® for two of her screenplays in a single year (1928): *Wonder of Women* and *A Woman of Affairs*. I don't know of any other screenwriter who has achieved that. She wrote such classics as *Ben-Hur*, *The Mark of Zorro* and *Strange Interlude*.

But what of Stewart's writing? Stewart, who was part of Dorothy Parker's literary roundtable sessions at the Algonquin, wrote *The Philadelphia Story* (that alone makes him a candidate for canonization in my book). He also worked without credit to co-write (along with Anita Loos and Jane Murfin) an adaptation of Claire Boothe's play *The Women,* which became one of the most blisteringly funny "women's films" (that's what they called 'em back then) of all-time.

1. Dinner at Eight
John Barrymore, Jean Harlow, Lionel Barrymore, Billie Burke (1933, NR, 110m)
This was adapted from the Broadway play by Edna Ferber and George S. Kaufman, but many fine plays have been fumbled in the pass from stage to screen. Stewart wrote the screenplay with Herman Makiewicz and Frances Marion for this witty and sophisticated high society comedy.

2. The Prisoner of Zenda
Douglas Fairbanks, Ronald Colman, Mary Astor (1937, NR, 101m)
Stewart came in to punch up this script by providing some additional amusing dialogue for this oft-filmed identity swap adventure. Stewart was an early "script doctor"—the Carrie Fisher of his day.

3. Escapade
John Mills, Yvonne Mitchell (1955, NR, 87m)
Stewart, while he was blacklisted, went off to Europe and wrote this satisfying drama under the name Gilbert Holland. Stewart channels his own experiences into this screenplay for this film, about a pacifist fighting hypocrisy.

4. An Affair to Remember
Cary Grant, Deborah Kerr (1957, NR, 115m)
Written while he was blacklisted, Stewart originally received no credit for his contribution to the screenplay for this classic romance, but his credit has been restored by the Writers' Guild of America (WGA).

5. Life with Father
William Powell, Irene Dunne, Elizabeth Taylor (1947, NR, 118m, DVD)
Adapted from a play which was in turn based on a Clarence Day story, this affectionate domestic comedy—about a turn-of-the century family headed by a less than enlightened patriarch—contains much of Stewart's hallmark wit.

6. Love Affair
Irene Dunne, Charles Boyer (1939, NR, 87m, DVD)
Another collaboration with Leo McCarey, this resulted in a romantic classic, as did their later film *An Affair to Remember*.

7. Summertime
Katharine Hepburn, Rossano Brazzi (1955, NR, 98m, DVD)
Written during the dark days of McCarthyism, Stewart worked without credit on this David Lean story of a spinster, played by Hepburn, who falls for a married man while on holiday in Venice.

8. Holiday
Cary Grant, Audrey Hepburn (1938, NR, 93m)
Adapted from the Phillip Barry play, Stewart co-wrote this excellent screenplay that has Grant and Hepburn starring as free spirits trapped in a stuffed shirt world.

9. That Uncertain Feeling
Merle Oberon, Melvyn Douglas, Burgess Meredith (1941, NR, 86m)
Another witty and stylish film, this one about a love triangle, is directed by Ernst Lubitsch.

10. Kitty Foyle
Ginger Rogers, Dennis Morgan (1940, NR, 108m)
Stewart wrote this one with Dalton Trumbo with whom he would later go on to be blacklisted. This soap opera about the love life of a secretary helped Ginger step out of Fred's shadow.

SEE ALSO:
The Philadelphia Story ("Delusional Cinema")
The Women ("Splitsville Hits")

WHEN TO WATCH
November 30. Enemy of the state Donald Ogden Stewart's birthday (1894-1980).

WHAT TO EAT
"Some caviar, sandwiches and a bottle of beer." (from *The Philadelphia Story*)

GREAT LINE
from *The Philadelphia Story* by Donald Ogden Stewart (uncredited), Waldo Scott, Phillip Barry (play)

"I thought all writers drank to excess and beat their wives.
You know, one time, I secretly wanted to be a writer."
—CARY GRANT as C. K. DEXTER HAVEN

P.S.
THAT'S INTERESTING

But wait, there's more! In this, the last chapter, I just wanted to toss in some fun and interesting movie tidbits. I hope you enjoy them as much as I do.

Beautiful Bombs

WHEN YOU FEEL LIKE ENJOYING SOMETHING NO ONE ELSE LIKES

It's a Wonderful Life, The Wizard of Oz and *Citizen Kane* were all bombs when they were released. Here are some more recent duds that need to be dusted off the video shelf and discovered. I'm not talking about obscure Brazilian art house movies here—I'm talking about big budget Hollywood movies that somehow, despite being excellent, were unable to find an audience.

1. Babe: Pig in the City
James Cromwell, Mickey Rooney, Elizabeth Daily (1998, PG, 96m, DVD)
The *Midnight Cowboy* of kids movies. The marketing department at Universal owes somebody an explanation. This is one of the best sequels ever, and they couldn't get anyone to see it.

2. Out of Sight
George Clooney, Jennifer Lopez (1998, R, 122m, DVD)
A cops and robbers movie with style, wit, substance and two great looking leads. I guess Universal was too busy bungling the *Pig in the City* release to give this film the attention it deserved.

3. Pennies from Heaven
Steve Martin, Bernadette Peters (1981, R, 107m)
Gorgeous Edward Hopper-esque settings frame the story of sheet music salesman who tries to lip synch his depression-era troubles away in this musical which I would describe as totally original, except that it was adapted from a British TV mini-series. It was a big gamble for MGM to make a big-budget musical in the eighties and unfortunately, they lost a lot of money.

4. Night Falls on Manhattan
Andy Garcia, Richard Dreyfuss, Lena Olin (1996, R, 114m, DVD)
This well-crafted police drama represents mainstream filmmaking excellence as practiced by Sidney Lumet. It's got a superb cast, and it's every bit as good as a dozen other movies I can think of which went on to become big hits. Why it made less than $10 million dollars at the box office is beyond me.

5. Tucker: the Man and His Dream
Jeff Bridges, Joan Allen, Martin Landau (1988, PG, 111m)
Director Francis Ford Coppola obviously relates to his main character, Preston Tucker, a man driven by his dream of building the car of tomorrow. Tucker is determined to finance his dream, come hell or high water, even if it eventually collapses. (Coppola raised funds for his own Zoetrope Studios which eventually failed financially). Great Joe Jackson score.

6. Stuart Saves His Family
Al Franken, Laura San Giacomo (1994, PG-13, 97m)
This seems to have been written off by the public as just another ill-conceived *Saturday Night Live* one-joke sketch project. But I'm telling you, this movie is good enough, it's smart enough...and doggone it, people will like it.

7. A Perfect World
Clint Eastwood, Kevin Costner (1993, PG-13, 138m)
A thoughtful manhunt movie with Eastwood as the pursuer and Costner as the pursued. It made $100 million outside the U.S. but was relatively ignored domestically, earning about $30 million. Normally $30 million is nothing to scoff at, but with stars like these and a budget of this magnitude, it's a disaster.

8. Dreamchild
Ian Holm, Peter Gallagher, Coral Browne (1985, PG, 94m)
If I ruled the world, this brilliant, original, little movie would be regarded as a classic. It's the enchantingly told tale behind the writing of "Alice in Wonderland." Though it does have pedophilia-esque undertones, it also has Muppets. See, something for everyone!

9. Matinee
John Goodman, Cathy Moriarty (1992, PG, 98m)
Only about twelve people saw this affable, coming-of-age piece set in Key West during the Cuban missile crisis. Goodman is terrific as the peddler of schlocky movies. The highlight is his film within the film: *Mant* (half-man, half-ant).

10. At Close Range
Sean Penn, Christopher Walken, Mary Stuart Masterson (1986, R, 115m)
This thriller about a rural Pennsylvania gang family is based on a true story from 1978. It made less than $2.5 million at the box office, though it seems to have had more life in video.

SEE ALSO:
Reds ("Writers")
One from the Heart ("Cult Classics")
Brazil ("The Future Looks Weird")
Dark City ("The Future Looks Weird")
The Iron Giant ("The Wonderful World of Animation")

WHEN TO WATCH
August 17. Underrated actor Sean Penn's birthday (1960).

WHAT TO EAT
A beautiful cholesterol bomb, like a super-rich double chocolate mud pie.

GREAT LINE
from *Out of Sight* by Scott Frank, Elmore Leonard (novel)

"Is this your first time being robbed? You're doing great."
—GEORGE CLOONEY as JACK FOLEY

Before They Were Stars

WHEN YOU FEEL LIKE DIGGING UP THE PAST

The great thing about *not* being a movie star is that you'll never have to go to a movie theater and see a slide of your high school yearbook picture projected onto the screen. These people, of course, don't have that luxury.

1. After Dark, My Sweet
Jason Patric, Rachel Ward, Bruce Dern (1990, R, 114m)
Before he was Julia Robert's ex-boyfriend, Patric starred in this really good movie.

2. Hairspray
Ricki Lake, Divine (1988, PG, 94m)
In this movie, Lake burst onto the scene with her first starring role and demonstrated her immense talent. Then she got her own talk show and we forgot she had any talent at all.

3. This Boy's Life
Robert De Niro, Leonardo DiCaprio (1993, R, 115m)
DiCaprio's first starring role has him playing opposite De Niro as Leo's wicked stepfather who tells him to "shut yer pie hole" a lot.

4. Hard Eight
Samuel L. Jackson, Phillip Baker Hall, Gwyneth Paltrow (1996, R, 101m)
Before he became the wunderkind who made *Boogie Nights* in 1997 (and then *Magnolia* in 1999), Paul Thomas Anderson made this (in some ways more interesting) Las Vegas character study.

5. Say Anything
John Mahoney, Ione Skye, John Cusack (1989, PG-13, 100m)
Mahoney was in a lot of movies before he found stardom as Frasier's sitcom dad. He's a great actor. If you need proof, check out this wonderful, original, thoughtful teenage love story with Mahoney as—what else?—a caring father.

6. Bottle Rocket
Luke Wilson, Robert Musgrave (1995, R, 91m)
Rising Hollywood Director Wes Anderson has only one career obstacle that might hinder his success: he is burdened by original thought. To see evidence, check out this quirky comedy crime caper. The full-length feature is expended from a short, also starring the talented Wilson and directed by Anderson.

7. A Nightmare on Elm Street
Johnny Depp, Robert Englund (1984, R, 92m)
Depp's first film and a credit of which he can be proud. This clever slasher movie about a group of teenagers' collective nightmare spawned an entire series and made Freddy Kruger a household name.

8. The Return of the Texas Chainsaw Massacre

Matthew McConaughey, Renée Zewelleger (1994, R, 86m, DVD)

Part four of this slasher series starred McConaughey and Zellweger. Within two years, these two were starring in *Lone Star* and *Jerry Maguire* respectively (and respectably).

9. Mermaids

Cher, Bob Hoskins, Winona Ryder, Christina Ricci (1990, PG-13, 110m)

Hollywood's newest offbeat sensation, Christina Ricci, was first seen in this Cher vehicle. The little smartass had a mouth on her even back then.

10. A Certain Sacrifice

Madonna, Charles Kurtz (1980, NR, 60m)

I like Madonna's earlier, sluttier movies.

WHEN TO WATCH
February 12. Bug-eyed sensation Christina Ricci's birthday (1980).

WHAT TO EAT
You might want to make up a plate of toothpicked canapés in honor of Cher's character in *Mermaids*, who cooks virtually nothing but hors d'oeuvres.

GREAT LINE
from *Hairspray* by John Waters

"Finally all of Baltimore knows: I'm big, blonde, and beautiful."
—RICKI LAKE as TRACY TURNBLAD

The Longest Movies
In the World

WHEN YOU FEEL LIKE SPENDING A WEEK
IN FRONT OF THE TV

For the record, these aren't literally the longest movies ever made. I mean, Andy Warhol made a movie called *Sleep* in which a guy sleeps for eight hours. In real time. (Of course, Andy Warhol also made a movie called *Blow Job* and appeared on the 200th episode of *The Love Boat*.) I've not seen the Warhol movie and I don't want to. You might, however, want to see some of the movies on this list because they're all great movies. They're just long. Very, *very* long.

1. War and Peace
Vyacheslav Tikhonov, Lyudmila Savelyeva (1968, NR, 373m)
Clocking in at six hours and thirteen minutes, some real wars don't last as long as this Russian film. In a country where they have to stand in line for bread, I guess they want to make sure they get their rubles worth if they're gonna stand in line for a movie.

2. Little Dorrit/Nobody's Fault
Alec Guiness, Sarah Pickering, Derek Jacobi (1988, NR, 369m, 2 parts)
Just over six hours, this is a Charles Dickens tale told in two parts, each half from a different character's point of view. It's really fascinating, if you've got the time.

3. Mary Poppins
Julie Andrews, Dick Van Dyke (1964, NR, 139m, DVD)
Although this is the shortest film on this list, I ask you, does this movie *need* to be two hours and twenty minutes? Then again, it takes an hour just to say Supercalifragilisticexpialidocious.

4. Shoah
Documentary, directed by Claude Lanzmann (1985, NR, 566m)
Nine and a half hours is a long time to do anything, let alone sit around looking at Holocaust footage.

5. Hôtel Terminus: The Life and Times of Klaus Barbie
Documentary, directed by Marcel Ophüls (1988, NR, 267m)
More Nazis. Why is everyone afraid to edit the Nazis? Hasn't there been enough suffering? This documentary of the former SS Captain is four hours and twenty-seven minutes long. That's a lot of "Heil, Hitlers."

6. Godfather Trilogy
Marlon Brando, Al Pacino, Robert De Niro (1981, NR, 570m)

In case you can't get enough of *The Godfather* (and who can?) here's nine and a half hours of *The Godfather*! This features all three films reedited into one with some additional footage. (Just a note: *The Godfather Epic* is a version with just the first two films and it aired on TV as the *Godfather Saga*.

7. The Thin Red Line
Nick Nolte, Sean Penn, John Cusack, Ben Chaplin (1998, R, 170m, DVD)

If you can sit through this two hour and fifty minute war drama, you should be awarded a medal of some kind. It manages to be strangely rewarding and tedious at the same time.

8. Greed
Gibson Gowland, Zasu Pitts (1924, NR, 140m)

The legendary Erich von Stroheim's masterwork. MGM released this two hour and twenty minute version after studio big cheese Irving Thalberg had it butchered. But who can blame him? The original was over ten hours long.

9. Tree of the Wooden Clogs
Luigi Ornaghi, Francesca Moriggi (1978, NR, 185m)

A three hour-plus examination of a year in the life of some Italian peasants which feels like you're watching them in real time. This film is an artistic triumph, but not for the faint of ass.

10. 1900
Gérard Depardieu, Robert De Niro (1976, R, 255m)

A mere four hours is all it takes Bernardo Bertolucci to relay the saga of the rise of fascism in Italy.

SEE ALSO:
South Pacific ("Desert Island Movies")
The Ten Commandments ("Spiritual Movies to Watch on Easter")

WHEN TO WATCH
Whenever you can free your schedule for a day. Or in some cases, a week.

WHAT TO EAT
Everything in your refrigerator. Believe me, you'll have the time.

GREAT LINE
from *The Thin Red Line* by Terrence Malick, James Jones (novel)

> *"What difference do you think you can make, one man in all this madness?"*
>
> —SEAN PENN as SERGEANT EDWARD WELSH

One-Hit Wonders

WHEN YOU FEEL LIKE WONDERING
WHATEVER HAPPENED TO...

Okay, so maybe you've never achieved fame or fortune in your life. The good news is you're still around and maybe you will some day. And if you do just one memorable thing before you check out, you'll be tied with a lot of famous people. Take Rosa Parks, for example—she just sat on a bus, and she sparked a nationwide movement. Or, to use a far less noble example, look at Monica Lewinsky. She climbed under the desk in the Oval Office and became an overnight household name. Here are a few other one-hit wonders:

1. Night of the Hunter

Robert Mitchum, Shelley Winters, Lillian Gish (1955, NR, 93m)

The only film directed by actor Charles Laughton is one of the all-time greats. It's a dark, brooding allegory about pernicious preacher Mitchum's pursuit of some innocent children.

2. To Kill a Mockingbird

Gregory Peck, Robert Duvall (1962, NR, 129m, DVD)

Mary Badham, who played Scout, Atticus Finch's daughter, created one of film history's most enduring characters in this gratifying courtroom classic. Yet she only made two other films.

3. The Best Years of Our Lives

Myrna Loy, Fredric March (1946, NR, 170m, DVD)

Harold Russell won an Oscar® for his role as a disabled vet but didn't win another acting job for thirty-four years.

4. The Killing Fields

Sam Waterston, Haing S. Ngor (1984, R, 142m)

Ngor took home the Academy Award® for playing a role that closely paralleled his own real-life harrowing experiences in a Khmer Rouge prison camp. He continued to work as an actor, but there were no significant roles. Sadly, he survived the killing fields but couldn't survive Hollywood. He was gunned down in his garage in 1996.

5. Kids in the Hall: Brain Candy

Dave Foley, Bruce McCulloch, Kevin McDonald, Mark McKinney, Scott Thompson (1996, R, 88m)

This movie landed in theaters with a thud and no discernible positive commercial or critical response. Too bad it probably ended the film careers of many involved.

6. Central Station

Fernanda Montenegro, Vinicius de Oliveira (1998, R, 110m)

Long-time Brazilian film star Montenegro made her sole U. S. splash with this very effecting film portrait of a flawed and lonely old woman. After losing at the Oscars®, she made comments about Gwyneth Paltrow winning because she (Paltrow) is a virginal and non-threatening fantasy of a woman. Apparently in Brazil, they don't have a "no sore losers" clause.

7. A Brief History of Time
Documentary, directed by Errol Morris (1992, NR, 80m)
A documentary about and starring scientist Stephen Hawking in his role of a lifetime.

8. The Passion of Joan of Arc
Maria Falconetti, Eugene Silvain (1928, NR, 114m)
There seems to be a Joan of Arc curse. The very next film after she played the "Maid of Orleans," Ingrid Bergman met Director Roberto Roselinni with whom she bore a child out of wedlock, resulting in her banishment from Hollywood for nearly a decade. *Saint Joan* launched Jean Seberg's rocky career which ended in suicide. We can only hope for Milla Jovovich, who divorced director Luc Besson during the production of 1999's *The Messenger*. The very best of the cursed Joan movies, though, is *The Passion of Joan of Arc*, a French silent masterpiece starring Falconetti, who is *stunning* in the role. It was only her second movie and she never made another.

9. Throw Mama from the Train
Billy Crystal, Danny DeVito (1987, PG-13, 88m)
Anne Ramsey didn't start working in films and TV until her forties, and then in small character roles. She finally got her big break as "Mama," a role which earned her an Academy Award® nomination. She died a year later.

10. Thoroughly Modern Millie
Julie Andrews, Carol Channing (1967, G, 138m)
And you thought Channing was just famous for being famous. Granted, she's had a distinguished career playing the character "herself." But she also had a significant film role as Muzzy in this Roaring Twenties farce.

WHEN TO WATCH
February 19. The anniversary of the 1955 release date of *The Night of the Hunter*.

WHAT TO DRINK
Pepsi One.

GREAT LINE
from *The Killing Fields* by Bruce Robinson, Sidney Schanberg (article)

"Nothing's forgiven. Nothing."
—DR. HAING S. NGOR as DITH PRAN

Movies in Which People Were Killed for Real

WHEN YOU'RE FEELING LIKE A SICK FREAK

What's wrong with you? Seriously? Do you really want to see these movies? Just because somebody died during the making of them? Well, okay, much like a school yard drug dealer, I'm not going to *make* you watch these. I'll just supply the information, and if you want to use it it's entirely up to you. By the way, despite what you might have heard about deaths on the sets of both *Mad Max* and *The Wizard of Oz*, those were rumors which are either untrue or unsubstantiated. However, the deaths in the movies on this list were the genuine article.

1. Ben-Hur
Charlton Heston, Stephen Boyd (1926, NR, 148m)
There were rumors that a stuntman was killed during the filming of the chariot race in the 1959 version starring Charlton Heston, but these rumors are false. The real death occurred during the filming of the chariot race for the original 1926 version.

2. The Crow
Brandon Lee, Michael Wincott (1993, R, 100m)
Lee, in his last starring role, died when a prop gun containing blank cartridges with too much firepower was fired at him during the filming of a gunfight scene. Lee's father, Bruce Lee, also died in a freak accident before completing the film *Game of Death*.

3. The Misfits
Clark Gable, Marilyn Monroe, Montgomery Clift (1961, NR, 124m)
On the last day of filming this picture, Gable reportedly described his working relationship with Marilyn this way: "Christ, I'm glad this picture's finished. She damn near gave me a heart attack." The following day, Gable suffered a fatal heart attack.

4. Brainstorm
Christopher Walken, Natalie Wood, Louise Fletcher (1983, PG, 106m, DVD)
Wood drowned under mysterious circumstances near the end of production on this expensive sci-fi thriller about virtual reality. For her remaining scenes they used a double, but the film was delayed for months.

5. They Died with Their Boots on
Errol Flynn, Olivia de Havilland (1941, NR, 141m)
They certainly did. In fact, three professional riders died during the filming of cavalry charges.

6. The Eiger Sanction

Clint Eastwood, George Kennedy (1975, R, 125m, DVD)

Extremely dangerous stunts were required for this authentic mountain climbing thriller, including star/director Eastwood dangling from a nylon cord 3,000 feet in the air. Eastwood survived, but a stuntman lost his life during production.

7. Twilight Zone: The Movie

Dan Aykroyd, Albert Brooks (1983, PG, 101m)

During the filming of the Vietnam action sequence in this movie, a helicopter, rocked by explosions, crashed and killed actor Vic Morrow and two child actors.

8. The Conqueror

John Wayne, Susan Hayward, Agnes Moorehead (1956, NR, 11m, DVD)

This film's greatest entertainment value is watching John Wayne try to play Genghis Khan. Its greatest tragedy is that it was shot near a nuclear testing site in Utah. A frighteningly large percentage of the cast and crew later died of cancer, including Wayne, Hayward, and Moorehead.

9. Vampire in Brooklyn

Eddie Murphy, Angela Bassett (1995, R, 103m)

Stuntwoman Sonja Davis died of a blunt force head injury after falling on an improperly inflated airbag while doubling for Bassett in this weird hybrid of comedy and horror.

10. Plan 9 from Outer Space

Bela Lugosi, Tor Johnson (1956, NR, 78m)

Lugosi allegedly died during the production of this notoriously awful Ed Wood film. (If drugs and booze didn't kill him, the embarrassment of appearing in this movie probably did.) Tom Mason finished playing Lugosi's role of the "Ghoul Man" by covering his face with a cape.

WHEN TO WATCH
March 31. The anniversary of Brandon Lee's fatal 1993 accident.

WHAT TO EAT
You won't be able to eat.

FAMOUS LAST LINE
from *Plan 9 from Outer Space* by Edward D. Wood, Jr.

"God help us in the future."
—CRISWELL, narrating

Copycat Crimes

WHEN YOU'RE FEELING LIKE A SCUMBAG

That's right, it's the end of the world. Morally bankrupt filmmakers are out there making movies that portray heinous acts of violence, which in turn inspire otherwise upstanding real-life citizens to skip their Boy Scout meetings and commit the same kinds of heinous crimes. But if violent movies really cause people to become criminals, how come comedies don't lead people to becoming comedians? Okay, sure, there *are* instances where people claim to have gone out and copied crimes they've seen in movies. But my bet is these idiots would be committing crimes anyway—they're just too stupid to think of any ideas on their own.

1. A Clockwork Orange
Malcolm McDowell, Patrick Magee (1971, R, 137m)
This movie about, in McDowell's character's words, "a bit of the ultra-violence," was banned upon its 1971 release in Britain after a rash of copycat crimes broke out. This film is still seldom seen in the U.K.

2. Pulp Fiction
John Travolta, Samuel L. Jackson, Uma Thurman (1994, R, 154m, DVD)
This Quentin Tarantino sensation was the most talked-about movie of 1994. Beginning with its winning of the Palm d'Or at the Cannes film festival, people couldn't stop raving about it or at it. Audiences ate up the brutal comedy about small time hoods, but the criticism of this ultra-violent film was equally vociferous. Some even saw it as a symbol of everything that's wrong with contemporary society, and there was an attempt by Australian law to ban the film for a scene described as a "how-to manual for shooting up heroin."

3. The Basketball Diaries
Leonardo DiCaprio, Mark Wahlberg, Lorraine Bracco (1994, R, 102m)
DiCaprio plays a guy who wears a trenchcoat and guns down some people at a high school. Allegedly, this film was a favorite of the two killers who carried out the massacre at Columbine High School in Littleton, Colorado, while both wearing trenchcoats. The movie was also blamed as inspiration for an earlier school shooting in Paducah, Kentucky.

4. The Matrix
Keanu Reeves, Laurence Fishburne (1999, R, 136m, DVD)
Many hysterical pundits wanted to assess this sci-fi thriller with a share of the blame for the Littleton killings. The movie was number one at the box office the same week of the Columbine tragedy and Reeves wears a black trenchcoat during a killing spree in the film.

5. Rebel Without a Cause
James Dean, Natalie Wood, Sal Mineo (1955, NR, 111m)
In 1953, a Boston judge wrote about the influence of this film: "We have the spectacle of an entire city terrorized by one-half of one percent of its residents. And the terrorists are children." I wonder what he would have thought of *Natural Born Killers*.

6. Natural Born Killers
Woody Harrelson, Juliette Lewis (1994, R, 119m)
This Oliver Stone mess about a couple of young people on a killing spree was loudly derided as an invitation to violence. The film is purportedly a criticism of the way the media sensationalizes and exploits violence. Ironically the film is, itself, sensationalistic and exploitive. It was linked to many crimes after its release, including the 1995 shooting of Patsy Byers, a case that went all the way to the U. S. Supreme Court.

7. Menace II Society
Larenz Tate, Tyrin Turner (1993, R, 104m, DVD)
A series of gang films emerged in the 1990s, including the landmark *Boyz N the Hood*. Unfortunately, some, including this one, were marred by violence that broke out in theaters where the films were playing. By the mid-90s, some theater owners became leery of booking black-themed movies amid charges of racism.

8. Scream
Neve Campbell, Skeet Ulrich, Courteney Cox (1996, R, 111m, DVD)
Gina Castillo, 37, of Los Angeles, was killed by her teenage son and nephew who both confessed to the crime. They claimed they were inspired by *Scream* and its sequel.

9. Money Train
Wesley Snipes, Woody Harrelson (1995, R, 110m, DVD)
Shortly after its 1995 release, crooks used this movie as a blueprint to blow up a New York subway train.

10. The Program
James Caan, Halle Berry, Omar Epps (1993, R, 110m)
A college quarterback leads his team in some stupid stunts, resulting in some stupid movie-goers copying the film and lying down in the middle of a highway. After several incidents led to serious injuries, the scene was cut from the movie.

SEE ALSO:
Taxi Driver ("Oscar® Whores")

WHEN TO WATCH
March 30. The anniversary of *Taxi Driver* fan John Hinkley, Jr.'s attempted assassination of then-President Ronald Reagan (1981).

WHAT TO EAT
Fries and a five-dollar milkshake. (see *Pulp Fiction*)

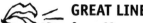 **GREAT LINE**
from *Menace II Society* by Tygert Williams, Allen and Albert Hughes (story)

"Went into the store just to get a beer, came out an accessory to murder and armed robbery. It was funny like that in the 'hood sometimes."

—TYRIN TURNER as CAINE

INDEX

HERE'S YOUR CHANCE

I don't know if you've ever written a book but now that you've read mine, I'm sure you're thinking it can't be all that hard. I'm sure I've left off some of your favorite movies and included a few that you hate. In the spirit of loving generosity that I'm pretty sure I am the walking embodiment of, I am now going to give you, the reader, a crack at it. Let me know what categories I left out. Let me know what movies I should have included. Why, for example did I not include movies like *Clerks* (it's lame), *Eyes Wide Shut* (never saw it) and *Men in Black* (Do you really need a book to discover this movie?) I'll even get you started with some ideas that I didn't quite have room for in the book: Movies about Talking Hamsters, The World's Greatest How-to Fishing Videos, The Best of the Weather Channel, Funniest Emergency Room Mishaps Caught on Tape, The Films of Judd Nelson, Movies You Thought Were Really Great Until You Sobered Up, Movies Where You Can See Harvey Keitel's Ass, Movies That Teach You Macramé, The Greatest Porn Screenplays, Movies That Would Have Been Better with Gary Coleman.

Send your suggestions to my attention by fax to 310-471-4969 or by email to info@loneeagle.com. Who knows, maybe your ideas will show up in the sequel: *2001: A Video Odyssey*.

Also from Lone Eagle Publishing . . .

ABOUT THE AUTHOR

Steve Tatham has performed stand-up comedy all over the world and has appeared numerous times in print, on the radio and on television. He is a writer at Walt Disney Imagineering. He has a long history of broadcasting his opinions about movies, beginning with his own college radio film review show as an undergraduate at UC Berkeley. He lives in Los Angeles with his wife, Mary, their son, Cole and their Australian Shepherd, Bailey. *1001: A Video Odyssey* is his first book.